Adventures
in
Zambian
Politics

Adventures in
ZAMBIAN
Politics

A Story in Black and White

Guy Scott

LYNNE
RIENNER
PUBLISHERS

BOULDER
LONDON

Every effort has been made to identify photographers and secure appropriate permissions, but we will be pleased to be alerted to any corrections for future editions.

Published in the United States of America in 2019 by
Lynne Rienner Publishers, Inc.
1800 30th Street, Boulder, Colorado 80301
www.rienner.com

and in the United Kingdom by
Lynne Rienner Publishers, Inc.
Gray's Inn House, 127 Clerkenwell Road, London EC1 5DB

Library of Congress Cataloging-in-Publication Data
Names: Scott, Guy (Guy Lindsay), 1944– author.
Title: Adventures in Zambian politics : a story in black and white / Guy
  Scott.
Description: Boulder, Colorado : Lynne Rienner Publishers, Inc., 2019. |
  Includes bibliographical references and index. |
Identifiers: LCCN 2018032409 (print) | LCCN 2018033096 (ebook) | ISBN
  9781626377752 (e-book) | ISBN 9781626377592 (hardcover : alk. paper)
Subjects: LCSH: Scott, Guy (Guy Lindsay), 1944– | Zambia—Politics and
  government—1964–1991. | Zambia—Politics and government—1991– |
  Politicians—Zambia—Biography.
Classification: LCC DT3117.S36 (ebook) | LCC DT3117.S36 A3 2019 (print) |
  DDC 968.9404092
LC record available at https://lccn.loc.gov/2018032409

British Cataloguing in Publication Data
A Cataloguing in Publication record for this book
is available from the British Library.

Printed and bound in the United States of America

 The paper used in this publication meets the requirements
of the American National Standard for Permanence of
Paper for Printed Library Materials Z39.48-1992.

5 4 3 2

You all did love him once, not without cause:
What cause withholds you then, to mourn for him?
O judgment! thou art fled to brutish beasts,
And men have lost their reason. Bear with me;
My heart is in the coffin there with Caesar,
And I must pause till it come back to me.

—*Julius Caesar,* Act 3, Scene 3
William Shakespeare

Is it not passing brave to be a king,
And ride in triumph through Persepolis?

—*Tamburlaine,* Act 2, Scene 5
Christopher Marlowe

Contents

Photographs

Foreword

THIS BOOK, YOU WILL SOON DISCOVER, IS UNLIKE ANY OTHER POLITICAL memoir you have ever read. Where retired politicians commonly use such books to retrospectively praise and justify their decisions and denigrate their enemies, Guy Scott, former Zambian vice president (2011–2014) and minister of agriculture (1991–1993), provides robust and insightful critical analysis of not only Zambian political life in general but also his own party and government. Where most memoirists focus only on themselves and their achievements, Scott situates his life's work historically in the history of Africa, of its peoples, and of its experience with colonialism, which was of course formative— but by no means determinative—of his own life.

This book is, as will now be clear, only partly a memoir. Scott ranges across the Zambian historical and political landscape, with insightful discussions of Bemba proverbs; Livingstone's explorations; the migration of African societies into what, fairly accidentally, became Zambia; the activities of Zimbabwean liberation movement forces within Zambian borders; and, in more detail, an effective assessment of the country's postindependence economic and political development. All of this is leavened with personal remembrance and anecdote, delivered in a typically witty, sometimes ribald tone. Scott discusses many issues that have been analyzed in more pedantic detail by academics such as myself, and he has therefore provided a selected bibliography for those who wish to explore further.

The book is also partly a biography of Scott's long-time collaborator and friend, the former Zambian president Michael Sata, who—to widespread international incredulity and equally widespread Zambian indifference—appointed Scott to be Africa's first white vice president since independence. Following Sata's untimely death in 2014, Scott served briefly as acting Zambian president, again a unique role in international eyes but one that Zambians largely accepted with little concern, at least on the basis of his race.

Racial difference, as the book's subtitle indicates, occupies a central but characteristically unpredictable position in Scott's life and in this work. Scott discusses his upbringing and education in a central/southern Africa marked by harsh racial inequality and violence and his family's attempts to navigate the politics of this conflict. Scott's father, Alexander, was a prominent journalist and leading figure in the liberal multiracial politics of the late 1950s and early 1960s that, although often derided by African nationalists then and subsequently, was influential on the markedly tolerant nonracialism of Zambian political life.

Scott rejected the conservative and racialized values he encountered both at school in (Southern) Rhodesia and at university in Cambridge (1962–1965), and he embraced the optimistic promise of African independence when he chose Zambian over British citizenship in 1965. Scott worked for the government planning office, but also became a journalist, participating in the vibrant intellectual discussions about the best way to ensure that political freedom translated into meaningful social and economic change.

In 1970, at a time when many Zambians were beating the path from the village to the town, Scott took the road less traveled into farming and became a highly successful commercial farmer. Scott provides a lucid and revealing account of Zambia's promise, the violence it experienced during the southern African liberation struggles, and the country's decline into economic depression and authoritarian politics. In 1982, Scott took his family to Britain where he studied for a PhD in computer science. Disillusioned by the failures and betrayals of Zambia's one-party state, he nonetheless seized the opportunity in 1990 to support the nascent Movement for Multiparty Democracy (MMD), becoming minister for agriculture in the new MMD government in 1991.

Scott, having witnessed the disastrous effects of state control of the economy under Kenneth Kaunda's United National Independence Party (UNIP), defends the MMD's program of economic liberalization carried out by the MMD in power while decrying the growing corruption and intolerance of MMD governance under President Frederick

Chiluba (1991–2001). Scott, like many original MMD supporters, left the government in 1993 but remained close to those in power. Here he sheds light on the nature of governance under Chiluba's presidency, in particular on Chiluba's attempt to secure an unconstitutional third term in office and the divisions and rivalries within the ruling elite, acted out in an unedifying manner with little or no consideration for the people who elected them.

Michael Sata enters and exits the story at instructive junctions. Scott is at pains to dispel some of the rumors that have attached to the legend of Sata's background and rise to power, but he equally understands the power of the Sata myth and doesn't make it his primary task to resolve or reject all of them. He provides significant new evidence on Sata's upbringing, his education and early political life, and his time in the UK in the late 1960s and 1970s, working in skilled manual jobs such as on the British railways. He also shows how in the early 1980s, Sata skillfully built up a political base within the ruling UNIP, first as a local councillor and then as a member of parliament and district governor in Lusaka. Scott reveals some of Sata's business backers and paints a persuasive picture of an intelligent and occasionally ruthless politician in pursuit of power.

While Scott was out of government for most of the 1990s, Sata rose to increasing prominence as Chiluba's key lieutenant, ensuring he retained his grip on power even as he alienated his supporters and ousted his rivals, often by underhanded and authoritarian means. This was a balancing act that couldn't last; when Chiluba, despite Sata's best efforts, was prevented from standing for an unconstitutional third term as president in 2001, Chiluba unexpectedly nominated as his successor not Sata but the lawyer Levy Mwanawasa. Sata broke away from MMD and established his own party, the Patriotic Front (PF), as a vehicle to run for the presidency.

It is at this point that Scott re-enters the political mainstream, summoned as Sata's own key lieutenant and trusted adviser. The central part of the book focuses on the transformation of PF from an also-ran party receiving 3.4 percent of the presidential vote in 2001 to the party that would carry Sata and Scott to power a decade later. How was PF able to distinguish itself from the many small parties that appeared at this time, and how was it able to overcome the huge advantages of incumbency?

The narrative Scott presents here is one of the most revealing "insider" accounts of electoral politics in contemporary Africa: he gives us a firsthand look at how PF gave popular expression to the anger of Zambians about the country's lack of development and how poor domestic governance, foreign exploitation (from so-called investors), and bad policy advice (from well-meaning Western governments) contributed to this situation. Although Scott shows how PF marketed itself as a pro-poor party, and was certainly understood as such by its supporters, there is little here about policy development or discussion of how to govern in the interests of the poor or what this might involve. Instead the focus is on techniques designed to win power, a Machiavelli's *Prince* for twenty-first century Africa.

Having recounted the excitement and controversies of PF's victory in the 2011 election in which he played a central role, Scott provides equally interesting insights into the PF in power and his significant role as vice president. Without blowing his own trumpet, he details his efforts in challenging corrupt land speculation, ensuring the immediate delivery of antiretroviral drugs to patients newly testing positive for HIV, and (admittedly less successful) reforming economic policy. Scott turns his analytical gaze to key policy questions for Zambia and much of Africa: the need to invest in infrastructure in a large and underpopulated country; the negative effect of the country's enduring dependence on copper and cobalt exports, specifically the problem of a strong currency; and the key question of Chinese economic and political relations.

As always with Scott, his focus on serious policy issues is leavened with his characteristically acerbic wit, which is particularly well applied to his vice presidential diplomatic adventures in Malawi, Zimbabwe, and North Korea. He writes movingly of Zambia's footballing triumph at the 2012 Africa Cup of Nations and of the funeral of Nelson Mandela.

What emerges from the book, despite Scott's argumentative and occasionally pugnacious style, is the obvious affection, even love he felt (and feels) for his late friend Sata. Their joking relationship clearly deepened during their long campaign for power and in office, and the book movingly reveals his pain and anger, not only at the ill health that affected Sata soon after he became president, but also at the unedifying maneuvering of senior PF figures as Sata became increasingly incapacitated. Here there is a barely stated but understandable sense of what might have been had Sata lived longer. Scott's own tumultuous time as acting president, a time of great controversy, is covered in less detail, and the book carefully avoids commentary on the presidency of Edgar Lungu or his reelection in 2016.

This book will hopefully be read well into the future, long after many academic studies of African politics or society are forgotten. More than anything, the clear-sightedness and focus on what works—

which has underscored both Scott's writing and political activism over his life—make this a deeply revealing and valuable study for those who wish to understand how politics actually works in Zambia and beyond and how it has been shaped by extraordinary individuals like Michael Sata and, indeed, Guy Scott.

—*Miles Larmer*
Professor of African History,
University of Oxford

Acknowledgments

A BOOK LIKE THIS, RECOUNTING THE EVENTS OF MANY YEARS, DEPENDS on the family, friends, and colleagues who in so many ways gave me encouragement, inspiration, ideas, advice, time, food and drink, campaign contributions, and so much more. A few people sucked into the endeavor of making sense of our country may be regretting their involvement, but somehow I don't doubt that they are generally pleased to be part of history—that's my guess.

The role of my friend and colleague Michael Sata has, I think, had enough space devoted to it here. This is a book about him after all. But there are many others now dead who gave unstintingly, whether or not successfully, to building our country. In writing the book, I have had the opportunity to remember their contributions and to remind myself again of how they inspired and helped me and others engaged in the same fight. I single out here for acknowledgment my father and mother, Alexander and Grace Scott; Valentine Musakanya; Emmanuel Kasonde; Anderson Mazoka; and, despite his flaws, Frederick Chiluba.

But the majority of the key political players are still alive, and far too numerous to list. I am also keenly aware that for those who are still active in politics, from all parties, being mentioned here might or might not be welcome in our highly political climate. To my fellow Zambian politicians, including those with whom I have been most closely associated and those with whom I have never agreed about anything, I want to thank all of you who are dedicated to making democracy a reality in our country.

I also want to mention those people who have supported my campaigns with generous resources, but they usually wish to be anonymous. Various people have been generous with fuel, loans, vehicles, T-shirts, posters, accommodation, bail, and all the rest that is needed for elections. Michael Galaun has died, sadly, so I can thank him publicly. Somehow we resolved the dispute between his father and mine over a generation of difference, and Zambia received the benefit. The late Mike Bush helped out once victory was secured: it's hard to plan a victory wardrobe in advance, so Mike's suits went to parliament on my back in 1991, and his dinner suit came with me to Perth to meet the queen for dinner twenty years later. ("The only shame was that it wasn't me that was in it," said Mike, before he died.) For the rest of you—you know who you are, and thanks!

Someone who was extremely important in my own life and who supported me at home for many years with unfailing kindness and the keenest interest in my political fortunes was Whiteson Nkazi. It is one of my greatest regrets that he did not live to see me become vice president, as I am sure his pride and pleasure would have been greater than that of anyone else, including me and all the other members of my family.

People with a national role dominate political histories. But the fun (and some of the frustration) of politics involves the great many enthusiastic supporters who throw themselves into elections—some sing, some drive, some tread the streets and paths, some pack hundreds of meals for polling agents or fold leaflets or cut up *chitenge*, while others put themselves on the line to ensure safety and success. My political adventures have been shared with Jimmy Nyirenda, Judge Ngoma, and Biggie Mwiinde, who have traveled the length and breadth of the country with me. At home, the late Rose Muteto and more recently Victoria Chivende have contributed their superb organizational skills to the many tasks needed to make campaigning a success. There are countless more activists at district, constituency, and ward levels who have also played a part in the events recounted in this book.

While I was in office, as vice president and president, there were many people around me who made it all possible. Without Attorney General Musa Mwenye, the civil servants at Cabinet Office and elsewhere, the staff of Government House, and my security detail, we would have gotten nowhere at all, although I am sure my neighbors don't miss the howling sirens that accompany the vice presidential motorcade.

Media is oxygen for democratic politics, and it is a shame when journalists have to be brave to do their everyday jobs. I'd like to thank the many enthusiastic journalists who have covered my career over the years, sometimes with great courage, especially many Zambian *Post* journalists. Photojournalism played an important role in getting my message across, and I recognize the contribution of these brave souls, especially Eddie Mwanaleza, who took many of the photos in this book—if I was wading through a river, Eddie went first to get the picture. While I was in office, Effie Mpande covered my work for ZNBC with great professionalism. (It is a shock to find that, as this book is being finished, the entire *Post* archive has disappeared from the internet. Not only are all references to the *Post* currently untraceable online, but a great record of Zambian political history—especially, and perhaps ironically, the documented history of the Patriotic Front—seems to have vanished.)

I have consulted many people during the writing of the book, although the mistakes and faults are all my own, of course. Whether they recognize what I've taken from their words, I would like to thank Peter Kasolo, Ian Dunn, the Mutima founders, and members of the Sata family.

The book does not fall clearly into any genre, which may or may not be a good thing. As such, it has made life particularly hard for those people who have generously given their time to review my manuscript and offer ideas and feedback. Vernon Wright gave me a lot of his time and very valuable advice based on his exceptional skills as a writer and editor, and I am most grateful to him. Thanks too to his pal, Terry Bell, and to my co-in-law, Lynn Barber, for her comments. I've also been helped or inspired by conversations with others who are writing about the history and current state of Zambia, including Miles Larmer, Marja Hinfelaar, and C. K. Lee. Particular thanks go to Miles Larmer for his time and for his generous foreword. Thanks too to Namwali Serpell, whose work also creates insights into Zambia through literature, for permission to use her article in the first chapter.

At Lynne Rienner Publishers, I was delighted to meet Caroline Wintersgill and Lynne herself. Their warmth, embracing me and my book with such enthusiasm, was extremely welcome. It has been a pleasure to get the book wrapped up with Caroline's help, and I greatly appreciate Lynne's decisiveness and commitment to this project.

It is customary in acknowledgments to thank one's friends and family for their support during the writing of a book. There are too many friends and wider family members to name them all, but I would be remiss not to thank Sarah Jane, Vernon, Gerri, and John. I would particularly like to thank my children, Sasha, Hugo, Sebastian, and Thandi, for their forbearance and understanding. My political career has not brought them many benefits and has certainly taken me away from them, but they have survived and made me extremely proud of

XX Acknowledgments

their many achievements, including making me a happy grandfather to Effie, Enzo, Salif, Twaha, Nia, Eva, and Luke. I also appreciate the years of support and kindness from Charlotte's parents, Janet and Robin, as well as Stephanie and Ivan, Lucy and Alan, and all their children; special thanks to Steph for her constant encouragement and care.

It ends—as it began—with my wife, Charlotte. Born and brought up in Britain, she has since lived for more than thirty years in Zambia. Michael was the one who introduced us—a fact for which he never failed to take credit. She was working for the District Development Support Program in his home district of Mpika, which fell under his responsibilities as minister for local government, and I was on the campaign trail standing as the MMD candidate for the area. I had already followed her trail up the Luangwa Valley, an adventurous journey even for a young woman who had already mastered the art of single-handedly winching her own car out of flooded rivers. She would be the first to say how much she has gained from her life in Zambia, but she has given back so much to our country, to her many friends and colleagues, and above all to me. It is hard for both of us to know where my work ends and her work begins. I am proud to have supported her in her outstanding work over many years for the poorest children and families in our society. I am also equally proud to say that my own work over the past thirty years, and much of the wider work that I cover in this book, would not have been possible without her intellect, her good judgment, her deep understanding of Zambia and its people, and her enthusiasm. It goes without saying that this book bears her imprint as well.

—*Guy Scott*

1

Prologue

WE HAD JUST COME BLOODIED FROM A PRESIDENTIAL ELECTION THAT saw us whimpering in seventh place, clutching only 3.4 percent of the valid votes cast. In the parliamentary election run simultaneously, we came up with one seat in remotest Bembaland, won by a once-upon-a-time agricultural officer whose name we didn't know. This single seat was all we had against 149 seats belonging to our enemies, spattered in big smudges on the national map in a sort of tribally tinged action painting.

Michael Chilufya Sata was unimpressed. "Rigging!" he declared. "The vehicle sent to rig our only seat must have broken the clutch plate and failed to make it to the polling center. Remember the trouble we had with that road? We will spend a lot of money on fixing roads."

Could things get much worse?

As soon as the election was over, I went in for a medical check-up in South Africa. There were no electrocardiogram machines around Lusaka in those days, and the Zambian response to such problems is to do nothing and change the diagnosis. It nonetheless was becoming obvious to my wife, Charlotte, that I was prone to angina and a heavy smoker and that the two facts might be connected. She put me on a plane to Johannesburg. Two days later I lay recovering from a triple coronary artery bypass graft (a CABG nicknamed "Cabbage" by the cognoscenti). I was nursing a vile temper but there was compensation in the attentions of nurses moving among us in the intensive care unit.

I did not get to see or even hear from Michael—"Candidate Number Seven"—for four weeks; this was when I was dispatched back to

"Africa," the new, politically correct name among South Africans for what used to be called the Black North.

On arrival, in a wheelchair on the apron, I heard that Michael was in jail, awaiting trial for "car theft." It was not possible in Zambia in those days, way back in 2002, to obtain bail while awaiting trial for car theft, the reason being as follows. The first post–one-party-state president, Frederick Chiluba, slayer of the long-standing incumbent Kenneth Kaunda, champion of democracy (we shall dig up some better stuff in due course), became incensed with his own inability to jail one Archie Macatribuoy, a used car salesman, on the basis of extant law. So he sent a bill to parliament, which declared that the mere allegation of car theft should be non-bailable. (He could have declared a State of Emergency and locked up Archie even without an excuse, but that would have been over the top even for a jilted president.) Archie's alleged crime was that he was rumored to be the lover of Vera Chiluba, a large, cuddly woman who had found herself first lady of Zambia. As soon as parliament passed the no-bail law, Archie was accused of stealing a string of sec-ondhand motors and disappeared inside. Has anyone heard of him since?

Unfortunately, once the *affaire* Archie was over, nobody remembered to restore the law to a less ass-like tendency, and it duly misfired, result-ing with Michael in jail. Michael had kept two ministerial vehicles and used them for the election campaign. I recall that one was a Japanese 4 x 4, almost brand new, in which we spent endless hours touring thousands of miles of very poor dirt roads up and down the country. Obviously, because he had to resign his position in government to campaign for the presidency as bona fide "opposition," he should have returned all govern-ment property, and his use of the cars could be construed as theft to some degree. One of his many less-than-deadly but more-than-mere-irritant opponents was appointed minister of transport in the new government. He was not slow to make use of the ability to throw Michael into jail, under the Archie law, as a putative car thief.

And so it happened that the now mythical grand reunion of the two leaders of the Patriotic Front—Michael and me—had to take place dur-ing visiting hours in the Kamwala Remand Prison. The prison officers were most helpful to me with my chair, and remarkably sympathetic about the cushion I carried everywhere. This was an aid that helped stop my chest from hurting whenever I laughed.

After greetings, I proudly handed over to my boss an automatic blood pressure measuring machine that his wife, Christine (a pediatric surgeon), had somehow procured from the University Teaching Hospi-tal. He had earlier expressed concern about his "BP." I strapped his upper arm according to the instruction pamphlet and turned it on. Within a minute it declared his blood pressure (high and low) to be 120:80, with two green lights to match. That's very good, perfect in fact, we shouted in unison, for a man in his sixties. Then it was my turn: 120:80. Just out of hospital and fine-tuned! It did not blink at Charlotte's perfect score either, nor at the doctor's, nor the gigantic murderer being prepared for release after twenty years of "life" and who had begged to be assigned to Michael as his bodyguard and had in turn been assigned to bring us hot water for tea.

"The machine is giving us a blessing in the coming battle," our leader pronounced.

"Michael," I said, "it is broken. It is not capable of making up any other numbers. If you strap up one of these rats here and manage to avoid squeezing it to death, it will tell you its blood pressure is 120:80."

"Let's catch one and see!"

"Nonsense," I said.

He responded sarcastically: "That's what you need a white man for in your political party, to tell you what the numbers mean. Let me tell you something about numbers: the only good number is one that is dead or at least wounded.

"In fact I am going to remove three zeroes from the currency. I want a strong kwacha."

"Well, please don't try it on your blood pressure."

And so we continued until I was looking too exhausted for Charlotte's liking. I stumbled to the car in acute pain, chortling. Michael of course remained behind but we were one in resolve:

> *Is it not passing brave to be a king,*
> *And ride in triumph through Persepolis?*

(You don't often get Marlowe in African narrative but it is a plus when the opportunity occurs.)

Time passed and then one morning they picked up Michael in the *kasalanga* (a truck that ferries prisoners) and, after visiting all the prisons in search of accused persons, took him to court. His fellow defendants sang for him as the truck, an old 15-ton cattle transporter, bore him to yet another session of the unassailable state versus the unbailable former minister. What anyone expected I do not know, but suddenly an unexpected, hitherto unseen little man popped up in the witness box. In retrospect he looked for all the world like those small mammals on guard duty over a burrow, such as are used for advertising cornflakes the world over. The small mammal gave it as God's truth, and nothing but the truth, that Michael had been authorized to take the "borrowed" campaign vehicles on account of his being a "Friend of the System."

Without a sign of thought, the magistrate wielded his ancient splintered hammer and struck the cracked colonial-era hardwood block, after which the accused and the friends and followers of the acquitted uttered a deep sigh and left the courtroom. Michael clicked his fingers for some money and commenced peeling off 10,000 kwacha notes (to be "rebased" in due course) for his fellow passengers in the *kasalanga*. After leaving the court we drove in my car through the town center as pedestrians and motorists alike waved to us in a friendly way. Everyone knew Michael but they could not see quite yet the added zero that would pump our votes from 3 to 30 percent. But we were not in a skeptical mood. We told ourselves that 3 percent is a good start.

"What on earth," I asked, "is 'the System' and how do you qualify as its friend, Mr. Opposition candidate?"

"Ssshhh, do you ask a mongoose that has come to rescue you, where it came from?"

"A mongoose? Is that a Bemba saying? How long were you in the slammer?"

"Forty days," he answered, "Forty days and forty nights. Like Jesus."

I thought closer to twenty, and I said so.

"What is the use of twenty days and nights?" he demanded, "It has to be seven, twelve, or forty—or none. Thank you for the lift and now go home to your wife."

In passing, it may help the reader understand Sata-matics if I recount "the tale of the corrupt farmer." Levy Mwanawasa (the new president, the one who had just beaten us) became very fond of boasting about his achievements in the agricultural sector. Shortly after his release from imprisonment and already on the campaign trail, Michael attacked Levy as a corrupt individual with eight farms! Levy promptly convened a press conference where he attacked Michael in return, declaring that he, Levy, had only six farms (and was thus pure as morning dew).

"You see," Sata said to me, "the guy rises like a tiger fish to take that bait. He thinks he can defend six farms against eight to a group of people who do not know what one farm looks like."

Didn't make sense to me. But I had at least five years to figure it out.

I went home to seriously recuperate and keep track of time. After some number of days and nights I abandoned the wheelchair, the crutches, and the smokes. I assiduously applied myself to walking: first 20 paces, then 200, then 2,000 daily.

Over a period of, let's say, forty days and forty nights I felt I was recovered.

We had endured the worst passage of our journey and we could sense the flavor of the future, all airiness and light and the painless variety of laughter.

And never mind the System, wherever It lives, however It works. With luck, It will not even notice us.

Michael was extraordinarily well-known throughout the length and width of Zambia, and was as much a part of folklore as he was a part of the political zoo. How it worked I could not figure, but I observed. Children as young as two recognized him instantly and stood fixated in awe. In fact, such was his "charisma" or his "presence"—which are inadequate words—that people would hallucinate his appearance in their home or workplace. Reports of Sata sightings frequently came from different locations simultaneously. He was our own Elvis and Lord Lucan rolled into one. It is not easy to capture such a character in the written word, especially if he is one who enjoys reinventing his past to craft better stories.

As for me, I am the product of "white settlers," although both my parents had good credentials as "liberals" (sometimes known as "communists" in the nomenclature of the confused and far-off southern African 1950s). My father represented African interests in various forums and also Lusaka's voters as an MP in the parliament of the Central African Federation. Like many politicians the world over, I acquired my taste for electoral politics while still a child from politically minded parents and prominent visitors.

We lived in a sprawling Cape colonial style bungalow outside Lusaka; all the rooms opened on to deep verandas, which provided access to a robust garden nursed by three streams that in their turn enticed you to follow them into evergreen forest. An arbitrary explorer—say a boy with dogs and a shotgun—could find in this vined greenery evidence of abandoned experiments in building and exotic agriculture. All this, it seems, inspired a chorus of small birds and mammals, themselves no more than nature's toys, to be conspiring to distract the hunter from his task.

Uwaningila mumushitu tomfwa inswaswa. Do not listen too closely to noises in the *mushitu* (dense rain forest); they will distract you from your goal.

Back on the verandas I might suddenly find myself face-to-face with prominent freedom fighters or nationalist "terrorists" of the day—Kenneth Kaunda, Harry Nkumbula, Simon Kapwepwe—needing my father's help or just somewhere comfortable to confer. Today they all have six-lane highways, international airports, and secondary schools named after them. One day I came back from the forest and found a gorgeous red-haired lady who introduced herself as Barbara Castle and her mission as the destruction of the British Empire. I could only gaze in wonder and take it for granted that this was a worthwhile objective. Wow, what hair!

Most communication with the outside world was by way of early electronics: the BBC news was miraculously accessible to people such as my father, who was prepared to put his ear to a huge loudspeaker and imitate the attentive dog of "His Master's Voice." The main machine was connected to wires festooned through the gum trees as well as tractor batteries to keep all those valves warm. You had to learn to ignore sounds like those made by manic electronic hyenas (real? imaginary?). We were also served by a "party line" telephone, number A3, with a ringing tone of three short rings. One day I answered it and was challenged to a duel by someone who turned out to be an angry Italian. My father had publicly denounced the federal policy of banning blacks working for the railway from ascending to the responsible position of engine driver. The state would import Italians and Greeks to do this job. The Italian man on the phone wanted to kill him, once he had chosen his weapon. My mother took the phone and explained that they were threatening her bambino and that she would call the police and that she was anyway a good shot and my father had no intention of dying like a Russian poet.

In retrospect, and before the election, it was obvious in the late months of 2001 that Michael and I had hit the wall—although in different places—in the multiparty democratic political system that had prevailed in Zambia for the previous ten years; we were now both gasping for air, if not dying in the water. What could be more obvious? The country's outgoing president Fredrick Chiluba had (to use his own soccer metaphor) "dribbled" Michael and prevented him from becoming head of the ruling party—and thence the next president of the country. (Like most Zambians—except Michael—Chiluba was a huge soccer fan. He reportedly sent ministers warning letters on yellow State House letterhead. I never got one, though, and my letter of dismissal was not red. He later likened his political skill in getting rid of his opponents as "dribbling." For the uninitiated, a yellow card in soccer is a warning, and a red card gets you sent off the pitch; dribbling involves using tricks and superior skill to retain control while getting the ball past your opponent.)

I had meanwhile hunted high and low for influence in the political world, having been comprehensively dribbled much earlier by the same cunning Fred. However, once he had accepted that he could no longer play the ball all by himself, Michael went back to basics. He phoned my home and got Charlotte on the line. "Tell your husband to come here," he growled.

I decided to join his secretly conceived and newly born political party and help him head for hegemony. I took about two weeks to wrap up my chores as a nonaligned "political consultant." Our new party was called the Patriotic Front. A boat was chosen for its symbol, ostensibly Noah's Ark, complete with dove and olive branch. (However, village voters found our picture of the ark incomprehensible, so we had the artists metamorphose it into a dugout canoe. Cartoonists needed no prompting to add dove-droppings.)

And then? Can I remember?

Just under ten years later I drove through the hallowed gates of State House to the smiles and cheers of the guards. As I found and entered the right room I was castigated roughly thus: "You, white man, late as usual, what would you be if you were not white? I think you would be dancing for coins outside the Post Office."

"Perhaps I would be president, Sir?"

"That job is taken. But I will give you the next one down. Pick up a Bible, read this sheet of paper and then sign it. Your *Honour* the Vice President, *Sir*."

What could I say?

"Thank you, your Excellency. I believe I am the only white vice president in sub-Saharan Africa. This is a tribute to your nonracial approach to nation-building."

"My foot," he replied, "I just want to destroy Obama's monopoly as the only black president in the world with a *mzungu chola* boy [white person bag-carrier]. And you'll do."

The diplomats present, including the US ambassador, laughed not entirely heartily; they were not sure in what spirit the words were uttered. Since this is a book whose author is striving to impart clarity in murky areas, I will seek to explain.

In Zambia the practice of *chimbuya* is widespread. When used literally as "cousin" it is no more nor less than it sounds; "I want you to fly to London tonight and bury your *mbuya* Mrs. Thatcher on my behalf" is plaintext. Coded, the word is translated in the academic literature as "traditional cousinship" or "teasing cousinship." Tribes or groupings of tribes who have fought each other and stolen each other's women and cattle in the distant past have considerable license to insult each other without usually provoking anything beyond a mocking response. It is said that if you find yourself in court, your most earnest hope should be that the judge is your "cousin," your *mbuya*. He will treat you more leniently even than a member of your own tribe will. That is the theory.

Marriage across tribal lines is common; a good place to observe *chimbuya* is at a wedding party in which the bride and groom are tribal cousins. Recently I was present at such a wedding reception for a bride who was a member of the Sala tribe, which is a component of the Tonga or "three tribes" grouping. The master of ceremonies was a Lozi from the groom's side. Constant jibes were aimed across the divide: "I will ask the band to play slowly so the Tongas can keep in step," "extra meat is available if you show your registration card proving that you are Tonga," and so on.

Chimbuya is easy enough to understand, but when practicing it, take care! This morning's paper, it just so happens, bears a photograph of a Bemba schoolteacher, handcuffed to a tree for attempting to play *chimbuya* with Paramount Chief Mpezeni of the Ngoni tribe. The two tribes are cousins, and one of the standard lines of mockery relates to the eating of monkeys by the Bemba versus the eating of field mice by the Ngoni. The formal mode of address to Mpenzeni is *Nkosi wama kosi,* "King of All Kings." The word for "rat" in both languages is *koswe.* The Bemba had greeted him with the pun *Koswe wama koswe,* "Rat of All Rats." Normally this might pass as a good joke, but Mpezeni was not in the mood for such a thing. He was still recovering from a tear gas attack by riot police who had broken up a meeting of Ngoni chiefs and subchiefs to discuss issues of contention with government. Lesson: before you open your mouth, try and be sure that you understand both the culture and the politics, as well as the neurological impact of a recent tear gassing on someone's sense of humor.

Zambian journalists, well acquainted with the *chimbuya* genre, used to laugh at Michael's and my cousinship jokes at public meetings or press conferences, but never bothered to publish them. Foreign journalists, alas, sometimes produced stories around "black president insults white veep" or vice versa. I tried to warn Michael of this source of misunderstanding but he ignored me. So far as he was concerned, all whites, nay all humans, were his cousins and he stuck to this position until his dying day. Visitors to Zambia's State House displayed variable rates of adaptation to learning they were Michael's cousins. I remember a high-powered delegation from Barclays Bank being totally bemused by Michael attacking me for being a racist when I complained about high interest rates for corporate agriculture. I attacked him back and the English bankers were plainly embarrassed. Conversely, George W. Bush, accompanying his wife, Laura, on a visit to her cervical cancer charity in Zambia, got in on the game very quickly. He had me nailed as a "scaly old dude" before I even had time to look up a few sayings from my Texican dictionary.

Back to my appointment as vice president. I declined to answer Charlotte's phoned queries as I guided my new motorcade to our farm. It took eight minutes from door to door without too much use of the sirens. The drivers and the security detail engaged in a constant advisory dialogue over the walkie talkies: "Mike Poppa at the lights!" "Charlie Charlie!"

"Who is Mike Poppa?" I asked.

"It means Mad Person, your honor.

"Charlie Charlie?"

"It just means 'copied' or 'Roger.'"

"How do you describe a road like this?"

"Shit, sir."

"What's all this?" Charlotte asked as our numerous scruffy dogs scrambled to make their mark on the sudden plague of new car wheels. "Don't tell me you're the VP!" We fell in each other's arms with the tears that mark the successful culmination of a long journey.

There was a surge of international media interest in the phenomenon of a white vice president in an independent African state. It was brief mainly because there was none of the controversy that contemporary journalism requires. Virtually no Zambian, not that I knew of anyway, disapproved my appointment on racial grounds. Most folks on the street shrugged and asked: so what? And why should you care if he is white if we don't? How do you make a controversy out of that? Go and hover with your microphone elsewhere.

The terms of reference of a vice president vary from country to country in line with constitutions and unwritten traditions. Generally, as the title implies, it is a supportive role to an executive president who may delegate responsibilities or not, according to whim. This has caused some to question the importance of the job; the most notable skeptic being one-time US VP John Nance Garner, whose scatological description of the job is easily found via Google.

So far as I can see, Michael had chosen me as VP for two major reasons. The first is that I had worked hard and earned the position. My involvement in the ten-year campaign was a key ingredient in PF's coming to power, and voters would seriously question my being sidelined. Indeed, Michael had promoted me to VP of the party four years earlier. Such an argument is not decisive in political reasoning, however, and I figure Michael also had something extra—a message he wanted to send to the world—perhaps a message concerning the need to end the sterile debate about color, colonialism, guilt, and compensation. The point was not that he too could appoint "technocrats" or minority representatives as Chiluba had already done with me, and as Robert Mugabe and others had often done, but that he could actually use a white as an emblem of the state. It added to his pride that what he was doing was decades ahead of South Africa, the self-styled trendsetter in our neck of the woods.

So those who criticized my posting as "ceremonial" missed the mark: that is precisely what it was intended to be. Never mind my day job in charge of famine risks and other looming disasters; never mind my leadership of parliament; never mind my use of convening power to

Official White House photograph by Amanda Lucidon

At the White House with Barack and Michelle Obama, attending the US-Africa Leaders' Summit, 2014

achieve joined-up government. Yes, I had power, and I enjoyed using it. But my primary function was to represent Zambia, as delegated by the Boss, and make Zambia stand out from the crowd of "can't quite remember which one that is" African countries.

Michael Sata was a delegator indeed. I danced with the Obamas on his instructions (alas stepping on the first lady's foot without his authority while getting down to Lionel Richie). I flew tens of thousands of miles around the world surrounded by pistol-packing bodyguards on the strength of his signature. To obey him, I was sleepless in Sri Lanka, baffled in Bolivia, and confused in Korea (North—he kept South for himself). As the official embodiment of the Head of State, I descended into hundreds of Zambian villages on a Chinese helicopter—sometimes with a door having fallen off in flight—to make promises and garner support for our party in by-elections. I can proudly say I did a good job of detribalizing voting patterns across the west of the country, in particular.

Mario Cuomo allegedly said, "You campaign in poetry, but govern in prose." I am not sure I can explain or teach poetry, but I am certain you cannot argue with it. There are other ways of describing the "emotional intelligence" content of political campaigning. Joyce Banda, the former two-year president of Malawi, described campaigning in her country as "falling in love with the voters and persuading them to fall in love with you." Unfortunately for her, she fell short of being reelected as only the second female president in Africa, despite the insight. Michael and I, during interminable outings on the campaign trail, decided to restructure the PF's campaign content and strategy along the lines of a Catholic church service: 50 percent music, 25 percent promises you can't quite guarantee to fulfill and 25 percent threats you certainly cannot enforce.

Sorry, Your Grace, only joking!

The bit about governing in prose has its meaning, but it should not be taken as justification for removing the fire from political activity and replacing it with whatever keeps bureaucrats warm. And when all is said and done, effective governing itself is part of campaigning for the next election. So while part of this book treats some of the "technical" aspects of running an African government technically, it is nowhere neglectful, I hope, of the emotional or poetic aspects that feed into policymaking and popular support.

A challenge for me with electoral poetry was that I did not speak Bemba, the language in which we were mostly campaigning. But I persevered with learning many of the subtle sayings to which the language has given birth. I have scattered some of our favorites liberally throughout this book because I cannot resist them either. Please note that I famously even invented one myself.

Alas, the fairy tale of the accession of a once-upon-a-time porter at Victoria railway station to state president by dint of sheer energy, cheek, and charisma lasted just over three years. Then Michael died, not far from the same Victoria station. We will find the body ahead.

We started with a mistake—it would be very un-Zambian to get it right straightaway. To a question regarding how far back we have to go to find a white president in Africa, I responded "to the Phoenicians," a pretentious reference to a pre-Christian Semitic civilization that hung out in the Mediterranean and circumnavigated Africa. The word was reported by a *Telegraph* reporter as "Venetians" and circumnavigated the earth by email, and we were all mocked. One newspaper ventured an apology to the effect that it is a good thing on my part that I read T. S. Eliot. I shut up and said nothing. It happens I found the Phoenicians strutting their stuff in a novel by Wilbur Smith (b. 1933 Broken Hill, then Northern Rhodesia, now Zambia). Thanks, man.

Upon Michael's death, the Zambian Constitution elevated me to the job of acting president. Contrary to some poor reporting and mud-stirring, there were no two ways about it. There was some political waffle to the effect that the Constitution was being wrongly interpreted, but not a single legal authority without political interests took that position, and neither did the chiefs of the security forces. So now I became the only white president in sub-Saharan Africa, though without much real power to counter the disorderly scrapping for succession that immediately broke out. This short-lived promotion provided the *Economist* with one of its more amusing punning headlines: "White Man, Burdened" (4 October 2014). Indeed, there was another brief media feeding frenzy about me, but after a couple of gaffs, subsequent severe reprimand from Charlotte, and some timely, firm advice from her sister Stephanie, I cut off communication with most of the international press. With tensions so high, trouble could easily arise from sensational and inaccurate reporting intended to amuse foreign readers—but it was potential dynamite when recycled into Zambian discourse, most especially by word of mouth and via social media.

The Constitution required that I act for no more than ninety days, within which an election was to be held to replace the dead president through the ballot.

THE DIFFICULT INTERREGNUM IS over, new leadership is in place, and I no longer have my job. Reasonable people have congratulated me on keeping the peace, while some who feel shortchanged think I should have done it differently. One helpful person volunteered a heavily annotated copy of *Hamlet*. I think it is fair to say that Zambian political affairs are returning to the condition they were in before Michael Sata (with whatever help I could give him) tried to change the game forever. But it is too soon to judge whether there will be another upbeat and interesting political story to tell about our country or not. Meanwhile, this is the story of Michael Sata, PhD (well, I will explain the degree), and his campaign and government. In both of these I am proud to have played my part.

Let's borrow some words from my Zambian literary heroine, Namwali Serpell, the winner of the Caine Prize for African Writing.

One of the most insidious forms of prejudice is the inability to see beyond one's own understanding of what prejudice even looks like. Consider the media flurry over the death on Tuesday of Michael Sata, the fifth president of Zambia. Major news outlets—the BBC, al-Jazeera and CNN—have dutifully reported the facts: Sata, who concealed his terminal illness for months, was known as King Cobra for his vitriolic tongue; his politics entailed aggressive, sometimes racially inflected, jabs at ruling and infiltrating powers (the Zambian elite, the Chinese); he did some good, he did some bad; he fell short, he will be missed. But most of these reports have also placed curious emphasis on Sata's vice-president, Guy Scott, who will now step in as interim president for the 90-day period mandated by the constitution before a general election is held.

Untimely presidential death by illness has happened in Zambia before, as recently as 2008. When Levy Mwanawasa died halfway through his second term, the vice-president, Rupiah Banda, stepped in and won the interim election. So why is the world so interested in this old story from this young country? Well, as the BBC put it: "Zambian President Sata death: White interim leader appointed."

Yes, Vice-President Scott is white—or what Zambians call, with a measure of fond condescension, a muzungu. He is the "first white president in Africa in 30 years," some say; "well, since South Africa's FW de Klerk," others report with a meaningful look; "Oops, ahem, sorry, the first one since Mauritian prime minister Paul Berénger," still others hasten to correct. Cue collective eye-rolling from Zambians at home and abroad.

As Scott said when he was elected in 2011: "I have long suspected Zambia is moving from a postcolonial to a cosmopolitan condition." Or, as a (black) Zambian tweeted yesterday: "OH MY GOD our interim president is white! Do not chat to me about Africa not being progressive."

But of course the UK, blinded by the paternalistic mists of postcolonial guilt, would worry about a backslide. And the US, which only sees in black and white, would find this state of things confusing. Instead of recognising, as the internet does, that Scott's position is a sign of political progress akin to the US election of a minority president, the mainstream media seems to be carrying that double-bladed hatchet of racial anxiety. Scott's interim position must be either a sign of black passivity or a harbinger of the threat that always hovers behind a black majority: the spectre of the black crowd, its riots and rampage and rage.

No matter that Guy Scott was born in Livingstone (in what was then Northern Rhodesia) and is a Zambian citizen. No matter that Scott has been our white Zambian vice-president for three years, or that Sata's death and Scott's constitutionally stipulated succession has been on our minds since Sata was first rumoured to be ill many months ago. No matter that Scott has been a major political player since the 1990s, shifting from party to party until he ended up in the Patriotic Front (PF) as Sata's running mate. The two men were already actual mates. An unlikely pair—Scott a PhD with a scathing sense of irony; Sata an outspoken populist with a reputation for stepping on toes—they spent more than a decade building the PF together and shared genuine respect. As Scott put it in a Guardian interview in 2013: "Michael's very clever, he knows people tend to regard him as a racist because he talks rough. He's usually tried it out on me already. He says things like, 'What would you be if you weren't white?' I said, 'The president?' That shut him up." Scott lost a friend as well as a president on Tuesday night. (Serpell, 2014)

There are many intelligent and well-informed people who have no idea where Zambia is, let alone how it is. We citizens sometimes like to boast that we are such a remote country that World War I lasted nearly a week of extra time thanks to poor communications. But there is or was another less amusing handicap. During the freedom wars of the second half of the twentieth century, Zambia was demonized by white suprema- cists in the south as the epicenter of "the Black North," a hot, violent, and disease-ridden land, full of terrorists. The manager of an animal res- cue center in Zimbabwe once refused to allow the wife of a senior UN diplomat in Lusaka to adopt a stray dog on the grounds that he could not permit a dog to endure the horrors of Zambia.

So I have taken it as my responsibility to give more background information than the reader well versed in Zambian matters might require. Some newcomers may even conclude, as have many others, that Zambia is one of the world's better kept secrets. (Though some colonial officers came to call it MMBA—a Million Miles of Bugger All—so we are not all in agreement.)

Last, let me confess that we were not, of course, just two of us even at the start. From the very beginning there were people who were already or quickly became supporters of and believers in Michael; some arrived some days ahead of me. There was Paul Lumbi, who was brought up with him in the domain of a left-wing British district commissioner; and Edgar Lungu, the future president (2015 until date as yet unknown), made-for-destiny, who stood for parliament in 2001 on a PF ticket. He came eighth in the Chawama constituency but he at least flew the flag in the faces of the mockers.

There were many who devoted their own time and money and ingenuity to organizing the Patriotic Front at various points in its ten-year battle for power. Michael was the commander and I his deputy. As former cabinet ministers, we were the two best-known and noisiest members of a venture that succeeded where many others, with apparently far better initial prospects, sank beyond the point of possible salvage.

Wise Bemba Sayings for the Campaigner in Poetry

In *modern* Bemba orthography, the sound usually denoted by "b" in writing is a three-way cross between "w," "v," and "b"—with the relative strengths in the mixture depending upon various factors. Thus, the word "bebele" is pronounced close to "vevele" by actual members of the Bemba tribe, while nonmembers may describe the tribe as the "awemba." There is no "r" sound in Bemba. The sounds rendered by "ng" and "nd" leading a vowel are as in "sing" and "sand."

Uwaningila mumushitu tomfwa inswaswa. Do not listen too closely to noises in the mushitu (dense rain forest); they will distract you from your goal. That is, do not pay attention to small distractions.

Kwindi ngaakokola alya namukasuba. Or Koswe nga akokola (munganda), alya nakasuba. The rat that stays (in the house) too long, eats even in broad daylight. Normally this is taken as a reference to relatives who stay too long and take over your house, but also used to refer to someone who has stayed in power too long and becomes corrupt. One urban version features a rat that changes the TV channels.

Sebana wikute. Necessary gratification without dignity. Loosely: A man has to do what a man has to eat. Even more loosely: Eating in the toilet.

Kolwe angala pa musamba anashya. The monkey plays on the branch that is familiar to him. A person when teasing tends to pick on someone who is used to being teased by him. More insightfully: you cannot joke with a person you do not know. If you watch vervet monkeys letting off energy, you will see that this saying also incorporates an accurate naturalistic observation.

Shaupwa bwino. I did not marry well. A witty apology for poor clothing or equipment (e.g., a cheap cell phone).

Elyo lwanya. Approximately: Now (a very large amount of) shit is about to be encountered.

Umuchinshi tabalomba. Respect cannot be imposed—it must be earned.

Ulelosha tabamucheba ku kanwa. Do not hold a man to account for what he says when you can see his face is twisted in grief.

Alanda elyo atontonkanya. He speaks and only then thinks.

Kuya bebele. They must go. The MMD (opposition party) slogan in 1991 against (ruling party) UNIP: "To go is a must."

Donchi kubeba. Don't kubeba. Do not tell them. This is my personal contribution to the Bemba language, meaning "it is only the vote that counts; you don't have to say how you are voting. Just accept all the bribes they give you." It became the title of a smash hit song.

Uwakwensha ubushiku bamutasha ilyo bwacha. How well you have been led in the night is apparent only when the sun comes up. Then you can praise or condemn the one you have been following.

Ukuteka mbwa mano. If you do not have the sense to feed it, even a dog will abandon you. Normally wedding advice to the wife about feeding the groom, it is also used to warn against driving away political allies.

2

The Plucky Little Devil

LET ME MOVE THE NARRATIVE BACK TEN YEARS, TO THE END OF 1991, when I was appointed by President Chiluba to the Ministry of Agriculture, Food, and Fisheries. While still trying to get my bearings as minister by walking around the vast Yugoslav-style building serviced by virtually zero water or waste disposal, I noticed a fair trickle of white men and a few women sniffing their way around the ministry building as soon as the doors opened each morning. They were predominantly dressed in khaki pants and shirts and were driving light pickup trucks. It seemed they were finding what they wanted, leaving after an hour or so with hope written on their faces. Enquiry revealed that their target within the ministry was the office of one of my deputy ministers. This, it turned out, was being operated as a clearing-house for foreigners looking for farmland in our Texas-sized country. Further enquiry revealed that they were paying a commitment fee as a guarantee of their "seriousness" in the hunt for land to settle and farm.

Huh!? Without me knowing??

There were few possibilities regarding identities of these people. I strolled out into the parking area and joined a group that was returning to their vehicle (all smiles). Two women had a lit a gas burner in the back of their truck and were preparing a camp breakfast—in a three-legged potkie pot—of maize meal and beef stew. When we each got a hot tin cup of coffee we walked back and up to my office (the lift was not working, nor any toilet, I distinctly remember about this solemn historic moment).

17

They passed without delay under the professional gaze of my secretary, Mercy, an air force widow who voluntarily acted as my public relations agent.

"You have come to the right place," she announced, "my boss knows everything and everyone."

"Well, gentlemen, you seem to have left your oxen behind. What happened?"

I am quite ashamed today of treating my guests sarcastically amid all that hope and scarcely suppressed enthusiasm. This was the South African radical right wing, in the flesh, pleading for hope and redemption from the government of *Zambia*. Some were so desperate, or perhaps just so devoid of irony, that they had not even completely torn the "AWB" badge off their khaki shirts. This wave of near-refugees—which continued for some months—was not a simple commercial "rush" for access to the warm earth; it was something more mystical than mere business and real estate; their quest was a sort of spiritual reboot of the Great Trek. And thus the search was not for a farm here and a farm there, one for you and one for me, mingled with the generally underutilized patches of gentle well-watered soils. It was a deferred search for a unified (if miniaturized) country—a replica of the original homeland—gone missing perhaps during childhood. Of course there were exceptional individuals or the odd corporation interested in doing business outside the *mythos*, led by the profit and loss account but these were not part of the mainstream. The majority, the true Boers, were trekkers engaged in a search for something held together in a shared dream. What they sought, I was told by their leaders, was quite frankly that their venture would culminate in at least one Dutch Reform Church central structure, adherent to Afrikaner traditions and language (above all language), morals, and culture, smiling on the seemingly endless *mealie* (maize) fields of Neuew Zambie.

"But what is your problem in the Old Transvaal?"

"We have released Mandela and the blacks have taken over the country," they explained. "We have to queue up with them in the banks and the co-ops."

"But the blacks have taken over here quite some time back, you will find. Mercy will take you shopping and show you how we do it without discrimination."

"Ah yes, but they are not the same blacks. We have never had to queue with our blacks; they knew us before . . . "

I am sorry, I told them, but you cannot set up your own country here just to avoid standing in line with people you have never met

before. You would have more luck on Mars. I am not even taking it to
cabinet as a note for information.

Where can we go? Congo? Mozambique? Kenya? Help us, Doctor!

Oddly, after all their vain effort, and the lack of sympathy, they
invited me to be guest of honor at the South African Fertilizer Association (the manufacture and sale of fertilizer is a largely Afrikaner-run
industry in SA). They kept toasting me in Cape champagne.

"You tried," someone said.

Who me? What did I try?

At one point in southern African history it looked as if the "Great
Trek"—actually a series of ox-wagon caravans big and small—would
lead to the occupation of the areas that became known as Rhodesia
(north and south). By 1850 or so, numerous Boers had decamped from
British authority and had effectively delineated two new countries—the
Transvaal and the Orange Free State. There was no obvious end in sight
to the expansion. Winding the time machine back and letting it run in
this expansionist mode, we would surely bet on the Boers as winners.
Even if the Brits managed to hold *southern* Rhodesia, the north would
surely become the Republic of Trans-Zambezi, stretching from the massive Kruger Falls—the world's largest waterfall—to the German East
African territory. But it did not happen that way. Why?

David Livingstone was probably not even the first white person to
trudge successfully through the Kalahari, to beyond the Big River, enter
what is now Zambia—and live to report on it. There are stories of
Afrikaner hunting parties going as far as the Zambezi—and reporting
the falls' existence—long before Livingstone got there. And in around
1850 the Portuguese were busy trying to build a bridge of human settlement connecting Angola and Mozambique stretching slap bang across
Zambia-to-be. It is hard to believe a clear picture of the falls was not
already in some private sketchbook.

But, whether the first or the tenth, Livingstone entered his and our
country-to-be on all three of his major African expeditions and finally
died here, ostensibly looking for the source of the Nile. This was some
two years after he was found by the journalist Henry Morton Stanley
whose actual words of greeting are not known—the famously understated presumption (Dr. Livingstone, I presume?) being concocted
later by a junior editor in Chicago. I was born in the town named after
Livingstone on the northern side of the Zambezi River, opposite the
Victoria Falls. The city retains its name today, and likely will for a
very long time, since almost nobody whose opinion matters seems to
have any issues with Livingstone and his waterfall, whatever may be

the case with the other famous pioneering white man, Cecil Rhodes, Man of Many Statues.

I had always assumed young David, on arrival in South Africa, hit the ground running, disembarking at Cape Town, heading north to be tutored by Robert Moffat in arts essential to the well-prepared missionary-adventurer. It seems he lost no time in acquiring Moffat's twinkling and immensely brave daughter (the image of her father), before marching forth into the dark interior. There is speculation that Livingstone had been rejected in England by the love of his life and married Miss Moffat on the rebound in desperation. Well, there is a lot of speculation about David and his motives.

It took Livingstone ten years to make his first "serious" incursion into the Kalahari Desert (i.e., beyond Boer country) and thence into the rainy flood plains and savannah that are today located in and around Zambia. During the decade of what might be called preparation, he engaged vigorously with the burning political issues of the day in South Africa.

One of these concerned the wars that arose as white settler responses to purported black uprisings whose consequence was inevitably the defeat and dispossession of the native inhabitants—all at the expense of the British government. The view of missionaries, who found that they could travel unimpeded through areas where these wars were supposed to be raging, was that they were fraudulent. Many British South Africans—including the famous governor Sir Harry Smith—struggled to bring justice and hard facts to the fore but the settlers had friends in London. The vocal opposition of the likes of Livingstone did not make him popular with the British settlers.

But his disagreement with the "English," as he described both the British and himself, was a mild matter compared to his open hostility to the "Boers" settled in the frontier area beyond the Vaal River, known until recently as the Transvaal. He seems to have wanted a fight—and he got one.

Livingstone hung up his shingle, as doctor and missionary alike, near the river Kolobeng. The site of his settlement and mission, called Livingstone-Kolobeng, is nowadays a private secondary school, and it is just inside Botswana thanks to minor adjustments in boundaries.

Livingstone in his first diary takes surprisingly modern politically correct care to avoid lumping all Boers together. He distinguishes between the Dutch Cape settlers who he deems a "sober, industrious, and most hospitable body of peasantry," and those, in contrast, "who have fled from English law on various pretexts, and have been joined by English deserters and every other variety of bad character in their distant localities, are unfortunately of a very different stamp. The great objection many of the Boers had and still have to English law is that it makes no distinction between black men and white."

Livingstone gives us a brief description of the capture of slaves by Boer raiding parties, just in case we are skeptical that we are dealing with "real" slavery:

> one or two friendly tribes are forced to accompany a party of mounted Boers. . . . When they reach the tribe to be attacked, the friendly natives are ranged in front, to form, as they say, "a shield"; the Boers then coolly fire over their heads till the devoted people flee and leave cattle, wives and children to the captors. This was done in nine cases during my residence in the interior. (Livingstone, 1900)

Livingstone encountered a range of obstacles to his aim of opening up the interior of southern Africa to the Western world of the mid-nineteenth century. Apart from the financial hurdles, these impediments included human and animal diseases that threatened to kill him along with his companions and their transport animals; the dryness of the Kalahari Desert, accentuated by decades of drought; and the hostility of many tribes and other population groups. Of these last, the *Trek Boers* in the Transvaal region were one of the most problematic at the beginning of his adventures. They were against any British traders and missionaries living at the northern-most limit of white settlement in South Africa and going on into the unsettled Kalahari Desert beyond. They feared such interlopers would become the forerunners of British rule from Cape Town, which had already "forced" them to migrate from the Cape by banning the capture and keeping of indigenous people as slaves. As the colonization of Rhodesia and the Jameson Raid later showed, the Boers indeed had grounds to be uneasy about imperial Britain.

But our feisty Glaswegian, unable to resist the temptation of throwing down a challenge, declaimed:

> The Boers resolved to shut up the interior, and I determined to open the country, and we shall see who have been most successful in resolution—they or I.

Ironically it was a Boer attempt to expel Livingstone that provided the sharpest spur to his move into the desert and thence into the moist interior of central-southern Africa. The Boers blamed him, wrongly he says, for arming and teaching the local Bakwain people to use firearms and thus resist slave raiding. The Boers uttered threats against him and his family. As a result, when he embarked upon his first trip from Kolobeng in the direction of the Zambezi in 1850 he took his entire family—his wife (pregnant) and three young children—with him. This was a precaution against them coming to harm at the hands of Boer neighbors if he left them in their home. His hope was that he would be able to settle with his family among friendly people and in a healthy area. (His fourth child, Elizabeth, was born but died after the expedition came back to Kolobeng). Upon returning, under a heavy hail of criticism for risking the lives of his family, he took them to the coast and dispatched them to Britain.

Returning from his "orphaning" of his children (the eldest was only six), the missionary found that the Boers had attacked his settlement with a force of 600 men in the so-called Battle of Dimawe; sixty Bakwain died resisting the Boers who had burned Livingstone's house down, killed his watchmen, and destroyed his library and his stock of medicines.

The Boer farmers who raided the settlement stole cattle, wagons, and women, but through the command of Sechele, the Bakwain successfully defended their own settlement. But the raid and the ongoing drought caused unrest among the Bakwain so they left the area of Boer settlement.

The trigger for the Battle of Dimawe seems to have been the Sand River convention, in which the British divested themselves of responsibility for events north of the Vaal and effectively gave the Boers independent status. But they did not cripple the limbs of the missionaries—the lowland Scottish mafia as it might be called today. The mutual mistrust between the English and the Boers lived long. In 1929 General Jan Smuts, the South African statesman who did much to bring the British and the Boers together after the Boer War (1898–1902), spoke in Scotland:

> I once took the opportunity to discuss the matter with President Kruger, and his explanation of the differences which arose between the Boers and Livingstone was that Gordon Cumming—another of your errant countrymen—had supplied the border tribes with rifles and ammunition in exchange for ivory, and the Boers, finding the natives armed, concluded—erroneously—that Livingstone had done so, and treated him accordingly. (Smuts, 1930)

Did Smuts really think he was telling the truth or was he consciously chipping away at the grounds for Boer hatred of the British—an agenda item that overrode all considerations of fact for him? But Livingstone moved on: "Yet, after all, the plundering only set me entirely free for my expedition to the north, and I have never had a moment's concern for anything I left behind" (Livingstone, 1900).

It strikes me that, apart from his own determination and that of his competent and frequent traveling companion, the English big game hunter William Cotton Oswell, Livingstone was at several advantages over the Boers in driving a permanent pathway to the Zambezi. Oswell nicknamed him "the plucky little devil" and the explorer reciprocated by naming his own son William Cotton Oswell Livingstone. Livingstone was equipped, for example, with an accurate chronometer and star maps that enabled him to determine his longitude with an accuracy not too far off a modern handheld GPS. (He took lessons from the southern royal astronomer, Sir Thomas Maclear, with whom he spent many hours in his coastal observatory, becoming familiar with the nocturnal southern sky and learning how to correct calculations that were in error.)

Livingstone's first breakthrough into the fertile heartland of Africa was achieved with good political and diplomatic handling of the people of the Kalahari Desert and across the upper Zambezi (diplomacy being by contrast not a Boer specialty). His venture was protected by well-organized armies and leaders, especially the Makololo king Sebituane who had migrated northward from the area now called Lesotho and invaded and settled what is now the Western Province of Zambia (sometimes called Barotseland). The Makololo were made up of a collection of small tribes who, like many other South African groups, were affected by the jostling for land triggered by the European colonial invasions. The Makololo proved capable of containing even the warlike Matabele and the Batoka tribe on the Zambezi. Thus Livingstone, for whom their chief Sebituane held evident affection, had access to the river, including Victoria Falls. In his own words:

> When Mr. Moffat began to give the Bible—the Magna Carta of all the rights and privileges of modern civilisation—to the Bechuanas, Sebituane went north, and spread the language into which he was translating the sacred oracles in a new region larger than France. Sebituane, at the same time, rooted out hordes of bloody savages, among whom no white man could have gone without leaving his skull to ornament some village. He opened up the way for me—let us hope also for the Bible.

Reading between the lines (Livingstone was in fact not very interested in bibles), it seems Sebituane's objectives were international in scope—he saw himself as a statesman to speak with foreign kings and queens—not as a potential subject but an equal.

Unlike several explorers before and after him, Livingstone did not shoot his way around Africa even when dealing with far-from-peaceable groups and their leaders. He had the advantage of being able to practice some medicine to good diplomatic effect, but what comes across clearly in his writings is his candid and friendly attitude to his interlocutors. They simply seem to have judged him as a good man and trusted him accordingly. Sebituane's opinion of Livingstone was greatly enhanced by the trust he displayed in traveling with his wife and three children through the desert on his trip to "discover" the middle Zambezi (well to the west of its suspected course) in 1850.

Livingstone has had more than his share of literary mauling by the "myth busters" of the twentieth century, who were conjured into being to puncture the original hagiographers. He has been accused of cavalier risk-taking with the lives of other whites (including most damningly his wife); he has been accused of being an ineffective missionary, perhaps not even a Christian; he has been expertly diagnosed as having bipolar disorder; he has been characterized as oversexed; and he has been accused of never discovering anything of importance. So if you have read all the books, you may be convinced we have on our hands a priapic, short-sighted, manic-depressive, crypto-pagan whose leadership qualities would have looked poor at, say, the contemporaneous Charge of the Light Brigade.

Perhaps, but our current interest has to do with his legacy, not with unknowable aspects of his personality. What we call human rights abuses today have been delicately downplayed by important actors. This is especially true of the slave trade, and we have seen the Boers (on Livingstone's definition) obtaining farm and domestic workers in what is now South Africa. And the slave trade was still very much alive in its commercial, international, "wholesale" form on both coasts (Mozambique and Angola) and throughout the land area between them. Portugal was highly active in this industry, despite being a signatory to treaties outlawing it, supplying African slaves to South America and the Caribbean; and Arab and mixed-race Zanzibari-controlled operations were likewise in full swing. The evil industry was far from winding down: indeed the most famous East Coast based slave trader, Muhammed Bin Hamid (Tippu Tip), was still in his teens as the middle-aged explorer got started on his exploratory life and war against slavery.

Livingstone lost little time in gaining the enmity of the Portuguese, saying: "Nothing can be done with the Portuguese—they are an utterly effete, worn out, used up, syphilitic race: their establishments are not colonies, but very small penal settlements" (Bayley, 2014). This must earn some kind of Guinness record for diplomatic blundering, given that Livingstone was at the time he wrote it the British consul in Central Africa. Though perhaps we should note in passing that the Scottish dialect of English is tightly coupled to the Scottish penchant for verbal abuse, and that it is quite difficult to be nice to anybody while using it.

It was Tim Holmes, author of *Journey to Livingstone* (unfortunately out of print) who first brought to my attention the problem of assessing the man's motives. Livingstone was not of the then widespread view that African people were intrinsically backward. He believed that foreign influences, primarily the intercontinental slave trade and associated abuses such as wars designed to yield up slaves, had undermined African society, showing up as a breakdown of basic morals and morale, self-respect, and self-confidence. In current times we might find an analogy with the highly cultured societies of the Middle East whose names were once bywords for civilization, but which today connote gratuitous cruelty, bombings, and ethnic-religious cleansing. From Livingstone's writings it is possible to argue that his primary mission was to restore peace, order, and dignity—and that his controversial espousal of "commerce" sprung from his observation that only legal unencumbered trade (albeit inclusive of ivory) would distract Tippu Tip's attention from human cargo. Livingstone makes this observation in the course of describing how even his friend Sebituane captured and surrendered a number of young boys to the Mambari slave-trading tribe (actually more of a mixed-race mafia than a bona fide tribe), in return for state-of-the art rifles that he believed he desperately needed to ensure his peoples' safety.

The stereotypical picture of Africa opening to the West as purely a matter of colonial invasion by ill-intentioned whites is under pressure from the few facts we have confronted already. The leading colonialists we have encountered are the Makololo, closely followed by the frontier Boers. The latter are also the leading purveyors of Christianity, in the racist and fundamentalist version of the Dutch Reformed Church. Livingstone (representing himself as "English") allied himself with Sebituane's campaign to impose what today would pass as good governance.

The excitement engendered internationally by Livingstone's travels, as well as his death and spectacular posthumous return journey to Britain in 1873, impelled thousands of imitators into the interior of Africa. Kenneth Kaunda, the first president of Zambia, famously declared that Livingstone "was the first African freedom fighter." As Zambian vice president, I attended a funeral in Harare and listened to Robert Mugabe giving an account of "mission boys," like himself, who in the days of white rule would keep their hats firmly on their heads when told by white shopkeepers or policemen to take them off. This infamous dictator—of whom there is inevitably more to come in this book—was crediting the missionaries with creating the belief in human dignity, the self-regard that underpinned the freedom fight that created Zimbabwe out of Rhodesia.

LAKE NYASA AND THE surrounding country now known as Malawi was "discovered" by Livingstone on his second expedition to the interior, which proceeded by boat upward from the mouth of the Zambezi, headed for the valley below Victoria Falls. As it happened, the Cabora Bassa gorge within Mozambique, which he had not examined in detail during his first expedition, proved impassable by boat, so he opted to turn north up the Shire (*she-ray*) River that, with some portage, let them on to the lake. Much enthusiasm was generated by the fact that the lake was accessible—in a manner of speaking—by boat from the sea. Unfortunately the Shire and some relevant stretches of the Zambezi are extremely broad, sandy, and shallow, and massive engineering works would be required to make them navigable to seagoing ships. The dream lived for many years, though, with Nsanje Port launched by President Bingu wa Mutharika of Malawi in 2010 in the company of Presidents Mugabe and Banda (then president of Zambia; more on him later). We are all still waiting for results, though, and progress hit the wall with Bingu's death in 2012. I think it's safe to say that we will never hear the strains of the hornpipe blowing in from the east.

The Scottish identification with Livingstone's lake was and still is strong. Livingstonia mission, in what is now Malawi, was established in 1894 by missionaries from the Free Church of Scotland. Earlier, "Wee Frees" had tried settling themselves along the edge of the lake, but they suffered too many deaths from malignant malaria (see Chapter 3). Without knowing why, they noted that malaria did not present such a problem at higher altitudes around the lake—and the final location of Livingstonia was sited three thousand feet up from the lake, on the side of the escarpment leading to the magical land of the Nyika plateau. Livingstone had much earlier recommended altitude as a prophylactic for malaria but for some reason dozens of Europeans died to prove his sagacity. We now know that altitude renders the environment too cold at night for the survival of the anopheles mosquito, the only effective vector of malignant malaria, as Ronald Ross in India was still a few years away from proving. It was ultimately the capacity to manage malaria through prevention and treatment that gave Livingstone his capacity to outrun the Boers and leave them cursing his name in the Transvaal.

Livingstone himself must have been infected with this disease many hundreds of times but he was protected by the Victorian wonder drug. It is not certain that it was the vicious malaria on the Bangweulu swamps that killed him (there is still some controversy as to the cause of death). Quinine is an extract from the cinchona tree indigenous to the New World. Although used to treat malaria in South America and Europe for centuries, a sufficiently pure and strong enough extract for African travel was not available until 1850—just in time for use as a prophylactic and treatment by Doctor Livingstone.

Tropical Africa was once nicknamed "The White Man's Grave," a grim acknowledgment of the lethal effects of *plasmodium falciparum,* the causative agent of what is usually distinguished from other species of the same family of bugs as malignant malaria or falciparum malaria. In fact there is one very obvious thing wrong with the nickname— malaria has killed and continues to kill many more black people than white ones. (Though note that some level of genetically transmitted resistance can be detected in a population that has some generations of exposure to it—thus there is a resistant core that may be small but is immune to extermination by the disease.)

Although the story regarding the transmission of "sleeping sickness" (trypanosomiasis) by insects (tsetse flies) was generally known by the time of Livingstone's first journey, the similar but more complex mode of malaria transmission was unknown and remained so until the turn of the century. The reason for the time difference seems to be the greater complexity of the life cycle of the plasmodium. Until the mosquito vectoring of malaria was established (in chickens as it happens) by Ronald Ross, the general belief was that malaria was transported and deposited in victims by the invisible "miasma" (the very "mal" + "aria" itself) that blanketed the ground in the night. The architectural response to this theory was to build housing on stilts so that the miasma could ooze harmlessly beneath the floorboards.

Houses incorporating this feature are still inhabited in Livingstonia today, though some people opine that the stilts were protection against snakes or scorpions or even lions. This proves people can quickly forget anything they once foolishly believed. You would never suspect that nature fooled them into constructing stilts as protection from bad air.

As already noted, mechanisms of resistance to malaria are found in populations that have lived for some generations with the disease. But these are disadvantageous in nonmalarial areas and rapidly disappear in a population that is not constantly confronted with the disease. Livingstone observed that the Sutu, pursuing their destiny moving northward, seemed to be succumbing to "the fever" that was unknown in their own country. Some decades later the Makololo invader-rulers themselves were decimated by the disease and were chased away by the "locals" with more exposure to malaria through their ancestral line.

Today, medication remains problematic to some extent, with strains of the plasmodium developing resistance to medicines as they are developed. Several drugs have psychological side-effects on some people taking them for prevention purposes, to the extent that several strange interventions in Zambian affairs by delegates from the World Bank and IMF have been ascribed to weekly prophylactic use of certain antimalarial drugs (sometimes referred to obliquely by a cryptic phrase such as "Ah! Of course: it's psycho Monday").

All in all, malaria has had two broad impacts upon the Zambian people. One is the reduction in life expectancy relative to those living in otherwise identical areas free of the disease. The misery caused by numerous child deaths cannot be understated, though antimalaria campaigns featuring diagnosis, treatment, and prophylaxis are frequent and quite effective.

The other impact upon the Zambian population is that malaria has protected it, over hundreds of years, from invasion and extermination by the kind of people who invaded, say, North America and left very few indigenous Americans alive. Just think: in a parallel world, a Zambia without malaria, a country the size of Texas, might be presided over by a parallel George Bush—or, oh my goodness, a Donald Trump—right this moment.

NOT EVERY BOER WHO wanted to move north of the Limpopo was content to be frustrated. In Zambia there are hundreds (but only hundreds) of Boers farming and raising families, accumulated over the decades. Some started as miners on contract on the Copperbelt or went into farming on saved or inherited money or the proceeds of hunting elephants. An intrepid researcher into Boer settlement in Zambia was Tim Holmes, the Livingstone historian whom we have already mentioned. He used to hammer his ancient Land Rover to remote stretches of partly cleared bush. When he died he was contemplating writing a book entitled "Boer Settlers of Zambia," and his first stage was to locate as many of them as possible. Once he stopped at a dilapidated gate and, before he could get to it, an old white man in shorts stepped into the road waving a 12-bore shotgun. "*Voetsak* man," he shouted, and with a sudden and unexpected blast of empathy for Greta Garbo, "I want to be alone."

Tim's investigations were fascinating. One farmer had a "routine" of coming to town only once in about twenty years—the mean lifetime of a John Deere tractor. Tim found him in an agricultural machinery shop in Cairo Road. The farmer was shocked to discover that in Lusaka the crew cut was nowhere to be found, the 1960s having disappeared, and even muscular white salesmen sported long Beatles-style hair. "I do not buy tractors from girls," he declared and left. We never got to the end of that story. Who was going to supply him?

One day Tim arrived on an isolated farm and, after prowling around, found the widow who owned the place and her twenty-ish son sitting patiently in a saloon car parked in the closed garage. The boy had never been to school but he knew enough English to explain what he and his mother were doing—they were insulating themselves from possible lightning strikes. Indeed there were some audible rumbles around, Tim told me, but nobody except an Afrikaner would shut themselves in a vehicle, in a building, on the edge of a bit of storm activity.

Just under fifty years later I found myself in a jet plane, my vice presidential party at the parking area of O. R. Tambo airport. Nothing happened for some time and I asked the steward what the problem was. "Lightning," he said, "we are not allowed to take off when it's about."

I have never found any other international airport in the world that subscribes to Boer physics.

In the 1970s I tried to isolate myself from politics involving foreign freedom movements in Zambia. I wanted to get on with enlarging my commercial interests, but the Rhodesians started bombing camps belonging to ZIPRA (the Zimbabwe People's Revolutionary Army, the freedom fighters associated with Joshua Nkomo's largely Ndebele political party, the Zimbabwe African People's Union). The procedure was nasty. The Rhodesian air force jets would first drop concussion bombs and then land ground troops from helicopters to kill as many concussed freedom fighters as they could find. Not everyone died, but it scattered the guerrilla survivors and further confused them. Some had lucky escapes but met unarmed motorists or ran on to commercial farms, typically terrified and armed to the teeth.

In short, travelers and farmers, black and white, were not uncommonly harmed in encounters with the shaken-up ZIPRA troops. The white farmers' Commercial Farmers' Bureau put up a loud howl of complaint directed at the government. The Boers were the loudest, or at least the most quotable; they threatened to destroy all the crops in the ground in order to starve ZIPRA out of the country (*I am not going to plant a pip!*) and called—in the farmers' magazine—for military action by Zambia against the "terrorists." And there was more noise. The Western press went bananas, writing about "scenes reminiscent of settlers demanding protection from the Mau Mau."

A group of international journalists warned me of the dangers in the situation. They happened to know that I happened to know many of the leaders of ZIPRA and ZAPU from my schooldays. Consequently, I became chairman and convenor of "peace talks," which concluded with an understanding that farmers and others would communicate with me by phone or radio when they had information or a threat from dispersed guerrillas, and I would in turn communicate with ZIPRA Military Police who would come and cope with their people.

It seemed to work quite well.

And I met the lightning lady. She did not say where her son had got to but she arrived at my office in her lightning-proof car, and reported that she had come to surrender some confiscated weapons. I put on my best patronizing face and opened the trunk. She had "confiscated" or otherwise indeed acquired the guns, ammunition, and rocket-propelled grenades—used and otherwise—of a platoon. She had locked herself in her house, which had been protected by very heavy diamond mesh to kept the grenades out. The windows and doors had been reinforced, but guerrillas had climbed on to the roof and started shooting down through the corrugated iron roof. She had returned fire with a 12-bore shotgun, aiming where she thought from the creaking sounds in the roof the attackers were. She may have winged one because the attack stopped. She collected the ordinance and brought it to me.

I think we were just lucky that Kaunda managed to keep his message about peace within Zambia audible for the duration. I persuaded the committee of the Commercial Farmers' Bureau to expel the chairman, a very aggressive Boer who made no bones about his support for the last of the whites in their *laager* (wagon encampment), even as a reliable means of making deterrent noises in the night.

Luckily, the membership of the CFB knew their chairman as a stroppy little bugger and a world-class *kakprater* (*prater* means talker; the rest you can add yourself) and the bureau expelled him unanimously (leaving as a mystery the reason why they voted for him in the first place). As he sucked his pipe up his hill on his *plaas* we used to remind ourselves that as a nation we liked Afrikaners. Had not Lusaka produced Corné Krige, the famous captain of the Springbok Rugby team? "Zambia produces the best Boers" was our slogan for a while.

3

"Northern Rhodesians"

UNDER THE MANAGEMENT OF THE REDOUBTABLE SURGEON DR. ROBERT Laws, Livingstonia developed an excellent school that took students from across southern Africa, not excluding South Africa, and also sent out "homegrown" missionaries—indigenous Africans—to neighboring countries. One David Kaunda was sent to Lubwa mission in the north of what is now Zambia and in the heart of "Bembaland." He was himself politically active in the Native Welfare movement, and passed this interest on to his son Kenneth—who of course became the first president of Zambia. "KK" thrived politically because he had support from Eastern Zambia (which is in tribal terms virtually identical to Malawi) side-by-side with support from the Bemba-speaking tribes who dominate much of northern Zambia as well as the political turbine of the Copperbelt.

My uncle Robert, my father's oldest brother, graduated as a surgeon in Glasgow and joined the medical team at Livingstonia in the 1890s, hoping to be exposed to advanced surgical challenges while still young. Many young Western doctors even today opt to work some years in Africa to get the accelerated medical experience. Unfortunately it appears that Dr. Laws was in the habit of keeping all the interesting cases to himself, so my uncle left, but not before inviting a fellow doctor, George Prentice, to visit the Scott family home when on leave in Scotland. Thus did George meet his wife-to-be, my auntie Agnes, better known as Moppy, a girl with a talent for driving a motorbike along bush paths between the Indian Ocean coast and Livingstonia, arguing that it was more efficient than being carried in a *machila* (a hammock carried by porters). George and family moved around the country, and he ended

31

his career as a missionary doctor (and a celebrated amateur conserva-
tionist and pre-dinosaur era paleontologist) in Fort Jameson, within
what is now Zambia.

It is part of my family's verbal history that Moppy employed as a
young "bottle washer" in the kitchen a teenager named Hastings Banda.
This is said to have been at the mission station in Kasungu. Although
the details are in dispute among historians, young Banda migrated to
South Africa and thence to the United States where he acquired a medical degree. He subsequently worked in Britain in private practice. Here
he revealed an extreme puritanical worldview, even denouncing the
Church of Scotland for permitting touching between dancing partners at
a convocation in Edinburgh. This was despite living with one of his
female and married patients. He returned to Nyasaland in time to
become the leader of the Malawi Congress Party and thence the first
president of Malawi, a post he held for more than thirty years.

With two alumni presidents totaling sixty years between them to its
credit, the Church of Scotland had done well, bearing in mind that they
started like so many missionaries and explorers as a bunch of amateurs
who knew no better than to pitch their tents on the shores of a low-lying
lake in the heart of anopheles country.

My father came out to visit his sister and promptly fell in love with
the country. He was both a doctor and a lawyer, and he expected to
inherit a reasonable amount of money. The country suited his fundamental goals in life, which were very similar to those of a political missionary in the Livingstone mold. His primary assumptions about the way the
world was, and should be, did not include a belief in God, which he had
abandoned during his time as a battlefield surgeon in the trenches of
northern France. Let us note again that in Livingstone's time, "opening
up" Africa required that one become a missionary, perhaps one specializing in medicine, though later you could just about make it for short
periods as a hunter, explorer, or seeker of concessions. For long-term
financing, medicine was pretty much the only game for adventurers who
needed the resources. These days your metaphysics are optional.

My father started two newspapers, one in partnership with David
Astor, the late London press tycoon (best known for *The Observer*).
These papers were aimed at black Africans and dealt with their aspira-
tions and associated political concerns (though one subscriber wrote to
commend the quality of the newsprint, remarking that it was excellent
for handrolled cigarettes).

In 1953 he was elected, by whites, Indians, and "coloureds" who
had the privilege of the vote, as independent Lusaka MP in the parlia-

ment of the Federation of Rhodesia and Nyasaland (aka the Central African Federation). This political abomination was an attempt by white settlers in the countries involved, but particularly Southern Rhodesia, to prevent the automatic attainment of independence and majority rule in the north, ultimately by making us all into one self-governing dominion.

Although only nine at the time, I recall with clarity accompanying my mother as she went to hang posters on tree trunks in what is now Independence Avenue in Lusaka. "Vote for Scott and Stop the Rot" sang one. Another was more subtle; it looked something like this:

PUT
DOCTOR
SCOTT
IN THE
FEDERAL
HOUSE

Doctor in the House was a best-selling novel, play, and musical of those days and an apparent advertisement for it (As a play? As a musical? As a film?) was designed to attract interest—the punters drew closer—only to reveal the political message. How could any kid who liked word games not get hooked on electoral politics?

My mother, Grace, was a nurse who had been expelled from Gibraltar during the war for being the object of affection of a Spaniard. When she rejected his advances, he discharged his pistol into the ceiling of the nurses' accommodation. While waiting to be interviewed in London for a new posting, she picked up a *National Geographic* featuring the cattle herds of the Barotse Flood Plain. She asked to be sent to Northern Rhodesia, where she met my father who was inspecting hospitals along the "line of rail" between Livingstone and the copper mines.

Among many other skills, she taught herself to write like a journalist and reported fairly regularly in the British press on political events on the margins of the Empire. She also wrote a book that has been "borrowed" by many historians documenting the racial integration of the public education system in the run-up to Zambian independence. Her book is called *The Fading Colour Bar* and is out of print, but some articles in the *Spectator*, written around 1960, are easily accessible.

Why my mother married Alec Scott is not obvious. She was twenty-eight years his junior, though that may have resulted from many men her age being away at war. This was almost certainly the case with her fondly remembered Norwegian sailor, the captain of the merchant ship who delivered her to Cape Town by sailing slowly and close to shore. And there is a statistical tendency for nurses to marry doctors—not always to good effect—but in my parents' case it seems to have worked rather well. He exuded warmth (though his table manners were of a miserably low standard, I have been told pointedly many times); and he gave my mother the confidence to write professionally and to run a farm worthy of being called one. She also acquired a degree of confidence in her own abilities as a teller of stories. She told tall tales on the radio and in the newspapers. Perhaps this is how she came to claim that, when she accepted my father's proposal, he had not yet told her that he had two previous marriages under his belt and two children.

My father had married and divorced his first wife, who was also a doctor but who did not wish to join him in Africa.

My father's second wife was a bewitching "bolter," by all accounts. Her first husband was an Australian with a farm in Zimbabwe. On the farm he apparently kept her under a prison-style regime, forbidden from communicating with the outer world while he had his way with her. Though there was one exception—the (unmarried, handsome) local doctor had to be sometimes consulted.

My father, the doctor of course, quickly became infatuated with Ming—the nickname presumably designed to capture her delicacy of feature, the translucency of her skin, and her sheer unaffordability. It was not long before a three-week visit to Durban with the doctor himself was prescribed. She oscillated back and forth—so far as I can gather—between the farmer and the doctor but ended up having children by the latter and moving in with him. Sufficient stability was achieved for the production of a boy and a girl—my half-brother and half-sister. Then Ming resumed her swathe cutting, taking her two children to London and settling in the embrace of Magnus Goodfellow, the chairman of Eveready batteries. (Honestly—life imitated art in those days.) My father obtained a court judgment ordering the return to central Africa of the two children. They caught the last civilian boat out of Southampton in 1939. My sister recollects being afraid for the entire voyage; she also recalls my brother cheering on the German torpedoes that for some reason failed to make contact with the ship's hull.

Goodfellow had cancer and booked a suite in Claridges in which he received his friends and prepared for his death. Ming had one son by Magnus—whose acquaintance I brushed at Cambridge. After Magnus, she surveyed the admirers, chose another doctor, and settled with him in Bermuda. According to my sister, who visited her in the 1960s and onward, the house on Bermuda was constantly occupied by admirers, old and not-so-old men whose only purpose in life was waiting for the current husband to die and for them to be the next in line. Alas, I never met her and have no firsthand evidence that this spell casting was for real, but its seems her age never became an object!

In 1890 THE AREA south of the Zambezi and north of the Limpopo, soon to be called Southern Rhodesia (SR for short), had been invaded by the agents of Cecil Rhodes—the "colossus" who bestrode southern Africa. After three rebellions, fierce resistance on the part of the two major tribal groups—Matabele and Mashona—was put down thanks to the business end of the famous couplet:

> *Whatever happens we have got*
> *The Maxim gun and they have not*

In fact the Matabele were the first victims of the Maxim—which performed far better as a killing machine than was expected by its designers and gunsmiths.

The Nabobs of the Imperial Office had little choice but to accede to full colony status for Rhodes's eponymous country. However, they wanted a more moderate approach to further expansion north of the Zambezi. Rhodes's high handedness had created considerable unease, both in the way SR was being forcibly settled and also in view of the Jameson raid, an unsuccessful sneaky assault on the Boers of the Transvaal by Rhodes's soldier adventurers. The result was that the British government allowed the next country up the railway line to be called Northern Rhodesia (NR) and to be administered by his British South Africa Company (BSAC), effectively as a labor reserve. *But*, and it is a very *big* but, they preserved it as a protectorate, ultimately under the wing of the British government and off-limits for large-scale land grabbing and the unconstrained use of Maxim guns. In 1924 the British removed the BSAC mandate and took over direct administration of NR.

That wouldn't have troubled any colonialist too much except that it became clear that Zambia's proven reserves of copper were burgeoning, and so was demand for the "red gold" in the heavily electrified and militarized late industrial age. Having failed to give NR colonial status in the first place, the Central African Federation was the next best thing, since the federal administration could move tax and royalty money south. (Malawi was added to the federation, allegedly at the insistence of Britain.)

So the fight for independence by black nationalists and their few attendant "kaffir boeties" (a pejorative term for white supporters of independence) in the 1950s and early 1960s became in effect the same thing as the fight against the Central African Federation. "The Unholy Deadlock" ended at midnight on New Years Eve 1963, and Zambia and Malawi both became independent within a year. Southern Rhodesia dropped the "Southern" from its name, while its white citizens stiffened the sinews, summoned up the blood, and allowed themselves to be led into civil war by Ian Smith's promulgation of a Unilateral Declaration of Independence, a famously ill-advised undertaking that resulted in an estimated 50,000 deaths and much rancor between the tribes and races (Chitiyo, 2007). Genuine independence only came to Zimbabwe in 1980. In retrospect, it is doubtful whether Ian Smith could have sustained his UDI for more than a few months had it not been for infrastructure and reserves syphoned from the north during the federal period.

It is fair to assert that some whites in a country like Northern Rhodesia, including missionaries, were and still are racially prejudiced or inclined toward a paternalistic view of "natives." But it makes a cliché out of a limited truth to take this as a safe generalization. Even colonial officers, who tended to be upper-class public school and Oxbridge graduates, and thus given to patronizing people regardless of their race, were influenced by the Livingstone ideology as well as by the postwar British Fabian socialist vision of an equal society.

Of course, missionaries and their relatives were not the only long-term white immigrants to southern African protectorates such as Zambia. Demobbed British soldiers looking for farms, traders, and officers of the colonial administration who chose to retire here all came in some numbers, as did liberal eccentrics such as Sir Stewart Gore-Brown, the mud-brick castle builder. The most right-wing influence in Northern Rhodesia, however, was the influx of workers on the mines and the attendant industries such as the railway. Often they did not settle permanently but brought a version of apartheid with them, complete with practices such as pushing blacks on bicycles off the roads with their own vehicles to "keep them in their place."

But whites in Zambia or Malawi never totaled more than about 10 percent of the white population of Southern Rhodesia. The reason was simple: SR had the status of a "self-governing" colony that might just manage to resist the process of giving control to the indigenous people, which was embarked upon by Great Britain after World War II. Northern Rhodesia and Nyasaland in contrast were *protectorates* under direct British rule through a governor and his officials. The attraction of the "self-governing" label was so potent to white immigrants that Southern Rhodesia was over-settled, with many native village farmers driven off the land and into Northern Rhodesia, where they have settled and effectively become a Zambian tribe, nominally the seventy-third; these days holding Zambian citizenship and known locally as the "Mazezulu."

(The political situation was homologous in East Africa at the time, where Kenya's status as a colony drained white immigration and investment and black labor migration away from Tanganyika and Uganda, which were protectorates destined for independence.)

Education was segregated throughout southern Africa, and those of us from NR whose parents could afford it were sent to all-white SR boarding schools. I have been castigated for publicly likening my secondary school—Peterhouse in SR—to a Hitler youth camp. Well, that is perhaps somewhat over the top; most of the ideas about racial supremacy came from fellow schoolboys (girls being prevented from mingling with spotty blokes in those benighted times) who presumably got them from their settler parents rather than from the teachers—they were mostly English and keen on the British public school as a model for rearing young men to run the Empire. I sometimes think the racial discrimination they found in SR did not strike them very forcibly, as they seemed to see it as they did the British class system with the additional feature of color coding.

For the record, whites of a liberal persuasion did something to contribute to the campaign for independence in Zambia, even if much of their support was of the moral variety and limited to racially detoxifying the campaign for majority rule. Electorally however they did not count for anything more than a footnote to history. My father was the leader of a political party formed in 1957 called the Constitution Party. It sought a middle, measured, and peaceful way out of the federation and into independence. Its most famous supporter was Colonel David Stirling, creator of the famed Special Air Service during World War II. The founding of the party took place at the residence of Dr. Charles Fisher (son of a yet another pioneering missionary) on the

Copperbelt. I sat with my life-long friend Stewart, Charles's son, in the garden as the stridulating darkness crackled about us. Stirling joined us during a break. We were well impressed, having seen his likeness only in war comic books before now. "Well, lads," he said in the tone one might use to address someone who is having doubts about jumping out of an airplane in the dark, "this is a revolution; if this party doesn't succeed, Africa is finished."

The Constitution Party bombed—it didn't win a single seat in the federal elections and soon disbanded to make way for a clone called the Liberal Party led by Sir John Moffat, great-great-grandson or there-abouts of Livingstone's father-in-law and husband to Moppy's daughter Peggy (my first cousin). This party was more "moderate" but also sank without a trace. It is only in quantum mechanics, I later learned, where you can do X and get Y then do X again and get Z. And yes, I meant to ask Stirling if Africa is indeed finished as per his projection, but never chanced to meet him again. A pity, since I have searched in vain for other militant liberals without much success.

The Constitution and Liberal parties failed for the same reason that Harper Lee could not sell her first book, *Go Set A Watchman* (except recently as a curiosity). The cautious protagonists who thought they would be welcome as wise moderators were out of touch: as unexciting in fiction as in reality. (Bemba: *do not look back when swimming the river*).

It is tempting to posit that the white missionary and associated liberal traditions in Northern Rhodesia came to an effective end with the sinking of such ventures as the liberal political parties (and the "Capricorn Africa Society" that preceded them). It is an easy place to draw the line in the sand for the end of a phase or process. But really, all that came to an end was the visible controlling influence of so-called moderate whites—and it was not even very difficult to spot. The black man who came to power in Zambia less than ten years later, in 1963, was an embodiment of (white as much as black) missionary values. He was born in a mission, to missionary parents, and felt most at ease with other missionaries and mission products. Although a strong nationalist, Kenneth Kaunda's government incorporated a remarkable bias toward white missionaries and such types, not excluding lunatics, whom he recruited in the course of his travels or who turned up on his doorstep. One of his team (the Reverend Colin Morris) even ghostwrote books on behalf of Kaunda, promulgating a non-denominational utopian philosophy called "Humanism" (not to be confused with the humanist movement). Many of these white helpers to KK had little clue about economics and governance, it must be noted, but their very existence on the bridge of the ship of state (in a landlocked country) speaks volumes about the interdependence of certain whites and certain blacks in the attempt to create credible societies out of a demoralized populace festering in poverty and insecurity. Sebituane and Livingstone would be right at home—and possibly more practical in addressing some of the problems.

Many of the new black academic elite, with their tertiary education, took a very dim view of Kaunda's missionary-state and have left their fury in books that smolder into the historical record as we turn their pages. Valentine Musakanya, who will pop into the story at various points, was one of this grouping and probably the most articulate and angry.

Whites, it might be said again, disappeared from the highly visible front ranks of the political struggle for nationalistic goals, but they remained a strong influence behind the scenes as technocrats. When I was appointed to agriculture minister in 1991, I was construed by many as a friendly "expert," not as a true home-grown politician. Zimbabwe and South Africa have both featured whites in the government—partly as goodwill gestures to white minorities and as technocrats. What was exceptional about my rise to the vice presidency in 2011 was the political salience of such an appointment, which could not be classified away as being purely technocratic or advisory or as a sop to a minority. It seemed Michael Sata wanted to make a statement, and I was it—even if just what he meant my presence to signify was not clear to me 100 percent of the time (even now).

THIS OBITUARY TO MY FATHER, who was discussed in the preceding chapter, was written by Tommy Fox-Pitt, who features in the next. It was published in a London newspaper in July 1960.

DR ALEXANDER SCOTT
AN APPRECIATION

Commander Fox-Pitt writes: Dr Scott would have liked people to think that he was a hard-headed man who never allowed emotion to desert him, but whenever there was human need he responded to it spontaneously and with genuine feeling.

Dr Scott would appear for Africans as a barrister in court and reprimand them in private. Unlike most Government medical officers who spent more time on paying European patients than on their many unpaying African patients, in those years when he was a private doctor he would attend to Africans and let his European patients grumble. They grumbled not at neglect for he was punctilious and careful, but because it was not very nice for hands that had dealt with a sick African to help them.

In that land of irrational prejudice he had his enemies. When he was editor of the "Central African Post" he paid his African compositors the nearest thing to European wages that the capital town Lusaka had ever known. The unpopularity which this brought him with the Europeans, who were the only people with votes, was not enough to stop his election to the first Federal Assembly. His initial doubts about the integrity and wisdom of the Federal Government developed into a distrust strongly backed with accumulated fact and experience.

Three years ago he became, when he stood alone in politics, the most trusted of all Europeans. Later he associated with the Central African Party with other Europeans who were trusted less and these associations undermined the trust in which he was held by the Africans. But much remained to the end.

Now where will Africans turn for advice and help? They have lost a genuine friend and an honest critic. Many will say they have lost their only European friend.

4

Sounds in the Forest

MOST TRIBES OR TRIBAL GROUPINGS IN ZAMBIA ARE KNOWN TO HAVE inmigrated in fairly recent times. Some tribes came from the south, driven ultimately by the white (that is to say Dutch and British) invasions of the Cape and adjacent areas. We have already encountered the Makololo and the Mazezulu in this regard; to these we can add a group of Ngoni, relatives of the Zulu and the Matabele, on the run from Shaka Zulu himself. For them we have an exact date of crossing the Zambezi—19 November 1835—thanks to a total solar eclipse that coincided with the event.

The Tonga with their related groups are the second-largest population group in Zambia. Their date of arrival is not known, so it is probably in excess of 500 years ago. Their early presence in the country may be the result of the phenomenal natural gift of the Kafue Flats, a vast seasonal flood plain that used to support massive herds of wildebeest and other wild fauna, but which came to support huge cattle herds accompanying human migrants.

However, the largest contribution to the present day population, in terms of a single language group, comes from emigration from what is currently called the Democratic Republic of Congo, the mostly rainforest territory made notorious by Conrad's novel *Heart of Darkness*. This southward migration is assumed to be part of the "Bantu explosion" process, which is assumed to have originated in West Africa adjacent to the DRC. Crossing into what is now Zambia took place along the entire length of the boundary with the DRC, which is some 1,000 miles long. Historical analysis puts the main thrust of the migration at

41

around 1600 A.D. Opinions differ, and the situations of different tribes differ, but my opinion is that the trigger for the Bantu influx into Zambia was the discovery of the Americas at the end of the fifteenth century. This made available numerous crops—including maize, cassava, potato, and sweet potato—which are today essential components of the typical agricultural economy of the central and southern African plateau.

If you contrast west and southern Africa you find that domestication of truly indigenous African crop species is far more advanced in the west than in the south. In Zambia for example, several species of yam grow wild and are used for food during hunger periods, but there is no sign of domestication as in West Africa where yam is a cultivated staple food. In the agricultural systems of the southern half of Africa, Columbian species dominate. Presumably, these were brought to our area by the Portuguese or Arabs or their agents. These newcomer species turned out to be more suited to the cool seasonal savannah than to the rain forest, with the consequence that some "Bantu" were impelled to leave the forest for the areas they now inhabit. I emphasize that I am guessing about some of the missing bits, though I am assisted by my personal knowledge of tropical farming in Zambia, in particular.

The largest tribal group or affiliation in Zambia is the Bemba-speaking group, which consists of eighteen distinct tribes, dominated by the pure "Bemba tribe," which some declare is the elite Bemba "clan" rather than a separate tribe. These "pure" Bemba make up only a few percent of the Bemba of the group and has its homeland in a few districts of northern Zambia. The Bemba are regarded by many as difficult people to understand and work with. The world's acknowledged expert on the tribe was Audrey I. Richards, whose anthropological studies of girls' initiation ceremonies (*cisungu*), primarily conducted in the 1930s in Mpika and other Bemba-dominated districts, set a standard in centers of Western learning. She was unlucky to be holding forth in Cambridge on this subject while Valentine Musakanya, Zambia's MI6 trained first black senior civil servant, was at college there taking a British district administrator's course (designed for prospective colonial administrators). He attended a lecture by Richards and found himself, a Bemba, in sharp disagreement with the distinguished lady. He retaliated in Cambridge style, claiming: "I advertised my own lecture entitled: The sexual habits of the English tribe. It was well attended and successful: it was convincingly anthropological" (Larmer, 2010).

Some otherwise very good accounts of Zambia's people fall short, however, on the question of the aboriginal population that the "explosion" encountered and its fate. The writer Dick Hobson, for example, an accurate and concise raconteur of Zambian anecdotes and historical yarns, fails to give the aboriginals any credit. He depicts them as mere primitive hunters who got slaughtered, dispersed, or absorbed by the superior "Bantu" farmers (who were also smelters of iron). This cannot be correct; hunting and gathering by stone-age people in the vicinity of Zambia had gone on for tens of millennia before the Bantu appeared; it would be impossible for invaders to simply "disappear" them, like so many political dissidents in a South American dictatorship, leaving a clean slate. We would expect the immigrants to pick up survival tricks from the highly skilled hunters they were certain to encounter. And indeed we find ample evidence of the descendants of aboriginals surviving alongside the aggressive farmers and ironworkers.

Livingstone remarks, in the course of one of his attempts to cross the Kalahari, that there are two types of bushmen in the area we now call Botswana.

> We found many families of bushmen; and, unlike those on the plains of the Kalahari, who are generally of short stature and light yellow colour, these were tall, strapping fellows, of dark complexion. (Livingstone, 1900)

Livingstone seems to be applying the term *bushman* to anyone with hunting and gathering as their dominant livelihood. The people he describes here are what some "experts" call river bushmen, perhaps a branch of what they are referred to in the politically correct term, San, but who are called from the Cape to well into East Africa and the Congo rainforest Batwa. The race or culture as a whole, and as it remains, is specialized in exploiting environments that are unsuitable for farming. Even if the agricultural environments are removed, there are still many offbeat environments or ecosystems left such as deserts, swamps, rivers, mountains, and rain forest for a good practical and fleet-footed naturalist to make a living as he or she moves about. In Zambia there are at least six identifiable groups who still call themselves Batwa. At least one group consists of classic hunters, running down and trapping game of all sizes. These are probably genetically close to the Batwa people of the deep forest—the pygmies. The other groups are river or swamp Batwa living either in the Bangweulu swamps or the Kafue wetlands starting close to the Lukanga swamp and continuing into Tonga territory in extensive Kafue Flats southwest of Lusaka.

We might expect DNA research to settle all disputes regarding genetics in the near future, and maybe it will. But even now the similarities in hunting techniques (poisoned arrows most notably), trance dancing, polyphonic singing, and a political structure with no chiefs (quite unlike the Bantu) are so marked that a person without a strong agenda to prove otherwise would have to accept they are at some level "the same people." They can take quite a lot of finding, given the remoteness they have chosen as their protection; and they may take a lot of persuading to tell their story as the victims of violence at the hands of agricultural militarists. They have "disappeared" themselves by impersonation, intermarrying, and the ability to vanish in difficult terrain. Some Batwa claim their people invented dugout canoes to escape the Bantu—incidentally disadvantaging anthropologists and explorers generally. But from my own experience of finding them, all it takes is a bit of perseverance, and a $30 million Augusta Bell helicopter. I cannot imagine why others find it so difficult.

(I have been subjected to some criticism that I devoted a tiny fraction of my office's budget to making contact with the Batwa. I protest that you cannot govern people if you do not even know who they are.)

The reason I have brought the Batwa into this story is because their culture and their skills have had a lot to add to the understanding of Zambia's society. The Bemba and the related Bisa tribes, for example, found themselves in a very game-rich territory, including what are today the north and south Luangwa National Parks, with some of the most magnificent herds of Cape buffalo and hippopotamus on earth. There are also the natural flood and swamp Bangweulu areas of the Chambishi River, featuring such tasty exotica as the black lechwe and the sitatunga water antelope. Naturally, the immigrants wanted to exploit this natural wealth, so they approached the Batwa. The Batwa's version of the story is that they were asked by the Bemba and Bisa to hand over their "hunting spirits." After some consultation, they agreed that they could easily do this, provided some hundreds of Bemba and Bisa girls of childbearing age were sent to join them in the swamp. And yes, you know what happened next.

The Batwa, whether you regard them as one race or several races, are scattered widely across southern, eastern, and parts of western Africa. One of their own myths of origin states that they were created by God to entertain Him with their dancing. One evening God sat in heaven for hours enjoying their music and movement; he then felt tired and tried to retire to bed. Alas, the Batwa could not stop; they became more and more absorbed in the dance and sang and beat their drums more insistently. Irritated, the Almighty gathered them all up in his huge hand and threw them like seed, horizontally across the earth where they landed unharmed and continued their dancing in the various places where they found themselves. Indeed, provided they know you are not enemies, they do in reality start dancing as soon as they catch sight of you.

Although the Livingstonia mission in Nyasaland positioned the black missionary David Kaunda close by in the district of Chinsali, this was not until 1904 or so. Earlier, there was a general mistrust and fear on the part of whites including missionaries and administrators about the Bemba. They were thought to be unpredictable and dangerous. It was not until in the 1890s that a French priest named Joseph Dupont, based in Nyasaland, bravely strode into northern Bembaland and introduced himself, and the Bemba and Catholicism fell for each other. In fact they got on so well that Dupont was appointed as acting chief Mwamba and in effect acting paramount chief Chitimukulu of the Bemba for the duration of a succession dispute beginning in 1896. To take his new temporary job while keeping his permanent employers, the Catholic Church, happy, he had to avoid certain practices relating to chiefly succession—for example, inheritance of and compulsory sexual "cleansing" of the deceased's harem. And again, the Bemba are said to practice regicide to avoid the slow death of the king, which would create risks for the whole tribe. Clearly he managed to evade these things, maybe by digging deep into his reserves of humor. Less fun, he feared that the kingdom would burst into flames of civil war (I know the feeling) and urgently invited the British South Africa Company to move in and take control of the Bemba lands. This is apparently the only known case of a Frenchman handing over colonial territory to the British.

During much of Michael's tenure as president he was engaged in a political dust-up with the chief nominated by the Bemba advisory group or council, the *bashilubemba*. A quick flip through the literature reveals that the Bemba almost always have a vigorous scrap over the choice of a new Chief Chitimukulu. It is part of "who they are" and "what the Bemba are like." Some think it must have useful functions relating to exploring and relieving stresses within society.

It is very tempting, considering their dependence on game meat for protein, side by side with some of the stories of agricultural failure in the Bemba area, to write them off as a hunting and gathering tribe masquerading as farmers. But that is flatly contradicted by their cultivation practices of *chitemene* and *fundakila*. I have not the slightest doubt that these are among the most sophisticated *practical* systems of arable agriculture on earth. White men in shorts have unfortunately denigrated these "organic" agricultural systems over the years and proven conclusively only that the white race is one of the least perceptive primate strains known—at least among the nonextinct strains.

The sandy, acidic soils of northern Zambia—say up from 15 degrees latitude—mainly support miombo woodland, made up of quite fast growing softwoods, shrubs, and some grass. Left to its own devices it falls into a cycle of some sort, usually involving fire. Woodland cannot just grow and grow, although it can "close ranks" and turn into an evergreen Tarzan type forest with liana creepers. But this is unlikely to happen if there is a possibility of fire sweeping through in some years. Fire that is too hot can destroy the forest, turning it to open grassland; if the fire is cooler it can modify the forest in various complex ways. Chitemene inserts itself into the forest cycle thus: when the forest has grown suitably dense, the farmers lop or "pollard" the trees to create a quantity of firewood which, when gathered and spread appropriately, provides the fuel for a hot burn that leaves a seedbed of wood ash overlying "cooked" soil. The word is appropriate since a test for adequate heating is to reach the point where a tuber such as a potato placed six inches deep is fit for eating. The "parent" trees are normally unharmed and will immediately start throwing replacement branches after the burn. There is never enough firewood to provide a good hot cooking over the whole area and part of the skill is to judge how much of the cleared area can be used. If you can cover a third of it you are doing well. The Bemba males are taught the climbing and axe-wielding skills required from a young age, though the children of royalty are excused from the dangerous activity.

The sterilization of the soil eliminates weed seeds, and indeed turns them into fertilizer. Seeds are high in all common nutrients since they contain the "starter" pack for the plant whose genes it is carrying. Other organisms including bacteria, termites, and roots also yield up nutrients when cooked. The wood ash contains nutrients as well. The pH of the soil (its acidity) is corrected in the right direction (toward alkalinity).

The favored first crop in the chitemene crop rotation is finger millet. "Millet" just means "small seed" so there are many millets, mostly unrelated to each other, and Latin and native names are useful: *rapoko* is a Bantu word common to several languages, the Bemba is *amale*, and the Latin is *eleusine coracana*. Maize is also grown in the first round, since soil nitrogen levels and phosphate availability are at their best. You can make porridge out of finger millet but most Bemba would prefer to avoid the need. It makes a popular alcoholic—and nutritious— drink called *katata*.

Other crops follow: groundnuts, various legumes, sweet potatoes, edible leaf crops, and finally cassava, which fits snugly into the regenerating forest, ready to harvest whenever hunger beckons. For a bonus there are finkubala caterpillars, whose parent moths have been attracted to the fresh leaf flush that comes after the burning stage. (Proper harvesting of caterpillars entails yet more dangerous climbing.)

The area of Mpika features several testimonies to the past glory of the British Empire. The Crested Crane hotel built about three miles from the *boma* (administrative center) was a stopover for Imperial Airways flights from Europe to South Africa. The price of an ordinary ticket was beyond first class in terms of today's money and the hotel was accordingly of an unimaginably high standard. Its toilets boasted a world record of some sort—it had all the latest papers from the UK bound onto wooden boards that were cleverly hinged to the wall so that the user regardless of shape or stature could select any page of any newspaper and pull it across his or her lap for absolute ease of reading or completing the crossword. Of course the hotel has gone very much downhill since the birth of the long-range passenger jet and the absolute abandonment of the grass airstrip.

The administration offices and senior officials' houses of Mpika boma have, since the BSAC administrators got their fears in order and moved into Bembaland, been on a line of hills marking the watershed between the Luangwa River (and thence the Zambezi River) to the east and the Chambeshi River (and thence ultimately the Congo River) to the west. The altitude is a congenial 4,600 feet, cool the year round despite being only 12 degrees south of the equator.

Commander Tommy Fox-Pitt was a noted colonial officer in the Northern Rhodesian administration. He was district commissioner in Mpika at the time that Michael was born there. Michael informed Charlotte and myself separately that his father Langton was Fox-Pitt's cook. There is no reason to believe otherwise, and it would explain a number of things. Langton would likely have been a political organizer (through the medium of the "Native Welfare" clubs), and he would have had strong support from his employer, who was a grassroots socialist of note (not a misprint!).

A quick scout of the larger colonial-era residential houses in the Mpika boma reveals what was almost certainly Fox-Pitt's house. With luck the DC might have visitors for breakfast, for example a lady in the shape of the ever-present Audrey Richards, come to ask a few questions about new and ancient hunting magic. She would likely be in the company of her friend Lorna, the young wife of the Old Rhinoceros, Sir

Stewart Gore-Browne of Shiwa Ngandu (recently restored to fame by the *Africa House* book by Christina Lamb).

Just to remind ourselves that we are aware we are in Wonderland and unable to detach ourselves without difficulty, behold this gravestone in the DC's garden:

TO THE MEMORY OF CHARLES LINDSEY ROSS,
ELEPHANT CONTROL OFFICER,
BORN AT PORT PIRIE, SOUTH AUSTRALIA 18TH MAY 1877,
KILLED BY HIS 350TH ELEPHANT IN KAMWENDO'S COUNTRY
29TH MAY 1938.

Most people who did not know Michael very well are surprised to find that he was quite at home in the engine room—or should that be on the bridge?—of the ship of British Imperialism. Partly this is because they have not really taken serious notice of his values; and partly because they have no knowledge of the values promulgated by the colonial service in even the lowly house-servant. Still fewer people know of left-wingers like Fox-Pitt who were the counterweight to the racially divided society that less liberal colonial servants believed in. He was a committed egalitarian, a Fabian socialist, at least after the war. He ran the international Anti-Slavery Society, and he organized links between trade unions in Britain and nascent (black) trade unions in Northern Rhodesia.

He was given early retirement, probably because he annoyed the Colonial Development Corporation over the racially discriminatory system of tobacco growing in the east of Zambia (and in Nyasaland). The system allocated land and other resources to villagers on the basis that they would at most be able to grow cheap air-dried Burley tobacco. European farmers, purely on the basis of race, were encouraged to opt for Virginia tobacco, which requires complex curing using artificial heat as well as very sophisticated grading.

As well as the cook, Langton Sata, the DC had an official messenger, Mr. Lumbi. His son Paul was Michael's contemporary, political ally, and supporter, and eventually became Zambian High Commissioner to London during Michael's occupancy of State House. Paul is one of the most dignified, disciplined, and efficient of men, so it seems he escaped the effects of early exposure to some of the less endearing habits of colonial Brits. But in Michael's case, it is worth wondering whether his bossy, shouty tendencies were at least in part the influence of his childhood proximity to British Servants of the Crown.

(It should be clear enough, but just in case, let me emphasize what I am not saying. I am not defending the politics of colonialism or the administration of the colonial structure. I am simply saying what Michael and Paul have said to me: that being raised in the DC's house, under the auspices of a man like Fox-Pitt, they count themselves very fortunate and very proud.)

And while we are at it, let me elucidate the information, intended by his enemies to be demeaning to him, that Michael was not a Bemba (which in the class system of the area would make him "upper class") but a mere Bisa (purportedly a "subject" of the Bemba). Michael was a Bemba. Paul was and still is a Bisa. However, there is a "deep issue" burning here which readers with Byzantine tastes in politics would not thank me for excluding.

Bembaland, understood as that area governed by Bemba chiefs, is roughly divided east and west by the Chambishi River, the longest tributary of the Congo River and therefore, pedantically speaking, its source. Mpika and Chinsali districts are to the east of the river, leaving four to the west. Around 1870 the western "government" of the Chitimukulu, the bashilubemba based at Mungwi close to Kasama ruled that the lineages of succession (which are quite complex) should be revised to exclude chiefs from the eastern Chewe and Chimbaka lines from becoming the paramount chief Chitimukulu. Various arguments in favor of this discrimination are routinely advanced by its proponents. These include the allegation that Bembaland East "Bembas," who are in the minority, are not descended from the same Kola ancestors as the Western Bemba. The east is also declared to be too heavily infiltrated by Bisa people and chiefs—to the extent that it can be written off as Bisaland not Bembaland politically. Indeed, the east has sometimes been called Muchinga and its people Ichinga by the "purists" of the west.

This is all very arcane and impossible not to get confused about, and I would leave it out of the discourse if that was where it ended. But Michael evidently carried a deep resentment for years over the second-class status awarded to the Ichinga—the eastern Bemba. He waded into the whole political swamp in his first year in power, firing the Chitimukulu he found on the throne, declaring Muchinga to be a new province, and generally going head to head with the Westerners. What were his motives? At least he was guilty of discriminating in favor of his own subgroup. Other people who knew him claim he was deliberately practicing divide and rule with techniques he acquired under Soviet tutelage. This second allegation is of concern because there are other allegations of divide and rule tactics by Michael elsewhere in the country and these allegations extend to his successors.

AFTER THE WAR, FOX-PITT was transferred to the Copperbelt, though it seems Sata senior and his family remained in Mpika. Michael grew up there and went as far as he could with his education. This was effected at Catholic primary schools, which were not entirely appropriately described by the missionaries as "seminaries," probably to encourage a better uptake of prospective local priests, but certainly not to commit students to the cloth. This linguistic quirk resulted in Michael's fictional history of intending to join the priesthood (with add-ons such as his getting expelled for getting a nun pregnant).

This is not to say that Michael was a conformist. Anything but. According to excellent sources while at school, he joined a local self-described Catholic cult called The Church of the Sacred Heart (in Bemba, the Mutima church) formed in 1953 by a trainee priest named Emilyo Mulolani, which effectively led to Mulolani's excommunication. The sect or schism was at variance with mainstream Catholicism and other sects in that it promoted a more "European" or up-to-date approach to worship. Features of Mutima including mixing of genders in church seating (like Europeans) and Lourdes style communal bathing (only much warmer and no smell of chlorine). This was in stark contrast to the contemporaneous Alice Lenshina's infamous Lumpa cult, which

Michael Sata puts up his hand to disagree with the preacher at
St. Ignatius Catholic Church, 2011

sought to return to traditional African beliefs and values. The Mutima were also famous for contesting the priest's teaching during religious services—not listening, but interrupting and debating any point where they felt the priest had got it wrong.

One of the iconic photographs of Michael during his presidency is of him raising his hand in church, looking for all the world like a cheeky schoolboy, to argue with a Catholic priest at St. Ignatius church in Lusaka while that priest was preaching.

When he married his first wife, according to one relative, the Catholics refused to solemnize the union. In fact the Catholics went farther and downgraded Michael's father by two years in the standing of their church as admonition for allowing his son to join Mutima. Michael was reaccepted as a Catholic in due course, and it is not widely known that he was ever an adherent to the sect. The Mutima church finally took an interest in politics and sided with the UPP (United Progressive Party), the anti-Kaunda party formed by his childhood friend and sometime vice president, Simon Kapwepwe. The Mutima church was banned, and it seemed to the unperceptive to have disappeared, along with its signature blue garments. The government knows of the continued existence, indeed growth, of the church under the leadership of one of Emilyo's children. In fact I have just returned from buying Emilio II lunch. Why not? The church has even been credited as one of the founding forces behind the PF. For reasons that are not clear to me, the Ministry of Home Affairs refused to register it recently. This did not prevent Michael from acting like a member of Mutima in his local church by arguing with the priest (see photo).

5

Young Michael
Heads for Town

WHAT WAS MICHAEL'S FIRST AMBITION WHEN HE LEFT MPIKA FOR THE bright lights? Age nineteen, fit, and self-confident, what could be more natural for a young man raised in the orbit of the colonial service than to join the national police force? He was part of the first intake of police cadets at Lilayi Police Training College in Lusaka in 1956. Upon graduation he was posted to the Copperbelt, where his British commanding officer was mightily impressed by his self-starting qualities. He was the best of the first batch of graduates, says his colonial era police boss Colin Dunn, who is still alive and living in retirement in Lusaka. He was quickly promoted to sergeant, the highest rank to which a black policeman could advance in those days.

There have been plenty of attempts to provide an accurate account of Michael's itinerary through life between leaving Mpika and arriving in Lusaka to start his siege of the citadels of (then Kaunda's) government. We know he joined the police and was not immediately sacked, contrary to some accounts. He seems to have served for at least three years. Whether he left the police first or not, he was arrested in 1960 for "proposing violence"; this was presumably a political charge against an African nationalist organizer/agitator although his enemies have over the years twisted it into a pure criminal matter. Some doubt concerns the time he spent in jail but it seems to have been at least six months. (In the language of the independence struggle he became a "prison graduate" or "PG," an unavoidable step in the road to a freedom fighter's credibility.)

Once he was out of jail, it seems he joined both civilian employment and the trade union movement. As a unionist he was working in close contact with UNIP (United National Independence Party)—the leading nationalist party. He rose through the union system to general secretary of the NUECGW (National Union of Engineering, Construction, and General Workers), and UNIP sent him to receive trade union training in the Soviet Union, says the official biography put out by the cabinet after his death. But it also says he went to "train as a political commissar at a military university." He told me he went to the Soviet Union for training in "party organization."

All accounts agree that Michael returned from his spell behind the Iron Curtain to the Copperbelt shortly after independence. He acted as a labor consultant and entered into various partnerships with Irwin and other businessmen.

In 1970 he went to the United Kingdom for further studies, essentially doing GCE A Levels (secondary school exams/high school graduation level) with politics and constitutional law. The physical location of some of his night schooling seems to have been the London School of Economics, giving rise to the red herring of a degree from the LSE. He earned money working for British Rail and at Vauxhall Car Assembly plant in Luton. The story that Michael was a lowly porter at Victoria station—and nothing further—is contradicted by Valentine Musakanya, who was governor of the Bank of Zambia in 1971. Valentine, according to the account he gave me, was traveling by night to Cambridge, and the train was stopped at Bishops' Stortford by the stationmaster whom he recognized as none other than Michael. They chatted away in Bemba, with Michael asking Valentine to facilitate an overdue money transfer from Zambia (evidently rent on his Copperbelt house was the source of his money remittances while he was in the UK). He then waved the lamp for the journey to proceed.

On his return to Zambia in 1973 Michael settled first in the Copperbelt but moved to Lusaka, accumulating property, setting up companies in advertising and property development. A poor cook's son brought up in the elite ambience of the top of the colonial service; a policeman who went to jail; a trade unionist and simultaneously an employer; a practical practicing capitalist and certifiable Anglophile trained in party organization by the KGB. Who can claim such a variety of viewpoints from which to look at the world around him? My friend must have had more eyes than a jumping spider.

An interesting question is what role, if any, did Fox-Pitt continue to have in Michael's career after the war when he returned to Zambia and was based on the Copperbelt? We know from living witnesses (of whom Simon Zukas is the foremost) that the colonial administration had positioned Fox-Pitt in the Copperbelt because there was strong demand from black workers for assistance in forming trade unions within Northern Rhodesia as the road to economic advancement. Despite such institutions being illegal in the late 1940s and early 1950s, Fox-Pitt was one of several progressive colonial officers who helped organize trade unions and even nationalist political parties. Any good joined-up fiction writer would include Fox-Pitt in the story of Michael as a "helper," the powerful and ideal figure in folk tales who proves to be on hand just when all doors to further adventure seem to be closed. Alas, this is supposed to be a book of history—or an attempt at one until someone can settle the details of Michael's expedition to Britain.

Michael was quite close to several white businessmen on the Copperbelt. The most prominent, already mentioned, was Oliver Irwin, known as OJ, an accountant/partner with Price Waterhouse and an investor in many lines of business. These included safari hunting and taxidermy; Michael was a senior manager in this firm. And he partnered with OJ in the field of "labor consultancy." If anyone could mediate between workers and management it was Michael with his multiple jumping spider eyes. He was a one-man conflict resolution committee—and he got paid by both sides.

It is difficult to assess the relationship between the "labor consultant" and hard-bitten capitalist Oliver Irwin. OJ's interface with the wide world was typically blocked by a typically "closed" expression that indicated a lack of humor or kindness. However, he fell out badly with both his wives at various times and the gossip that hit the cocktail parties made Dallas look extremely tame. But he did leave a testimony of Michael and his relationship with him, though his sons have not yet released this document.

In one story that obviously has some truth, Irwin taught Michael to fly (Irwin kept a small air force through much of his business life). Michael told me the story and added that he had in fact been trained in East Germany but not sufficiently to pass a private pilot's license to Zambian standards. He did not want to tell anyone about his German experience and therefore had to meet the challenge of hiding the fact that he had flown before. It is very difficult to fake acquired lifesaving reflexes!

But a complementary relationship between workers and employers was not the sole dimension in which Michael "clicked" with his friends. He noticed that many rich people, especially white people, spent a lot of money and effort supporting "charitable" works for the (black) poor and the otherwise disadvantaged. The common belief is that charity tends to be provoked by a feeling that one is making money out of the people and the country and one ought to make a bigger contribution than arises from taxes and the like.

A sound example of a successful bloke trying to do the right thing by the local community is Cedric Whittemore, a Londoner who as a young man established a livestock farm just outside Kitwe. Whenever "Ceddy" would be producing more than his butchery could clear he would divert the surplus—eggs, meat, milk whatever—to the Kamfinsa prison close by and carefully supervise that it reached the intended targets (i.e., generally the prisoners not the staff). When Cedric met Michael for the first time, he was initially unimpressed by such a loudmouth, but became fascinated by his genuine concern for the prisoners of Kamfinsa.

Michael indeed had some magic with children. I recall the two of us dropping in at Rolf Shenton's house, which was halfway from Mpika to Lusaka, when we were returning during the campaign. We were making a lot of noise—laughing and shouting like warriors who have escaped death in a hard battle, not shy about laying into the hooch (and riding in triumph of course through Persepolis).

Rolf's wife, Linda, suddenly emerged furiously from the master bedroom holding a baby. "You seem to be the noisiest one, Mr. Sata; perhaps you would care to put him to sleep." Michael did not even stop in midflow; he took the proffered child and turned it to face him; the instant result was that the child was asleep before its mother had returned to the bedroom. "Madam, one sleeping child," he said.

As MENTIONED ABOVE, Tommy Fox-Pitt was repositioned on the Copperbelt upon returning from the war. The reason for this placement was to provide an answer to the demands of African nationalist politicians whose interest was to find a mechanism for boosting wages. There is no reasonable doubt that Fox-Pitt was a left-winger, Fabian socialist or whatever, before the "buffalo incident." In about 1948 a rogue Cape buffalo—potentially a killer—started troubling the villagers and townsfolk around Ndola. Fox-Pitt, a keen hunter, well equipped and expert with guns, undertook to deal with the beast. His first shot evidently wounded but did not kill the marauder, who charged, head up, in his turn. Fox-Pitt did not get in a fatal shot, but his tracker drew the buffalo's charge away from the white man toward him, to the fundi. Fox-Pitt could not intervene in time to save his colleague, who was gored to death. For years his fellow whites attributed Fox-Pitt's liberal tendencies to his burden of guilt at not being able to save the life of the man who had saved him. If only the psychology of politics was always so straightforward.

The picture of Michael as a sort of interracial multicultural consultant worked in Lusaka. (Irwin moved down to the capital as well.) I have never carried out anything resembling a deliberate census but Michael had dozens of business friends whom he found in the capital. There were Greeks (particularly shop owners, millers, and other medium-sized entrepreneurial ventures). Michael also had a close relationship with many business professionals of Indian origin. Of course, he was not the only black Zambian with political aims in life and the financial relationships between the givers and the takers must have been quite complex.

It is clear that he expanded the "labor consultant" financial relationship with a mixed bag of clients, with which he could and did harvest quite heavy flows of political funding. But in acknowledging this we should at the same time allow for the real affection of his contributors toward him and a shared belief that he was what Zambia needed more than anything else because of Michael's ability to get things done. In a sense he had populism thrust upon him.

Some people who knew Michael were nonetheless more cautious. Simon Zukas, undoubtedly Zambia's most eminent "white freedom fighter," says, "I always praised him as a man of action and said so at the [May 2011] Oxford seminar before he arrived and turned it into a party rally. [But I had] my misgivings about Michael [in] the period before he became President. I found him often erratic and I doubted his sincerity. In the period of Chiluba's attempt at a third term, Michael was associated with physical violence in Lusaka, especially during the by-election which FDD won" (Zukas, 2016).

6

The First Wind

HAROLD MACMILLAN'S FAMOUS PRONOUNCEMENT OF A "WIND OF change blowing through Africa," made in 1960, provided unanticipated impetus to the black nationalists of Britain's protectorates throughout the continent. At the same time it strengthened resistance to the same nationalists among white settlers, and among right-wing Western politicians. The local white hostility to British surrender was largely focused on Macmillan and his colonial secretary Ian McLeod. To this the settler wags added a third "Scotsman" named Machiavelli. Less wittily, the white settler position was very succinctly put by one of our governing United Federal Party stalwarts named John Gaunt: He reputedly declared that he would "rather shake hands with a black mamba than with a black nationalist." When I reminded Kenneth Kaunda of this recently he remarked: "Oh him—that man certainly knew his racialism."

Essentially, the wind of change blew strongly enough to liberate all African countries within ten years, save for the Portuguese territories, South Africa, South West Africa, and Rhodesia. It is an open secret that developed Western countries, despite imposing visible sanctions, covertly ensured that this bloc of minority governments was able to survive for some years as a perceived bastion against "communism" in the Cold War. The white nationalist regime in South Africa developed atomic weapons with the connivance of the West and the active cooperation of Israel. The Americans classified the South African ANC (African National Congress) as a terrorist organization, and Margaret Thatcher described Nelson Mandela as a terrorist. But the wind blew inexorably, and Thatcher eventually became a vital part of the process of change.

Independence confronted the new government of Zambia with the need to make an absolutely crucial decision. Are we at peace or at war? What is our stance with respect to the five minority white governments with which we coexist in southern Africa (four of which are literally neighbors)? It was not a semantic or symbolic exercise; other countries in our situation had to face the same questions and make their own decisions. Malawi under Hastings Banda decided to ally itself with the white regimes and to withhold any kind of assistance to the political and military structures of freedom fighters in the relevant countries. The South Africans rewarded him by building a new capital city in Malawi—Lilongwe. Botswana, along with other black states geographically captive to white states, struggled with the dilemma, sometimes turning a blind eye, but sometimes even handing over guerrillas fighting against the South African regime to their very enemies.

Tanzania under Julius Nyerere was part of East Africa and abutted only on Mozambique as a white-controlled neighbor; geographically Nyerere thus had an easier task taking the hawkish view than his bosom-buddy Kaunda. Tanzania's distant geographic position made it suitable as a rear base in which training could be provided to ANC and other freedom fighters with minimal interference from attacks from land, air, or sea. And quite by chance it turned out that the tracts of cleared but vacant land, housing, and other infrastructure—the abandoned sites of the infamously failed Tanganyika groundnut scheme—were ideal for military training purposes.

The position Zambia did finally take ought to be well known to every child in Africa. Well, perhaps it is, if dimly. When, aged ninety, KK accompanied me down to South Africa for Nelson Mandela's funeral in 2013, it was impossible to move through the airport in Johannesburg, or indeed through any public space at all, as he was blocked at every step, instantly recognized by young and old begging to be photographed with him. (To reduce the pressure I volunteered myself as an alternative subject, even offering free selfies in keeping with the fashion of the times, but hardly anyone recognized me. They thought I was Kaunda's bodyguard.)

Kaunda took the hard option. We would provide a base and resources for the freedom movements of southern Africa. We would not, however, commit our own armed forces unless we were attacked (it would have been suicidal to do so anyway). Soon we had the South African ANC headquartered in Lusaka; we had its leader, Oliver Tambo, accommodated at State House for his safety and comfort; and we provided training camps for its military wing. As well, we played host to liberation movements from Mozambique, Rhodesia, South West Africa, and Angola. Keenly aware of a possible de facto takeover of the host country by freedom movements, as witnessed in Lebanon, Kaunda laid down one rule: no internecine fighting or executions to take place inside Zambia. This stricture led to the expulsion from Zambian soil of Robert Mugabe and his ZANU/ZANLA organizations (the Shona-dominated Zimbabwe African National Union and its armed wing, the Zimbabwe African National Liberation Army), following what was judged (by investigators, including Scotland Yard) to be an internal killing effected by way of a letter bomb. This left only the Ndebele-dominated ZAPU/ZIPRA of Joshua Nkoma to represent the Zimbabwean freedom fight.

Let us note in passing that what Kaunda was doing by opening his country to being a "front line state" made historical sense. We were not

© Charlotte Scott

Former president of Zambia Kenneth Kaunda greeted by president of Zimbabwe Robert Mugabe in Pretoria, while Nelson Mandela lies in state

just an independent country deciding to interfere with its neighbors' affairs in the name of some incidental selfish cause; we were Pan-Africanists—all citizens of one country that essentially had been chopped into arbitrary pieces by our colonizers. The first version of the African National Congress, the SANNC, was created in 1912. At its very inception it was a broad southern African organization—with trustees from several countries including Northern Rhodesia—though this international aspect has been forgotten by most commentators. Viewed on the ground, the gathering of southern African forces was not a bad approximation of the political and historical truth. It is also worth noting that Kaunda's relationship with Mugabe also softened in time, as shown in this unusual pose taken while waiting for the viewing of Nelson Mandela's body to commence.

Settler children raised in overseas dominions or other extensions of an imperial power generally have identity problems and, more to the point, practical decisions to confront. The choices are made all the more difficult if the territory in question ceases to be part of the mother country.

My siblings and I were three boys and one girl. My older brother, John, studied at the University of Cape Town to become a surgeon. He worked for a while in Zambia after independence but then "took the gap" (a rugby term) and emigrated to Rhodesia after the Unilateral Declaration of Independence (UDI). I tell people what he told them: he wanted to help Ian Smith in his struggle to maintain standards, echoing a common Rhodesian excuse for continued white rule. This must have been in about 1966, and I did not see him again until 1979 or 1980, before the elections that put Smith out of the picture. He had allowed his oldest son to leave school at fifteen in order to join the Rhodesian Light Infantry and jump out of helicopters in order to "scribble [shoot with an automatic rifle] terr- [-orist]s in the gomes [hills]." I had to learn this argot (which originates with the colored population in Zimbabwe) in order to communicate with my nephew.

"Which of the two armies do you have more trouble with on your operations?" I might ask.

"Ahhh, Uncle Guy, ZANLA just run away; ZIPRA stands and fights. You rev them, they rev you right back." As he said this he brought the fingers of one hand together to resemble something like a flower opening and closing; perhaps a pulsating anemone? I looked again and realized his hand was representative of his arsehole during an encounter with ZIPRA. "You get spatter bum," he explained unnecessarily.

"So how many of you get actually killed by ZIPRA?"

"Oh, none at all. We call for a plane and it drops napalm. They do not run away. Finish."

There is very little doubt that ZANLA won the Rhodesian war. Disrupting the peace and running away—preferably in your hometown—is the way to win a guerrilla war.

The impression I got was that the bitterness of the Zimbabwe war would render the country ungovernable after its end. But I knew nothing. When the Rhodesians lost the war and election in 1980 Mugabe appeared on the television to preach reconciliation—my brother was very much taken by him. He stayed on in Zimbabwe in private practice, before becoming disillusioned twenty-odd years later by the breakdown of the rule of law and the economy, taking the gap to New Zealand. (Though nowadays there is no gap left to run to so "taking the gap" has been replaced by "packing for Perth.")

My younger brother and my sister both entered academia and apparently painlessly integrated into Britain as if it were their own country. However, I was instantly alienated by Britain, and I could not bear the feeling of abandoning my old country. (I tried the same route again in the 1980s but did not succeed in permanently abandoning Zambia.) I would guess that one in four staying behind, whether in body or spirit, while the others go to hell or Perth, is close to the statistical norm.

Let us roll back time a little more.

Most of the lifetime of the Central African Federation, and the run up to and beginning of the independence period, coincided with my formal education. This was entirely in Southern Rhodesia and in Britain. White Southern Africans' imaginings of Zambia seemed to feature a strong belief that Northern Rhodesia had a very hot climate, to the extent that it was unsuitable for whites to study at school. Schools for whites were hardly built at all in Northern Rhodesia, whereas there was a veritable epidemic of them built in Southern Rhodesia —to cope with the heavy white immigration and to displace the South African schools that the generation before mine had attended.

(The cause of the temperature myth seems to be that early visitors by oxcart, car, or train from the south to the north had to cross the Zambezi and thereby experience some low altitude. Temperature in the tropics is almost entirely a function of altitude—the so-called adiabatic gradient of about 3 degrees C per 1,000 feet approximately applying most of the time. Crossing the Zambezi is therefore generally a hot experience—in whichever direction you travel—as you dip down below the Central African plateau and up again, back into the cool sparkle or misty mellowness according to season. If you want to satisfy yourself that closeness to the equator is not a factor once you are in the tropics, consider Mounts Kilimanjaro and Kenya, which are on the equator and about the only places in Africa where you can find naturally occurring ice, and where local Bantu languages have an original word for it.)

My brother and I were sent to a junior boarding school called Springvale and thence to a secondary school called Peterhouse. Both were in Marandellas (now Marondela), an hour's drive from Salisbury (now Harare). These were both very much in the English public school tradition, Peterhouse being modeled self-consciously on Winchester, recruiting its teachers from Britain and seeking to send its alumni to Oxford and Cambridge (there were six of us from the first graduating class of fifteen in 1961). We studied, inter alia, Greek, French, and Latin. Attempts by boys, typically farmers' sons, for the school to include an option of Shona always came to nought. We played cricket and rugby, the point I suppose being that black schools would trash us mercilessly at any sport we had in common. (Thus most particularly we did not play soccer at secondary school.)

Racial discrimination was as absolute as gender discrimination, and I still joke (at least I think it is a joke) that keeping us away from blacks and women led us imaginative white boys into suspecting there was something really interesting, exciting, and possibly dangerous about the two groups; and that is why I seek to be in the company of both to this day. Can such a simple-minded theory be true?

I was quite openly against racial segregation. It is amazing in retrospect that I was not taken into the bush and beaten up by some of my contemporaries.

In any event I spent weekends and vacation time working for the NDP—the National Democratic Party, which was soon banned and replaced by a series of differently named replacements. As often as I could I made my way to the NDP's pokey office in downtown Salisbury, close by the *kopje* that marked the initial touchdown of Rhodes's blatant colonialist occupation. I operated the Roneo copying machines of the day and drafted calls to arms. This was not a common activity for a white teenager, but was that a bug or a feature of my taking sides?

The teachers could hardly constrain their delight as an acknowledged countrywide "emergency" evolved following Macmillan's speech. This provided the opportunity to construct and use a shooting range and to oblige all of us to sleep with hockey sticks under our beds in readiness for an assault (I do not think we used the word "terrorist" or even "communist" at first—they were just "them" unless they were serving the tea). The bell for assembly in each school's house was rung at random hours on random nights. I still have an almost eidetic image of small sleepy boys trying to decide which end to hold their hockey sticks, ranged along the veranda, backs to the "toyes" (group study rooms), staring sightlessly into the darkness. I wish I could report that the line-up ran from Aardvark to Zulu, as per the famous joke, but alas, the first is a Dutch word meaning "earth-pig," and we had very few Boers in our posh British school—I think the parents preferred to send them to boarding school in the old Transvaal where their ancestors had locked horns with David Livingstone. As for Zulu, he was just a poorly defined shape out there in the night, manning the machine gun that would take all us Anglo-Saxons out—from Avogadro to Zisserman or vice versa—if it was working.

I was given the status of a conscientious objector when I complained about being disturbed in the night. For once my colleagues were amused rather than outraged. Perhaps things were changing and the absurdity in our situation was beginning to become obvious.

One day in mid-1960 a teacher told me and my brother to get into his car, and he drove us to Salisbury airport. My father was unwell, he said. We flew to Lusaka, where my father was in a coma from a staphylococcus infection acquired during a more-or-less routine prostate operation. The bug was drug-resistant and nothing could be done as we watched it appear as boils on the skin. He was seventy-five.

The funeral had everything—or nearly. The governor sent an aide de camp (ADC) with a wreath; the various churches that had been on the same side as him appeared and had nice things to say. Kenneth Kaunda and company turned up, but Harry Nkumbula stayed away on account of the rift between himself and KK. He turned up later at our house in Lilanda, drunk and copiously weeping. His daughter Ompie, who was in the car with him, has precisely the same recollection as myself.

I fought my own tears with a slogan: *Unfinished business.* We returned to the backwoods of Rhodesia the same way we came.

Cambridge turned out to be a bit of a disappointment. Based upon the visitors who came to Lilanda, red-haired empire-busters and the like, I was expecting Britain to be full of radicals and revolutionaries. Instead, I could almost have not left Rhodesia. I found very few black students, lamentably few girls, plenty of snobs, and personal servants who tugged their forelocks. (I was at the university from 1962 to 1965 but the 1960s did not start swinging until 1965. So life was not yet in technicolor.) But there was always the train and I had friends in London, including black ones, with whom I could hopefully participate in the revolutions of the times. I learned a few things about politics. One is the meaning of "politics is a game of numbers." My African friends told me there was a massive demonstration demanding the liberation of a country called Upper Volta in French West Africa taking place on Sunday; would I like to participate? I duly turned up at Piccadilly Circus to find myself one of only about thirty protestors. The police were present in hundreds or thousands, lining the way to Trafalgar Square. We marched between their protective cordons shouting "We demand Freedom for Upper Volta!" to the mockery from the Londoners, and eventually sat down and listened to a passionate though incomprehensible speech in strangely accented French. There was no need to use the PA system. We went home. "Where is Upper Volta and what is wrong with it?" I found myself asking. (It is now an independent country called Burkina Faso and generally loses to Zambia at football.)

Perhaps global issues would be more engaging and generally important? I joined a Ban the Bomb sit-in outside the American airbase at Ruislip. We sat down on newspapers—the *Guardian* mostly—spread on the wet road. We shall not be moved!

"Excuse me, sir," said the policeman, "are you aware that you are obstructing the free passage of the Queen's Highway contrary to section garble, sub-section something of the Roads Traffic Act of 1958?"

"Yes, and I shall not be moved until Uncle Sam takes his nuclear bombs back where they came from!"

"Hey, Fred, there's a big one over here! Come and give me a hand. Now Sir, shall we throw you in the van or will you get into it under your own steam?"

As the Black Maria chortled along in the dead of night, depositing us in cells with prisoners' inscriptions on the walls (such as *"Oh my God I have killed a man!"*) I found myself wondering if, one day, I would ever be a head of state and what, when that day dawned, would be my view of nuclear weapons. Quite handy for intimidating bothersome neighbors, I concluded, provided they were not liable to go off spontaneously. I pleaded guilty and parted with some of my federal bursary as a fine for wasting her majesty's time.

It was thus I arrived at the point of discovering that I was not an ideologue or an extremist. I was not a socialist or a pacifist. It was quite a shock to discover I was only a liberal—a wishy-washy liberal driving down the middle of life's road. But perhaps I was being hard on myself. Were David Stirling or Commander Fox-Pitt wishy-washy? What was my father? How about "militant liberal" as a flag to march under?

Some of my fellow colonials along with other "foreigners" did not survive Cambridge. I was not happy, but I did survive—thanks partly to Stewart Fisher, who seemed to fit in well with the rowing crowd, even though he still denies participating in an expedition to leave Stephen Hawking stranded in his wheelchair overnight at the top of a Trinity Hall staircase. But he was also homesick much of the time, and we composed and sang calypsos to the departing swallows and the dangers of the women we left behind on the banks of the Zambezi (we would be so lucky!). I also formed a close friendship with Mario Nuti, an Italian economist who had made it to King's College after a spell with the Polish economist Michal Kalecki.

And there was the keen intellectual interest I developed in Keynesian economics. The great man himself was dead but our teachers had themselves sat at his feet and had by and large developed the skill to impart his insights to spotty youths. My supervisor, the mathematician Frank Hahn, made it all stand out in its subtle mathematical clarity. By contrast Keynes had made elegant use of plain language to get his thoughts across:

> [The Capitalist System] . . . depended for its growth on a double bluff or deception. On the one hand the labouring classes accepted from ignorance or powerlessness, or were compelled, persuaded of, cajoled by custom, convention, authority and the well-established order of Society into accepting a situation in which they could call their own very little of the cake, that they and Nature and the capitalists were co-operating to produce. And on the other the capitalist classes were allowed to call the best part of the cake theirs and were theoretically free to consume it, on the tacit underlying condition that they consumed very little of it in practice. The duty of "saving" became nine-tenths of virtue and the growth of the cake the object of true religion. (Keynes, 1919)

Keynes's *General Theory* was published more than eighty years ago. Its objective was to win a long-standing argument between economists concerning whether the level of economic activity in a country automatically adjusted itself via market mechanisms to a "full employment" condition, or whether it was necessary (or possible?) for government to take steps to ensure full employment—to interfere with natural processes. The reigning belief in the years before the *General Theory* was that attempts to interfere with the "macro economy" were doomed but that was not a real problem since supply and demand—market forces—would ensure an expansion of the labor force to keep close to full employment (famously "in the long run").

The arguments on both sides were not frivolous. Some markets may work optimally if left alone but many others demonstrate pathologies inviting intervention; but intervention does not always bring about any improvement. Often the treatment has worse side effects than the illness, pure and simple. Traditional views tended to be very conservative; do not interfere, even if the market has brought about unemployment and a lower rate of growth. The Liberal view, that Keynes personified, believed that the mega money markets such as those matching investment to savings, lending to borrowing, were too erratic and slow in their restorative potential once they had gone too far off track to rebalance quickly. Hence the state must take the bull by the horns and steer the economy back to normal within an acceptable amount of time.

I graduated from Cambridge in 1965, after three years of maths and economics, and headed for home. When I gaze from Mount Hindsight at the just-graduated "sunshine experts" of fifty years ago, myself included, some of us still virtually pubescent, our self-confidence was amazing. You would have thought from our cockiness that launching a new country three times the size of the UK into the infinitely prosperous self-sufficient future was child's play—you would have thought we had the understanding and the tools for the job. It only remained for us to acquire a hobby or two, like golf, to help us relax in the spare hours of the afternoon.

Part of our mistaken attitude was that it was widely thought that economics was now a "solved problem." The classical micro-economics of Marshall and others, combined with Keynes's insight into the existence of "stable unemployment" and "liquidity preference" that had dragged the world through the misery of the prewar Great Depression, meant we need never be materially miserable again on planet Earth. Furthermore, even the idea of commandist economic management did not make our blood run cold as it does today—we were all-knowing commanders ourselves. We were not even twenty years from the world war that definitively killed the Depression with efficient state control of the means of production—even the Russians, who built endless numbers of tanks in their hastily thrown together factories east of the Urals in the war. What would stop them switching their output to washing machines or sports cars come peacetime? (Imagine a Soviet sports car! I could once but cannot today remember what it looked like—nor how fast it moved.)

Meanwhile Keynes's insights were put to work in the postwar period to accelerate growth in the developed capitalist countries and achieve near full employment, while governments negotiated with the trade unions to hold the threat of excessive inflation at bay.

Who would have believed that fifty years thence—a full eighty years since the publication of Keynes's *General Theory*—we would be confronted with a recession to rival the Great one, apparently unable to shift gears? And an Africa that could seemingly only progress by selling its natural resources and by begging and guilt-tripping rich countries to give them back? All of us sinking into the Slough of Despond on the inside pages every day whenever world economic conditions were not optimal?

I recently read more of Keynes's work than I did as a student (you can decide what that means yourself . . .). It seems he was well aware of the dangers of believing economics to be an easy subject, even after his simplification of the issues:

> The master-economist must possess a rare combination of gifts. . . . He must be mathematician, historian, statesman, philosopher—in some degree. He must understand symbols and speak in words. He must contemplate the particular, in terms of the general, and touch abstract and concrete in the same flight of thought. He must study the present in the light of the past for the purposes of the future. No part of man's nature or his institutions must be entirely outside his regard. He must be purposeful and disinterested in a simultaneous mood, as aloof and incorruptible as an artist, yet sometimes as near to earth as a politician. (Keynes, 1924)

With that tall order, which I was deluded into believing I understood, I returned to Zambia, renounced my right to British citizenship and collected my Zambian passport. The Constitution of Zambia allowed that for eighteen months any adult born in the territory could do the same thing—but there was no dual citizenship until very recently, when it was included in a constitutional amendment. An indication of the way most whites and Indians viewed the options is to be had from the fact that the British High Commission had to devise a new form especially for me, although it was almost a year after Independence. I duly signed "Renunciation of British Citizenship Form RBC1/1." What was worrying many other locally born residents was that Zambian citizenship might prevent them from remitting funds to their "home" countries, and also that these countries might renounce *them*.

But I had deliberately made the decision to "stay behind." A factor that reinforced my resolve was the decision made by the Zambian government to take over responsibility for the scholarship awarded me by the outgoing federal government. My father had recently died, leaving us financially strapped (never put money in newspapers), so the cessation of the federal government's funding was an issue. Valentine Musakanya was secretary to the cabinet, and he pronounced very firmly that Zambia would honor my scholarship. If Zambia could do that for me, what could I reasonably refuse to do for Zambia?

Upon landing in Lusaka, I was employed by the government planning office in the section dealing with human resources. The colonial government had generally been benign toward the people in its care, but in the field of education it had been extremely neglectful. The missionaries tried but focused mainly on early education. It is frequently claimed that Zambia had fewer than 100 university graduates at independence— plainly orders of magnitude short of the requirement for the management of the country. Yes, we could start with helpful people coming from the developed world, but we needed to train and deploy our own sons and daughters—that was the thinking, and it was difficult to fault.

However, I was not cut out to be a civil servant or a central "planner." Under central planning, Mario Nuti (by then of King's College and later of Florence, Sienna, and other wonderful places) told me the future is certain; it is the past that changes every day. So I wandered off and started dividing my time between working as deputy editor of a monthly magazine entitled *Business and Economy* (in small print grandly "of East and Central Africa") and producing all manner of agricultural products that were being denied us by the trade disruption with Rhodesia.

The magazine was edited by Anthony Martin, perhaps a manic-depressive and certainly a heavy drinker, but the wittiest and best-read journalist I ever met. Toward the end of the month we interviewed capitalists and captains of government over liquid lunches, as well as eccentrics like René Dumont (author of *False Start in Africa*) and Edward Makuka Nkoloso, a primary school science teacher who launched trainee astronauts in oil drums straight down hills and in parabolic orbits from tall trees, all as a build-up to a Zambian-manned space program. We wrote our stories and laid out "the rag" in a haze, as was the Fleet Street norm at the time. We would sometimes accidentally swap pictures and captions, so that for example the official price controller would turn out to be a cow, apparently staring from the page unhappily at the hyped price of its milk or flesh. One day *Business and Economy* was accidentally bought by Tiny Rowland (the famously "unacceptable face of capitalism"), as part of a larger package, and far less accidentally closed down by him a few days later.

I don't think, in retrospect, that most of us economists took sufficient notice of the Rowland phenomenon and others like it. In an environment with strong centralist-socialist features and chips on political shoulders he managed to get his operation moving and making money, and thus providing sustainable employment, where others ground to a halt or were nationalized. I spent some time in more recent days with former senior managers of his, listening to their analysis of how the

Lonrho group worked. They point out that he correctly foresaw the massive government bureaucracy that would try and control the economy. He met it with an army of accountants and lawyers who, instead of fighting government, helped the bureaucrats do their almost impossible jobs. When import licenses were a constraint, when foreign exchange was strictly controlled, it was a pleasure for government to do business with the ever-thoughtful Lonrho, with its mightily acceptable capitalistic face. I made some use of this insight when I was vice president, keeping two Lonrho veterans on my book of advisers.

Another aspect of practical capitalism was dependent on Kenneth Kaunda's temperament erupting from time to time. The old man would fire some senior civil servants and make no provision for their earning a living, their kids' education, or whatever (he really was extremely harsh in this regard). But fired civil servants and multinationals quickly learned that they could "insure" each other, given foresight. So long as the fired government officials took care of the big company's permissions and requests—in anticipation—they would almost automatically be taken on in the private sector as soon as KK applied the boot.

Although Zambia was rolling in money in its early years, as the result of a worldwide copper boom and the redirection of royalties into the country's own coffers, we were dependent upon our southern neighbors for the supply of most basic commodities. Rhodesia, having sanctions imposed upon it by the UN, retaliated by imposing them in turn on us. The joke of the time was "Sanctions are finally biting; Zambia is on its knees." We were short of fuel, cement, a range of foodstuffs, even maize—the staple food we were accustomed to importing from Rhodesia. I decided farming was the key sector for development in landlocked Zambia. By 1970 I had taught myself enough about agriculture to go for it.

Despite the fact of a racial war taking place in neighboring countries and spilling over into Zambia, social peace and harmony by and large prevailed among the different groups. Even the few Trek Boers who had somehow managed to follow in Livingstone's footsteps with their cigarette packets stuck in their long socks were invited to official cocktail parties, along with ZIPRA, ANC, and other freedom leaders, to underline Kaunda's message of peace *within* our country.

But if physical insecurity was not a very big factor, economic security was. Kaunda and some of his missionaries (who sometimes were crazy to an almost clinical degree) tried to set us on the path to "scientific socialism," then as now a serious threat to successful life as we know it.

It was probably inevitable that most African nationalists became proponents of public ownership in key industries. It was still widely supposed even among academics in the West that some sort of state governance scheme could enable the public sector to take over swaths of industry, even agriculture, and create an egalitarian society without too much loss of efficiency. Even recent graduates of British universities—drafted as economic advisers and who would have been colonial officers were it not for the "wind of change"—held state ownership and control, along with efficient state intervention in trading and production, to be feasible. Kaunda did not understand business, but his political incentives were obvious: the copper industry and much else in Zambia was effectively owned by capitalists in the south. Indeed the country itself had been founded and originally named after a capitalist based in Cape Town. Nationalization was easily seen as the next stage after nation*alism*.

The impetus toward socialism had nothing to do with Cold War alignment. Zambia and many African countries were chary of political alignment with Communism. They regarded the idea of switching from West to East as a formula for changing from one colonialist arrangement to another. And they had recently witnessed war between the big rivals causing mayhem in the Congo. When members of the South African Communist Party arrived in Lusaka seeking asylum, they were surprised that Zambian Immigration refused them residency in Lusaka as SACP members (but helpfully suggested they announce themselves as ANC members). Globally, Kaunda and some of his many personal friends—Josip Broz Tito, Nicolae Ceausescu, Saddam Hussein—were founders and promoters of the Non-Aligned Movement, an international "third force" nowadays vainly looking for relevance in the post–Cold War world. (Contrast the fates of his friends with that of Kaunda, now lionized once more as the father of the nation; Africa is far more forgiving than some of these European and Middle Eastern countries.)

When I attended the funeral of Margaret Thatcher in London in 2013 one of the (more genuine) mourners was F. W. de Klerk. While we waited for buses he told me he was proud of delaying South Africa's day of freedom because it provided time for communism in Eastern Europe to definitively collapse and discourage Mandela et al. from taking the communist line to which the ANC was committed. In other words, he, de Klerk, had saved his country from Communism ("saving from Communism" being the standard defense for apartheid). Even taking into account the historical differences between us and our southern cousins, I cannot believe any South African nationalist was in danger of going in a different direction from those in the rest of southern Africa. Some academics, predominantly white ones, might have retained an ideological

commitment to Communism or Marxism but they were not a factor. I
wanted to remonstrate with de Klerk but unfortunately, I lost track of
him in the unseemly prostate-propelled sprint of grey-suited middle-aged
men from St. Paul's Cathedral to Mansion House across the road.

There is a tale that Kaunda had agreed with the international owners
to hold back on nationalization of the mines: taking ownership of the
assets but leaving the private owners to operate under management contracts. This is the highly successful route taken by Chile. However, the
white mine workers from South Africa had invented a slogan with
which they taunted their black counterparts: *Lo Zambia ena kawena; lo
mali ena katina.* This is in a South African creole called variously Funa-
galo, Kitchen Kaffir, or Chilapalapa, used as a lingua franca on southern
African mines and farms. It means "Zambia is yours; the money is
ours." Kaunda was reportedly so incensed when he heard the slogan that
he gave orders for instant and total nationalization. I hesitate to declare
this story apocryphal since KK had an awful temper that frequently
prompted him to take precipitate actions that he would only find the
humility to regret when the damage had well and truly been done.

Components or correlates of KK's heterodox regime included a ban
on all political parties other than his own UNIP, price controls, foreign
exchange regulations, conscription into the military, a government
takeover of all media, fuel rationing, a ban on foreigners operating
many kinds of small business, and the construction of a personality cult
(*Lesa pamulo, Kaunda panshi*—God above, Kaunda on earth). These
were some of the features of Kaunda's one-party and one-man state;
experts on the genre will gloomily recognize all of them. Looking at it
twenty years after the last white minority government in southern Africa
collapsed, it seems rather bizarre, but on Kaunda's behalf it should be
said that in those days there was no guarantee that the freedom wars
involving our neighbors would not escalate out of control. Most of
Kaunda's "socialist" measures are more or less standard for any country
regarding itself as being at war (Ian Smith's dispensation was actually
similar in many respects). And "war" was not an unreasonable description of the situation, especially toward the end of the Rhodesian fighting, when Smith's near-obsolete Hawker Hunters would streak in broad
morning through the Zambian sky. In those pre-GPS days, these were
apparently controlled visually by a high-flying small plane. My oldest
son, then nine years old, would shout "Spotter!" and we would share the
binoculars and listen for the sound of ZIPRA guerrilla camps being
bombed and strafed, in turn followed by the roar of trucks carrying the
injured to hospital. (During one strike the Rhodesians deposited boxes

of counterfeit medicine labeled in Russian as antibiotics; these were eagerly pounced upon and used by the Zambian medics who discovered that the "medicine" was in fact poison—too late to stop many of their patients dying in agony.)

There were comic episodes such as the "Green Leader" take-over of Zambia's air traffic control system, when some laconic Rhodesian version of Biggles came on the radio and grounded all civilian planes at the Lusaka airports. But the blood and the bodies were real enough. So forgiveness for those in the system is arguably in order, even for the British "overseas assistance" boys fresh out of university who designed laws to regulate the price of tomatoes—a logical impossibility—and the Irish policemen who hunted those citizens who were in possession of a few US dollars. Perhaps we can even look with equanimity at those who invented the "one-party participatory democracy" and invited us to go to the polls and choose between Yes to Kaunda (represented by an eagle) and No (represented by a frog). All was forgiven; we were at war.

Then Rhodesia cracked.

One of the truths of electoral politics is that right-wing governments can more easily implement left-wing policies than can the left itself—and vice versa. A Conservative voter could not protest about Britain giving away its Empire by switching to the Labour party on the left (which obviously espoused the same policy); whereas a Labour voter could meaningfully punish that party by moving his vote to the right. So with respect to UDI, for example, we were treated to the confusing spectacle of Harold Wilson miserably chickening out at every important showdown in the saga, and we had to wait for a Tory government to come along and call the Rhodesians to heel. It was Margaret Thatcher who brought Ian Smith to the negotiating table at Lancaster House. Kenneth Kaunda claims some credit in his own opinion for stepping out to dance the quickstep with her at the Commonwealth Heads of Government Meeting in Lusaka in 1979. "I softened her heart to Africans," he likes to say.

What to do with Zimbabwe sorted out? It is very tempting for a government to retain its powers of intervention and generally undemocratic arrangements even after a war has ceased. Many one-party states seem set on remaining so forever by perpetuating citizens' belief in a state of war or incipient war. If I had not known that many years ago by reading Orwell's *1984*, I would certainly have learned it when Michael dispatched me to North Korea to help the population of that non-aligned state celebrate the sixtieth anniversary of its victory [*sic*] over the Americans.

But in Zambia the problem was slightly different. We were much exercised by the question of when a creeping advance of the frontier of majority rule was effectively over (from our point of view). By 1980 many of us Zambians with liberal educations nursed the conviction that since the Portuguese territories had gained independence and the Rhodesian war had come to an end, we could get back to democracy and business. South Africa and its appendage South West Africa (Namibia) were obviously just a matter of time, and they were a long way from Lusaka.

Kaunda took a different view. He stuck to his guns. The "Boers" were still in power and Mandela was still in prison. Fight on! The Zambian economy suffered badly, the government had to wrestle with the IMF, employment sank, inflation went up to 200 percent. Next door the Zimbabweans seemed to forgive each other and get on with an economic boom. People in Zambia were fed up, and if a multiparty election had been held in, say, 1979, Kaunda would have tumbled, even if his opponent was a frog. But KK would not budge, and who knows but that he was right to hold out until he was sure Africa was free down to the last acre? He was no economist, that was certain, but you can argue that economics is what happens after a war, not during war—think of Germany, Japan, and Taiwan.

Perhaps the time has come to admit that we unjustly thought KK was just hanging on to power like so many of his dubious pals. It was much to our surprise that, when it became unquestionable that the freedom struggle had ended in South Africa, he readily agreed to sign away the one-party state and hold an election. He did this in 1990, the same year that Mandela was released from prison and flew straight to Zambia to visit his exiled colleagues and thank Zambians for their sacrifices. Although it was still four more years to a free election in South Africa, it was now plain that the war was as good as won. So to do him credit KK did not delay our own return to freedom once he was convinced that there were no racists—especially of the Boer variety—left for him to sort out. Conversely, he was convinced he would win the new election by a landslide—he could not understand the resentment of his own people and how sharply it contrasted with the admiration and thanks toward him of neighboring freedom fighters.

GOING BACK SOME YEARS, in 1980 some friends of mine, including Valentine Musakanya (but not including me), concluded that a coup would be both feasible and morally justified. Some of them were lawyers representing rebel Congolese gendarmes who had taken refuge in Zambia from Mobutu during the "Shaba 2" civil war. The plot was discovered when one of the plotters spilled the beans and most of them, including Valentine, were captured and tried. He had a lengthy trial and spent several years on death row, though the sentence was overturned by the Supreme Court on the grounds that evidence was obtained under torture. This exposed the cruel nature of Kaunda's fight against his political foes within Zambia—the One-Party State is a primitive beast.

He was released by Kaunda as part of the run-up to the return to what passed as normality in 1990. Valentine's spirit was broken and he passed his time drinking with his friend and fellow alleged coup plotter Pierce Annfield.

Back in 1980 I was very unhappy with the situation my family and I were in. I did not want to use my energy and intelligence to support some version of unscientific nonsocialism in a country without a war to excuse it. I had lost all faith in the running of my country by experts, donors, consultants, or professionals from home or abroad. As a country it seemed we were going backward, and the theories of how you build a backward country into something worthwhile were getting sillier by the day. Zambia needed a return to democratic governance—letting the people speak, and letting them reward and punish their leaders. That was my view.

Also, I did not want my three boys to grow up in a third-rate country in which they would flourish only because they were part of an elite class (i.e., white). I quoted Calvin Coolidge on Billings, Montana: "a good place to come from and a good place to go home to die." Was I really that depressed? Perhaps it was just an end-of-war reaction, the sort of thing you read about, a sudden loss of meaning or of temporary depression induced by the end of a life-threatening crisis. You might think human beings would dance away from concentration camps or battlefields when war ends, but in reality they just go flat for a while.

In 1982 I decided to exile myself and my family to Britain and get myself a doctorate in the then new field—opened up by computers—variously called "artificial intelligence" or "cognitive science" or "robotics." It offered change and a new intellectual challenge. "Don't forget to phone me when the day of democracy comes!" I said to one of those who stayed behind. It took eight years but he actually remembered.

MEANWHILE, BACK IN 1981, in a far-sighted move to position himself for the inevitable end of Kaunda, a certain noisy fellow joined UNIP "by the backdoor" of becoming a councillor and working his way up the party ladder. He had first wanted to stand as an MP (against other contestants all belonging to UNIP) but was vetted by the Central Committee on the grounds that he was loud-mouthed and critical of Kaunda and spent too much time hanging loose with whites (so it was said by some). But those who would censure him relented somewhat when he lowered his ambition to that of becoming a councillor. Once a councillor he made a lot more noise and gained fame and popularity, managing to speak through the screen of a state-owned press and electronic media. This is a rare skill, difficult to emulate. He became a specialist in local government, making councillors and officials work extremely hard by "bollocking" them in public. Sympathetic journalists found ways of sneaking his message through. When a disc jockey said "this man strikes like a King Cobra," the name stuck. They could not muffle him; he became an MP, the senior governor of Lusaka, and the minister of state for decentralization. When the Movement for Multiparty Democracy (MMD) was born in 1990, Michael Sata was ready for it. He had already thrown down the gauntlet: There I am, inside, now just watch me!

7

Chimwela:
The Second Wind

I DULY OBTAINED MY DPHIL FROM THE UNIVERSITY OF SUSSEX, BUT despite years in search of artificial intelligence, I had virtually given up hope of imparting anything resembling even a little grey matter into a machine, and my robots routinely crashed. Several conversations and some correspondence with Gaetano Kanizsa, the Italian Gestalt psychologist, plus the writing of many sophisticated computer programs that signified nothing and did less, had turned me into a phenomenologist (in my quest to understand the word I have reached the stage in which I do not have to use spellchecker). I wanted to go home, but Kaunda was resolutely hanging on, seemingly unwilling to give us the freedom to elect ourselves a government of our choice. I removed myself to Oxford, working as a researcher in the Department of Engineering, representing the male sex as a fellow of the otherwise all-female Somerville College.

It so happened that I knew the principal, Daphne Park, from the early postindependence period in Zambia. Raised in Tanganyika she had first been British high commissioner to Zambia from 1964 to 1967 and one of her protégés was Valentine Musakanya. At the time Daphne and I crossed paths at Somerville, Valentine was still in prison on death row for his role in the 1980 coup attempt. She was known to be a "spook" back in the early UDI days, regardless of the later loyal denials of the fellows and

---

Chimwela means "wind" in the CiBemba language of northern Zambia, often used to mean "a wind of change."

79

students, whom she referred to as "her girls," at Somerville. In later life and beyond, she has in some eyes assumed the role of a British "queen of spies." It was rumored that her main task was to see if, out of the anarchy in the Congo, the copper mines there could somehow become part of a sort of Greater Zambia and thence part of a Greater British sphere of influence. But it was not to be. I would guess her main worry concerned the Rhodesians and South Africans trying something similar.

But at the end Daphne confessed, over tea to Lord Lea, to being a party to the 1961 assassination of Patrice Lumumba, the pro-Soviet but freely elected president of the Congo (Lea, 2013). This crime was thought to have been a culmination of two interrelated assassination plots by the US and Belgian governments, which used Congolese accomplices and a Belgian execution squad to carry out the deed. She was at the time MI6 controller in Congo, masquerading as the British envoy in Leopoldville. This "confession" is held in some informed quarters to be bogus. Anyway, she had not yet confessed or "confessed" to being party to the assassination; this was still years off and nothing prevented our celebrating our reunion. Besides, she was partly raised in Nyasaland and Tanganyika and thus virtually a cousin of mine.

Some years passed in Oxford as my first marriage deteriorated and my interest in robotics followed it downhill. I took up a fraudulent persona as an expert in Congolese music and dance (I failed to make it popular among students but it turned out many years later as a moderately good defense and therapy for Parkinson's disease). What would have happened if the phone had not rung? But it finally sang in north Oxford in the small hours of the morning. . . what a sweet song. KK had agreed to hold elections, and the Movement for Multiparty Democracy (MMD) was the political party that was going to take him on. "You told me to phone you when he caved in," I was reminded. "Now where are you?"

I bought enough pairs of shorts to keep me traveling in cool comfort around a country three times the size of Great Britain and bought a one-way ticket to Zambia. I dropped into my office to collect my things, giving Robbie the Robot a hefty kick by way of farewell. (It was only a virtual kick because Robbie was only a virtual machine—like Super Mario—but the release of long contained frustration was surprisingly, non-virtually gratifying.)

In my now neatly folded memory, it seems I took a taxi direct from Lusaka International Airport to the first MMD national convention. (In literal point of fact I am sure I must have allowed a gap of some weeks.) I arrived at the conference center where would-be leaders of the new party had assembled to compete for positions on the National Executive

Committee, and—most importantly—to elect one presidential candidate to wallop Kaunda and lead us into the glorious future.

We were a motley bunch: politicians and officials who had fallen afoul of KK over the course of his interminable reign; pardoned coup plotters; parliamentary floor-crossers; alleged this, alleged that; trade unionists; exiled academics; and *kwasa kwasa* or *quoi ca* dancers. There were four white Zambians including me (one of whom claimed God had ordered him to go to the convention but had withheld any hint as what to do on arrival), and a similar number of Indian origin. Every variety of potential politician was there, and the wind of change almost blew us off our feet.

In the conference hall, I saw a man walking toward me whom I recognized from the press. He was very short, about five-feet one-inch, dressed in a posh black suit (Armani most likely), discreet platform shoes, and a silk floral tie with a matching handkerchief carefully tucked in the breast pocket. This form of dress had already been christened the "new culture," replacing KK-style safari suits. "Good morning sir," I ventured. He scowled at me and made to walk past. "This is the son of Dr. Alexander Scott," a passerby interceded, "he has come home from Britain to help." Fredrick Chiluba humphed, stopped, shook my hand, and thanked me in an American accent that he must have spent months of Sundays practicing in the bathroom.

Fred was a trade unionist who, under Soviet tutelage, had started his career as a keen Communist. He gave his first children names like "Castro" and "Mikoyan." Somewhere down the line he was converted, by US trade unionists, to the free market system. So his later children were given names like "Henry" and "John." (I never met Henry or John, but I certainly met Castro: about two years later, the manager of a bar hid me, Charlotte, and our friends in his office while Castro, wielding a pistol and stoned on imported drugs, trashed the place. Some weary looking cops eventually turned up and took him home.)

Fred was in first position to be elected as the MMD president in April 1991. He had openly fought Kaunda, using the unions' structures for support, for over ten years; he had been jailed for some months in 1980 on suspicion of being involved in the coup attempt already mentioned; he was a Bemba (or so he and his supporters claimed—others alleged he was Congolese); and he was a fine orator in a TV evangelist sort of a way. He easily won the poll to become the MMD's candidate, sweeping the floor against one pardoned coup plotter and a couple of elder statesmen, one retired, who had jumped the UNIP ship. Nobody was in the mood for "playing"—we wanted change, and Fred was the man to take on KK.

As I moved among the 1,600 delegates at the conference center, I noticed that there seemed to be something like a source of gravity traveling around, pulling people toward it. There was something exercising an attraction, leading to the formation of a crowd, without itself being immediately visible. A black hole? I elbowed my way into the thick of the crowd until I found myself face to face with its cause: a fifty-something black man of unexceptional stature and appearance.

"Sata," he said to me, "Michael Sata."

Bond, James Bond, I thought. "Guy Scott," I said, "pleased to meet you."

"Good to see you, Mr. Scott. We can do with a white man in this party; they sometimes come in useful in African politics you know. What position do you want?"

"Chairman of Agriculture."

"Done."

And so it was done, and I won the position to loud acclaim. One would have thought I had saved every man, woman, and child in Zambia from starvation. But I had not done anything like that, at least not yet. My enduring "achievement" that day was that I had been accepted into what its members came to call the "Michael Chilufya Sata Academy of Political Science," the great panjandrum that one day would roll into State House in a bid to rescue Zambians from anything evil you could find a name for or point a stick at.

It seems in retrospect that *everyone* who knew Zambian politics believed Michael was going to make it to the top. His charisma—to use an inadequate word for want of a better—simply made it obvious. (His gravitational field?) But not yet; first we had to have Fred. Enduring Fred was our penance for being late on the battlefield. For all his scrapping with Kaunda and his reputation as the hardest working governor and minister in Zambia, Michael could still be faulted as a latecomer to the opposition. Compared to Fred, he was sullied by a too recent association with UNIP despite having crossed the floor in parliament.

"Fredrick can have his maximum ten years, as the new constitution dictates, and then we will take our turn," he advised. If only it had turned out that simple.

To say that Michael was a controversial figure in some self-styled "educated" or "middle-class" circles is a gross understatement. He was regularly likened to Idi Amin and Robert Mugabe. And Michael's presumed similarity to Donald Trump is a popular theme of second-rate journalistic "think pieces" despite the time warp in between them.

He was described as uneducated, offensive, and a danger to foreign investment flows. Civil servants—especially council workers and hospital managers—regarded him with deep dread; and his Elvis-like unaccountable "appearances" to otherwise sane people made him feared even when he was out of the country.

"I saw him just there, behind the door."

"Rubbish, there's nobody there."

"I *saw* him!"

As governor for Lusaka and as a minister, his genuine appearances had a sound track of barked orders and palpable threats. He constantly railed at the laziness and incompetence into which the work ethic had transmuted since independence. And the nostalgia for well-run hospitals and schools and police forces resonated with the great majority of Zambians, especially if they were not directly in the line of fire.

But the educated or middle class, while they tended to fear and oppose him (though far from always), were not Michael's target audience. He knew on which side his votes lay, and he knew how to coax them into the ballot box. He certainly had respect for education, but he knew that most voters wanted to hear something more tangible than a political treatise or economic theory. A good example of his difference with "intellectuals" was provided by one Dr. Ludwig Sondashi, who has a PhD from Warwick University. In the 1991 election campaign—which simply took off as a continuation of the convention until we arrived at an election date—Sondashi joined us at a rally on the Copperbelt. He addressed the crowd in English and accepted Michael's offer to translate into Bemba. One fragment went as follows:

> SONDASHI (in English): When MMD comes into government we will strengthen the enjoyment of human rights by domesticating the relevant international conventions into our national statutes.
>
> SATA (in Bemba): When I was put in prison by the British, I was given three meals a day. Today, a prisoner is lucky to get one meal, unless his family provides it. We are going to reinstate the British system.
>
> SONDASHI (in English): That's not what I said. Where is the mention of human rights?
>
> SATA (in English): What is the Bemba for Human Rights?
>
> SONDASHI (in English): Then say it in English.
>
> SATA (language indeterminate): Human lights.

In the last election for the presidency in which he stood (in 2011), Michael got 43 percent of the vote. In the last presidential election in which Sondashi stood (2015), he got less than 1 percent of the vote.

You might venture that Sata had an instinct that directed him to take on any form of authority that lay in his path. The more formal and the more powerful, the more irresistible. He took tremendous pleasure in tripping them up. As a young man courting his first wife in Malawi he took some photographs of Kamuzu Banda's motorcade—strictly forbidden in the place and time. A policeman told him to extract the film from the camera. Sata pointed to a small hole in the camera and claimed it was a keyhole: "I can only open it with a key but I have forgotten the key in Zambia." The policeman was convinced by this lie and his tone of contrition.

Improvising our way into and out of potholes and obstacles was something we did virtually every day during the campaign period in 1991. This was most gratifying when the victories were on behalf of the underdog—the poor, the weak, the excluded. Our sense of moral righteousness needed to be fed, as did our appetite for votes, and the weak were the numerous ones.

One day I woke up to find I had lost my national registration card, an essential document for anyone planning to stand for parliament. I was worried that if I filed a declaration that I had lost it, the registration system would deliberately delay replacement. I confided my worry to Michael—what to do? The King Cobra leaped from his desk and marched me down to the registration office.

"Give this man a card!" he shouted imperiously. "He has been in England and never had one before."

It blew up in our faces, as one might expect in the days before the really nasty computer viruses hit town. The registrar general phoned us and asked why I had not reported my loss, ending with "Come and collect your replacement." We were lucky he was one of us. But the UNIP controlled press had a field day:

SCOTT NOT A ZAMBIAN!

This was my first, but very, very far from my last experience of Action Man's propensity for ill-considered and precipitate action and consequent public embarrassment.

As we turned to leave the registration center Michael spotted at the end of the queue a young woman of perhaps twenty, who was heavily pregnant as well as carrying a young baby.

"Why has this girl not been attended to? How can you tolerate to see her waiting for her turn? Come here *Maiyo* [mother]!" He led her by the arm to the photo booth.

"Bring chairs! We are not leaving until we see her leave this place with her card." We sat. She got her card.

I like to ask people who call Michael a populist what exactly they mean to imply. Do they mean that he was insincere when adopting the persona of a "man of the people"? This small incident of the girl and the card was not a big deal—even as campaign material it may have influenced only a few hundred people who got to hear the story (in the days before Twitter). But it captures very simply Michael's main message: the government does not care about the people and it is not doing its work properly. We intend to change that. We need to make the government work, the people who work in it *care*, and the ordinary people feel looked after.

A common conception of a populist is one who makes promises he cannot fulfill, but Michael was not promising anything unattainable; he was just emitting a sympathetic reminder that the government must treat the smallest people well. In this vignette there is no false promise for the future, no utopian vision. As someone said to me, Michael's actions were simply an illustration of "applied fatherliness." The Zambians who miss him today, and they are very, very many, nearly always talk of him being "my father."

The campaign period, between the national convention and the election, lasted more than six months. I addressed more than 100 rallies in Zambia in seven of its nine provinces. We started in Lusaka, conveniently, and I found myself among the elected national leaders standing on a rickety wooden stage surrounded by a crowd of people who had walked from all parts of the city to be there. I could not see clearly the edge of the enormous crowd, and I decided to do something that a retired Oxford don in the circumstances might easily do. The speed of sound in Lusaka is about 330 meters per second. When it came to my turn to address the crowd, I sang the first line of a song: *Tichose Kaunda ndi mtima umo*. The sound was promptly thrown over the crowd, eliciting an almost immediate response as it reached each listener. There was about a four second delay between the end of me singing the line, and the dying out of the returning sound. Call it 600 meters to the furthest member of the audience, and 600 back. Allow one square meter per person in the crush; that makes a million people out of a population of well under two million at the time. That cannot be right can it? But it was very big. Eat your heart out, Mick Jagger, I thought as I finished off the song that was a mockery of Kaunda's signature song *Tiyende Pamodzi* ("Let's go together with one heart" transposed into "Let's get rid of Kaunda with one heart").

As someone said to me around that time, politics is show business for ugly people.

On occasion my being white was an advantage, and I cannot think of any incident where it was a significant disadvantage. We went up to Mpika, Michael's home district in the Northern Province, to set up a command post for the MMD. Northern Province was increasingly focused on change, and the work started well. We became more concerned about what we heard from the east, though. Kaunda's UNIP was still in firm control, and taking heavy-handed action against any attempts to establish MMD structures. We decided to take a trip across the Luangwa Valley—a remote southern tendril of the east African Rift Valley—and sneak up on UNIP by finding a way to cross the river and enter the Eastern Province by stealth. This would give us some hours to appoint MMD officials and generally organize our support before the UNIP heavies up on the eastern plateau heard of our presence and were able to find and confront us. These considerations were not trivial—they were a very rough lot who had already lobbed big rocks at us when we had taken the main road. We duly overloaded my secondhand Land Cruiser with about ten passengers, and traversed eight hours of very bad road. The young girl "cadres" sang political Bemba songs in entrancing harmonies all the way.

We crossed the Luangwa River close to the National Park by commandeering a hunting company pontoon, and set off for an "eco-tourism" camp in which I had somehow acquired a share. It was the end of the dry season, and the long grass was brown. The sight of it evidently annoyed Michael, perhaps because it betokened yet another system that he had not broken, and he made me stop the Cruiser every few miles so that he could jump out and start a bush fire. After a while we had developed a smoky trail like a burning aircraft crash landing in painfully slow motion.

"This is against the law," I admonished.

"Stop!" He struck a match and started another one.

After dark we arrived at the camp and drank it dry (it rarely had any paying clients so all the drink tended to go down the manager anyway). Away from any hint of light pollution, the stars and the Milky Way were garishly visible as they set off on their dusk to dawn march across the sky ("an army with banners" the Song of Songs calls them). A young spotted hyena started its calling, whooping like a novice cowboy disappointed in love, as we sat close to the fire, which projected us as giants against the trees. At peace with all nature if not Kaunda, we distributed ourselves in the "eco-huts" with doorframes but no doors. All was peaceful until, after midnight, a lion that sounded to be about ten yards away and ten feet tall started to roar. The girls all squealed, jumped out of bed and ran for Michael's hut—the VIP suite with an extra-large door frame but still no door. Then the male cadres followed. For a while I stuck my heels in—shouting about lions not coming into huts and always being further away than they sound.

"Are you coming, Doctor Scott? Our people need to be comforted. I am told lions prefer to eat whites first."

I gave in and joined Michael's pride of dependents. How to redeem myself?

On the way back, around lunchtime, we used the hunter's pontoon again and pulled into their lodge (at least $1,000 per person per day for the package). We went to the kitchen to beg for food. The camp cooks apologized, saying that they only had food for the clients. "But this one," said Michael, pointing at me, "Does he not look like a client? I am sure he is one. You had better serve him."

The upshot was that I got to order a giant lunch for myself—ten steaks, a case of beer, a sack of potatoes, and a 25 kilogram bag of mealie meal. When the owners and clients of the lodge eventually returned from their sport—shooting a variety of antelopes as lion bait—they were very disappointed to see their lunch away in the distance, climbing slowly up the escarpment to the western plateau. Michael was in good spirits. "Was taking all that food legal?" he asked. He had saved his protégés from the maw of the lion, as well as from an uncomfortable day with empty stomachs. And he had made a system—a white man's system what's more—work for him. Then I remembered who he reminded me of: Oskar Schindler, who looked set to end his life as a petty con man and purloiner of ash trays from hotel rooms, but who famously turned his talents to rescuing Jews from the death camps in Poland. Michael would have been ever grateful to God for the gift of a *Sonder kommando* or two to screw up. But God had given him instead the challenge of a broken country full of people with a poor sense of self-worth. If anyone could take that on with success it was Michael. And if I did not do my best to help him what would that make me?

"Stop!"

"You're not lighting another fire; anyway, you did this area yesterday."

"No, I am just going behind that anthill to shake hands with Kaunda."

He even looked the part of national liberator as he cleaned the .375 hunting rifle that Saddam Hussein had given him (he claimed) when he paid an official visit to Iraq. He carried this with us, despite protestations that he had left it behind in Lusaka. Of course.

The safari operator (the former owner of ten steaks) came to see me in my office as agricultural minister some weeks later. He started off looking rather cross but by the time we parted we were having a good laugh.

Michael and I reviewed the electoral situation in Mpika and made a decision. I had been complaining that I would feel embarrassed as chairman of agriculture if I went to parliament representing an urban constituency. I had to find a rural one. Michael suggested that I stand for Mpika Central, where he was born and his parents and brother still lived. This is where he would stand if he did not have a reliable substitute but once I nodded my head he switched his attention to taking a seat in Lusaka where he could keep up his surveillance and defiance of the enemy (i.e., anyone still with Kaunda). Mpika seemed a bit precarious to me—there was not one voter who was white out of 20,000 on the register, and I hardly spoke a word of Bemba. But Michael was confident he could sell me.

We held a public rally on a football field in the middle of Mpika for him to introduce me as MMD candidate. As we approached the podium we saw that hundreds of people, mostly male, were dancing wildly to a group of ten or so drummers. There was something unusual about the coiling rhythms that I could not put my finger on; both Michael and I joined the dance. Suddenly one of the dancers fell to the ground and was unable to, or uninterested in, getting up again. He lay there panting and gabbling while the others simply stepped aside and continued. Then it happened again.

"Do you know what's happening?" Michael asked.

"Yes," I replied, "The *ngulu* [nature spirits] are taking over. These must be trance drummers."

"So you know something about your country. We had better stop them."

"Why?"

"Because you or I might be the next to fall over." Yes, what would people say if prominent politicians were to be felled by their *ngulu* set loose by drums?[1]

They would say we were drunk.

The rest of the meeting proceeded uneventfully, though with terrific enthusiasm for the next MP. I managed two songs, a couple of jokes in Bemba, and received a confident slap on the back from Michael. I had a strong spasm of Imposter's Syndrome at that and many subsequent points in the campaign.

I was not of course the first white man they had seen in Mpika, but I was the first who asked for the vote, for the mandate to represent its people in parliament. In fact they were quite used to whites. Sir Stewart Gore-Brown lived at Shiwa N'gandu (Lake of the Crocodiles), a gothic English castle cum stately home set in Zambia's largest private estate, about an hour north of Mpika boma (the estate came to international fame through Christina Lamb's book *Africa House*, 1999). I have long since given up trying to figure out what "statement" Gore-Brown was trying to make with his mock castle with its crenulations. By 1991, he was long dead and his daughter and son-in-law were in residence. The castle was threatening to crumble from a lack of Portland cement in the foundations and towers.

There was a large aid project based in Mpika, aimed at developing infrastructure and capacity according to whatever paradigm was current in the discourse of British and international technical assistance. The District Development Support Program or DDSP ran a guesthouse and club, which is where we stayed when in Mpika. This was where my wife-to-be Charlotte was employed as a monitoring and evaluation (M&E) expert. Michael described in his last opening of parliament speech the story of my good fortune in finding Charlotte at the DDSP and persuading her to stick around as the revolution developed and propelled us into the new Zambia.

The first time Michael and I visited DDSP together, we had stopped off earlier that day at a village in which the villagers were making clay bricks, without pay, as their contribution to the construction of a teacher's house. Michael stood on an anthill and addressed the locals—calling them suckers for making bricks for free. They all cheered, put down their tools, and declared that they were on strike.

"Was that a good thing?" I asked, "Now they will be without a teacher."

"The country is covered with piles of clay bricks, which never get used because government doesn't do its part."

"Surely the right approach is to lobby government? And anyway the British are paying for this one," I said.

"You want to go back to Oxford? We are here to win control of the country and that involves stirring up the people and breaking the system."

Later we confessed to the British DDSP director what we had done. He was furious, complaining that we had undone months of negotiations with the villagers regarding "self- help."

Michael adopted a hangdog expression and whispered: "Sorry."

The DDSP is long defunct, and there is only a little of enduring value to show for it. I doubt this negative outcome is attributable entirely to our intervention with the self-help scheme.

Some of the things I did and said upset foreign whites aiming to "do good" in Africa. Conservationists, for example, disliked my sympathy for poachers and my insistence of their being protected by the rule of law. (And they needed protection from abuses such as "shoot on sight"—an accepted policy in several countries at the time, and apparently on the up again now. But I will leave this subject for the time being; wildlife politics and policies are worth another book.) More generally, however, I found the skepticism and even hostility of foreign officials quite puzzling. Coming from countries where political rights are held in high esteem and that insisted upon the restoration of multiparty democracy in Africa, their double standards have at times felt surprising. I have been berated by ambassadors on countless occasions for being in the opposition and for speaking out on policies that I believe to be damaging; Charlotte has similarly experienced discrimination working for various aid agencies simply because she was married to me, a Zambian enjoying his right to speak his mind!

But I was not seeking a mandate from whites, not even the Indian shopkeepers in Mpika. I was seeking the support of the indigenous population, most of whom were extremely poor and surviving on dangerous and marginal activities—like illegal hunting, illegal *chitemene* gardening, and illegal prostitution based on the custom of truck drivers.

What they wanted to hear was that, despite the impoverishment of the local population via the regulatory environment (for example as applied to wildlife in the parks and reserved management areas), we who cared for them would find a way of squaring the circle—of letting them eat the cake and save it. Of course there is no simple or cheap solution, indeed there may be no solution conceivable, and the voters know it in their bones. However, they also know that the regulatory authorities do not care, but they want their elected representatives at least to "share our suffering."

Efforts by aid workers to introduce large livestock have been generally nugatory among the Bemba. Once a small group of trained oxen from the southern end of Zambia—where cattle dominate the economy and culture—were introduced as draft animals to help the local farmers to plough, harrow, transport, and do other tasks. Be that as it may, they were swiftly eaten, every last one (this was my Charlotte's first assignment as an evaluation expert—a sad zero).

The village of Kaole, just outside Mpika, has a reputation as the source of more big game poachers than anywhere else in the country. I was told they don't farm, unless you count growing cannabis. I was told that they divide their time between making money from poaching in the valley and spending the money in the village while stoned. Attempts to extend "development" have been reportedly unsuccessful; the half-life of the last batch of breeding "super-goats" introduced in Kaole was even less than that of the draft oxen.

One Sunday morning I drove to Kaole for a public meeting. Some women from the village walked up the road from the village to meet me. "We want to see you!" they cried ecstatically. "You are seeing me now!" I answered. "No, we want to *see* you!"

I had got out of the car to greet them so they had little difficulty undressing me—to see me—and hoisting me shoulder high for the triumphal march into the village. I sang a song to the effect that this year Kaunda is going home (to Malawi) with his material possessions on his head. This bit of hypocrisy drove everyone wild. "Show me your voters' cards!" I shouted. They had none; they had lost them or, more likely, smoked them. They heralded my departure with as much enthusiasm as they showed welcoming me.

A quick count at the rally in Kaole revealed more women than men in attendance. Where are the men? In the North Luangwa, it would seem, poaching. I did a little research and discovered the following account. The people of Kaole were by and large not Bemba but of a tribe relocated from Tanganyika to make space for the Ruaha game reserve. They were genuine pure hunters. The colonial authorities of both countries had agreed that they would be given the run of the North Luangwa, then an open hunting area; but the Northern Rhodesian authorities subsequently took this area as yet another game park and they were moved again—to the plateau. So the idea that they were committing a crime hunting animals in an area originally designated as their source of food was not convincing to them.

Toward election day, Michael came to visit and over lunch we were accosted by a well-known radio reporter/disc jockey called Chela Katwishi, a roving observer on the upcoming elections.

"How are you doing?" he asked.

"Who have you asked so far?"

"The district governor—he says it is 50:50."

Michael took him by the hand and led him to the car. "Let's see!" As we drove around Mpika boma we waved the MMD's "Hour for Change" hand gestures at everyone who looked our way. Overwhelmingly they answered with the same sign. Michael counted them up to 50. "There," he said, "is our 50. Now let's find the district governor's 50." On the spur of the moment he had invented a new method of polling.

We switched to the UNIP (and Churchill's) two fingered "V for Victory" sign and kept driving. After half an hour we had just three positive responses. "Go and tell your boss."

Katwishi claimed later that he had gone to report the result of the experiment to the governor and was slung in jail for the night for his trouble. Somehow I doubt it.

A couple of days before polling day I was urgently summoned by a supporter who told me a tale to chill the blood. Her son had been wandering around town and been accosted by a stranger who asked him whether he knew my whereabouts. He was a Tanzanian mercenary who had been hired, he claimed, by the UNIP government to assassinate me.

Shaking, I sat down and ran a titanic boxing match in my head: Primal Dread versus Oxford Reasoning. I knew that Oxford provided good reasoning because I had read in a prospectus that it had "given the world Reason." (I found it very encouraging to know this after four years at the place.) Notwithstanding Oxford's modest claim, Dread walloped away for a while before the thinking part of me warmed up and started to dominate the proceedings. Why would anyone give me priority on a hit list? Why would anyone tip his hand in this way? Why a Tanzanian? Surely, driving me out of town was the only hope they had of defeating me, wasn't it? That's what they're trying to achieve! Calm down, calm down, dammit.

Oxford reasoning eventually gained control and then quite characteristically went over the top. I dragged my bed out of Charlotte's house and parked it in the middle of the lawn. (She was in Lusaka going crazy on the receiving end of half-baked rumors about the hit man—we had no cell phones as the older reader will recall.) I rigged up a couple of bulbs to assist the aim of any wandering Tanzanian with his muzzle loader or WWI Mauser (which would have been originally liberated from the German army under the command of General von Lettow Vorbeck when it reached the Chambeshi River and discovered that World War I was definitively over).

Meanwhile, the story of the Tanzanian assassin had got round the town, and every off-duty watchman working for DDSP turned up with spears and knobkerries. The bloke, had he existed, would have been lucky to fire off a single round. Thus I was saved from Nemesis and Hubris both; but I still secretly wonder whether I would have survived the night on sweet reason alone.

When I phoned Michael in Lusaka to tell him this tale he just laughed. He assured me it was in the bag.

His confidence was well placed. I got 90 percent of the votes cast against an incumbent opponent who hailed from the place and whose extended family was largely intact and in possession of voters' cards.

Clearly there was no way I could have lost, even if I had been a sack of sweet potatoes.

Out of 150 parliamentary seats in Zambia, the MMD took 125, most of them by indecent majorities. UNIP's 25 came from the east—the province next to Malawi and still loyal to Kaunda. And so we took over a whole country, a country of around nine million people at that time.

On the wider scale, traveling around Zambia, even during my Mpika campaign, was unavoidable. My local campaign was disrupted now and then by urgent requests to join the "victory parade" of Fred Chiluba's progression round the country. The reason given was straightforward, "We want the *muzungu* to be seen." I interpret the meaning thus. The point is not that a *muzungu,* a white person, is seen as an intrinsically more honest person than a black. The point is there are tribal differences and fears afoot among the blacks, and one tribe cannot wholeheartedly believe the other where a change of tribal dominance is taking place. A *muzungu* has no reason to be tribal, so he is automatically a person to take down the pressure and ease the advance. A similar logic presumably lubricated the appointment of Bishop Dupont as virtual paramount chief of the Bemba.

During one of these trips I was sitting with Fred in his car, some ten kilometers from the town of Mwinilunga, close to the point at which the borders of Angola, Congo, and Zambia fuse to a point. Suddenly we were ambushed . . . by a welcome party not too dissimilar in its scale or intentions to the Kaole ladies who had wanted to see me naked. It was dusk and we were slowed right down to below walking pace.

"I will need a hot bath," Chiluba said, "in about four hours!"

I took a separate vehicle and searched the celebrating town for a missionary with the rare facility of a hot bath. Mwinilunga is high (outside mosquito range) and it was chilly despite the time of year. I located a hot bath with the infinite hot water capacity of a petrol drum, and went on over to the rest house to wait for Fred, but I was told he was already in. Listen! Fred had run himself a freezing cold bath and was apparently teaching himself to swim in it, giggling like a small child. "I can swim," he shouted, "Ba Guy I can swim!"

Note

1. This is not a textbook of pagan animistic (or otherwise non-Christian) perceptions and beliefs, but a few comments might be welcomed by some readers to clarify the "spirit possession" episode in this chapter. *Ngulu* is the Bemba word denoting a "nature spirit" arising from a natural phenomenon like a waterfall, or a

living or mythological creature such as a hippo or a mermaid. It is sometimes translated as "genius loci" ("spirit of the place") but that is not satisfactory. *Ngulu* is also not to be confused with ancestral spirits, *imipashi*, which have the social and environmental tasks of looking after the tribe's interests, interceding to modify the weather, and reducing tensions between families. Nor is it to be confused with *inkalamo yakutuma* (the evil "sent" lion of the witchcraft domain—the lion with an agenda—dispatched to harm an enemy).

The *ngulu* may be visualized as a creature with its own wishes, fears, needs, feelings and so forth—it is in other words an organism, not a mere mechanism or image, and it can come into conflict with the owner—upon whose shoulder it is often visualized as sitting.

Although possession by external entities is denied by mainstream Christianity, it is key to the pagan take on the world and developments of it—for example, the phenomenological thinking of Pablo Picasso.

Ngulu comes to the notice of the traditional spirit doctor—*nganga*, usually a woman who has been treated herself—by manifesting symptoms of its presence. These include a range of behavioral changes, sensorimotor abnormalities, and distorted perceptions that bring to mind fairly common Western addictive and obsessive conditions. In particular, the most common presentation of *ngulu* is a persistent refusal to take food. This manifestation occurs in the same proportions of age and gender groups as anorexia nervosa in the first world. The treatment applied in Zambia involves inducing a state of trance through music, dance, and the use of naturally occurring drugs of which the preeminent one is cannabis (presumably partly on account of the appetite boosting effect commonly known in the articulate and rational town of Oxford as "the munchies").

In the traditional pagan frame of thought, the point of the treatment is not to expel or exorcise the *ngulu* but to get it to cooperate with its victim or "owner." This contrasts with the approach of certain fundamentalist churches that use exactly the same methods of "raising" *ngulu* but then attempt to exorcise them using fire and images of fire.

Bemba *ngulu* speak when they are in a trance, whereas those of other tribes dance and mimic.

The Reign of King Fred

CHILUBA DULY CALLED HIS FIRST PRESIDENTIAL PRESS CONFERENCE, MADE his immortal declaration that "I never knew power was so sweet," and appointed his ministers. I was appointed to Agriculture, Food, and Fisheries, upon which Michael started clapping and hooting like a child overcome with sudden joy. He got Local Government and Housing—exactly in line with his experience and ambitions—and we were set to put the country on fire, and not just the game parks.

Being in the same cabinet as Michael, I had plenty of opportunity to study at the feet of the political genius known as King Cobra. I was naïve and academically overtrained, prone to support positions that were politically, or even logically, impossible from the start; prone to writing papers that were too complex or arcane. "Drop it, *mwana* [kid]," he would say, "let's go and have a cigarette outside."

I was a slow learner and got attacked quite often by my fellow ministers, who clearly saw me as one chick who could safely be pushed out of the nest. At least in part, the fact that I was white meant that I did not belong to a large and influential extended family (or tribe). Sometimes, Michael had to come to my defense in roundabout ways. For example, on one occasion, Fred used a meeting to engineer a set piece three-pronged attack on me (though he kept primly quiet himself). It was supposed to end with my dismissal. Just before it was launched, a note from Michael landed in my fist saying, in capitals, DO NOT REPLY TO THE NEXT SPEAKER. The next speaker duly assaulted me over some quite serious breach of procedure in my ministry. I tried to protest but got a ray gun glare from Michael who then begged for the floor. He spoke to the effect that my behavior was shocking to him, who had once called himself my friend, especially as he had recommended me for a ministerial position. He now wished to recommend that I be very severely admonished and suspended for a month. "Anyway," he declared, "it is too late to undo the damage." To my amazement the lined-up attackers started interceding on my behalf. We are being too intolerant toward our *mzungu*, they said, but let his friend's anger serve as a warning. Yes, the damage is done. Next item!

After ten minutes I got another note: Let us go and smoke. We lit up among the monkeys and the peacocks.

"Mwana, never forget how stupid some people are," he said.

Fredrick Chiluba lived with at least three chips on his shoulder. He was very short, he was raised in poverty, and he was uneducated. You might think that, having ascended despite these handicaps to the top job in a nontrivial country, no greater pleasure could be obtained in life than to smile pityingly at the 8,999,999 of your contemporaries who failed to make the grade.

But this was not the way Fred saw it. What he saw was that, given he now had the power—how sweet!—he could *correct* the past. Let me be clear: he did not want to rewrite the past (as many leaders have done and will continue to do). He wished to change the facts in solid reality. Uneducated? He could arrange to be educated. (He did not need any patron to mint him a PhD in Life History to compensate for his failure to attend university.) Poor? He could arrange to have more dosh in his account than any other Zambian—or any other African with luck. Even height? He could order handmade shoes, hundreds of pairs, to add a couple of inches and order carefully crafted suits which used tricks from the camouflage craft to add another couple of inches in the visual judgment of the observer.

Education-wise, after placing enquiries, Chiluba made an arrangement with Warwick University to study by correspondence the works of the great pioneer of democratic theory, John Locke. He would first aim to produce a master's dissertation and then, assuming it revealed sufficient academic ability, continue to a full doctoral thesis and associated degree. He would then be one of many people called "doctor" in African leadership (including Dr. Kaunda) but his doctorate would be the genuine article. A supervisor was assigned to him, who had to fly out to Zambia at intervals (first-class on the state-owned Zambia Airways, says the gossip from inside the plane) to put the proverbial red pen to Fred's drafts. In due course the master's thesis was produced and turned into a book: *The Challenge of Change.*

I tried to remonstrate with Fred with all due respect. There was once a group of professors who tried to appoint Vladimir Nabokov to head the English Literature Department at Harvard University. They gave as an argument his achievements in writing English fiction. Indeed, the sardonic exile from Old Russia, ever in natural beauty's pursuit, is arguably one of the best English-language prose stylists who ever lived. But the successful counter-argument was that the department was looking for literary criticism and teaching, not literary performance.

"What then gentlemen; are we to appoint an elephant as professor of zoology?" was the reported response of Professor Roman Jakobson.

"You are an elephant, Mr. President, an object of fear and wonder; why do you want to be a mere *zoologist*?"

Fred did not pursue his research but I doubt this was due to my Byzantine elephantine argument. Eventually he followed in Kaunda's footsteps, accepting an honorary PhD from a university in Malawi. Whether a deeper understanding of John Locke's ideas would have led to fewer violations of basic democratic principles on his watch is not known to science.

An extract from an eyewitness of Chiluba's private wardrobe:

> But most remarkable are the more than 100 pairs of size 6 shoes, many affixed with Mr. Chiluba's initials in brass. He is just a little over five feet tall, and each pair has heels close to two inches high. They are a riot of color and texture: jade-green lizard skin and burgundy suede, cream-color ostrich and lustrous red silk. (Duggan, 2009)

(At one point, one indignant taxpayer complained about the number of shoes, not pairs, showing Chiluba as even more extravagant than perhaps he was. But this went wrong when the number announced came out as odd, and confused a lot of people. But Chiluba was greatly annoyed at the exaggeration, as anticipated).

So it was in the business of allegedly converting state resources to his personal use, and particularly his purchasing of phenomenal amounts of very fancy clothing, that Chiluba ran into public opprobrium and international notoriety. "Chiluba's thinking is as tall as he is. . . . We are not going to steal money, we are not going to plunder, we are not going to buy suits, we are not going to buy shoes. We are not going to give girls houses," Michael said years later.

Chiluba, his intelligence chief, and his favorite tailor in Switzerland were sued by the Zambian government for the return of the money. The legal operation, including the cost of the lawyers (including Tony

Blair's brother), was funded by Britain. Mr. Justice Smith found for the plaintiff, though it is not clear what was recovered. What is also not clear is what was actually illegal in Zambian law and what was just extremely bad taste.

Sata was nothing like Chiluba. He proudly described himself as "ugly." While he dressed tastefully he did not do so to disguise himself or show off his wealth. He did not care about money, except as a means to his political ends and his family obligations. He lived in an unspectacular house in a second-rate suburb of Lusaka, or else in government accommodation when he was on the governing side. In all the finagling he and I had to do to raise money for the MMD in 1991 or the Patriotic Front from 2001 onward, I never noted a money junkie's gleam in his eye.

And as to education—well, Michael held education in very high regard; both his wives (not simultaneous) were university graduates, the first in education and the second, Christine Kaseba, in medicine. But at the same time he was very anxious not be seen as too well educated (and presumably alien to the masses he was aspiring to lead). So his many, many outbreaks of uncouth behavior in even the most diplomatically constrained circumstances worked to ensure he was not perceived as a "refined" member of the elite or, conversely, as someone intimidated by the elite. There was no posh person you could count on him being respectful toward.

Actually, Michael seems to have had as good an education within the country as was available to someone of his generation and his father's circumstances. He had received a good primary school education at Catholic schools. And Michael had gone further. At one stage, after 2001 when we were in opposition, the MMD government under Mwanawasa raised the possibility of amending the Constitution to exclude those without a full secondary education from standing for election as president. It was obviously a move tailored to exclude Michael specifically from the presidency—but he was prepared!

One day he called me and handed over an envelope of GCE A-level and O-level pass certificates in his name. "Keep these," he told me, "and only use them in emergency." Unable to complete his secondary education in Zambia in the 1950s, he had taken himself to Britain, famously surviving by working for British Rail, and studied night school courses in politically related subjects. He had put me in charge of this information because he did want to be the one portraying himself as above "his" people. As it happened, the scheme to bar candidates on educational grounds was abandoned by our foes.

However, the narrator is getting ahead. Let us go back to the MMD government in the early days when we were part of it.

As we took our oaths in November 1991 to uphold the Constitution and observe the State Secrets Act, the way ahead looked pretty clear for Michael, if a bit steep and strenuous in patches. To get the presidency in 2001 it would be necessary to ensure that Chiluba quit after his constitutional ten years. It would be necessary to ensure that competing parties did not steal the baton from the MMD, and it would be necessary to ensure that all of about six people in the party who were more senior than him were compromised. And all along it would be necessary to maintain the support of the voters countrywide and particularly the party officials who voted at the five-yearly national convention. To maintain this he had to remain well known—which in Michael's case was an objective best acquired by picking quarrels with his potential opponents, winning those quarrels, and making the wins famous.

It was a tall order but Michael embarked upon his ten-year odyssey with vim and vigor. One evening I thought to give Michael's expertise a little boost by making him a gift of Machiavelli's political handbook *The Prince*. He flipped through it in silence for ten minutes and then enquired: "Who is this amateur?" He left the book with me.

On the principle of big things, Michael first took on Levy Mwanawasa, Chiluba's lawyer from Ndola on the Copperbelt who had won the post of vice president, and Michael engineered a confrontation quite early in the ten-year campaign for his presidency. First, Michael paid in full and in advance the rental bill on his downtown office (from which he ran a private advertising business). He then summoned the head of one of the companies run by the Ministry of Health (to which Sata had been shuffled) and ordered him to pay the rent on the same private office. He then had the instruction leaked to Mwanawasa, who had an extremely loud mouth on the subject of corruption and a deep loathing of Michael. Mwanawasa ran to Chiluba, showed the instruction, and declared that the two men could not exist in the same government. Michael was called; he marched in to Fred's office and showed the original receipt for the rent that he had prepaid, asking, "Why would I get the rent paid corruptly if it is already paid from my pocket? My accusers are tribally prejudiced." Thus, collapse of the stout party, who had no choice but to resign and return to his law firm.

This is a somewhat convoluted tale but I have presented it to give a flavor of the trickiness that characterizes the deep end of the political swimming pool in an African country. You don't even need sharks to keep the adrenalin flowing. Next please. (The story recounted here is the version he personally told to me—there are others the reader may have heard.)

My opportunity to observe and chronicle Michael's not-always-honorable progress toward his lifetime goal varied over the ten years of Chiluba's reign. I started as a cabinet minister with very good access to him and a high profile of my own due to it falling to my lot to manage a massive food relief exercise following a weather-induced crop disaster all over southern Africa. Although he had nothing to do with this scary problem Michael was not slow to bathe in the glow of our unprecedented African famine logistics. We moved a million tons of maize into the middle of Africa from the other side of the world without losing a single life to hunger or even an outbreak of panic buying. I was lucky that point-men in the operation were one-time senior officers in the British army. Despite this Michael was quick off the political mark. "This has all been done by *us*," he declared, while our slow-witted opponents, inside and outside the MMD, wasted their time trying to trash the operation as inefficient and corrupt. I was initially very annoyed with these attacks, some from close colleagues, but Michael calmed me down. Never respond to allegations, he told me, because *they* will benefit from the free publicity. Concentrate on feeding the people you are supposed to be feeding, doing the job you are supposed to be doing.

I sometimes get compliments on the thickness of my political skin. Well, I am a graduate of the Academy.

The threatened food shortage, in contrast to the average "drought" or "famine," turned out to be quite genuine, not just a panic engendered by inexperience. With the recent change of personnel in government it was difficult to manage, particularly in respect of theft of money and maize. But we involved bodies like the Anti-Corruption Commission to good effect. Less widely known is the involvement of the South African government, which had been complicit during the freedom war, facilitating contacts between grain and transportation companies that thrived by corrupting Zambian (and other) leaders to slow down the eventual victory. Now that the war was over we were gifted with a list of those who had been traitors to their own countries.

It was a great honor for me to speak at the annual Consultative Group at the World Bank office in Paris after the drought. Carried away by my enthusiasm I declared that we would not have succeeded had we not received $400 million in aid. The Japanese delegate interrupted, "$300 million." "OK," I replied, "after all, what is $100 million between friends?" This throwaway line became famous beyond both arctic circles.

AFTER SIXTEEN MONTHS in office I was sacked by Chiluba as he started his internal cleansing of the MMD of potential rivals to himself. He chucked out Arthur Wina and Humphrey Mulemba, both of whom had stood against him at the convention. He also threw out Emmanuel Kasonde, the minister of finance, who had been heard (most likely on a hidden microphone in his home) making fun of Chiluba's dubious grasp of economics and making no bones about his intention of replacing him. At the time I assumed I had been targeted as a supporter of Kasonde, with whom I got on extremely well. However I did not know the game of African politics half as well as I know it now. Chiluba of course had identified Michael as the key potential threat and would have put him out with the others, except that Michael was too risky to leave outside the tent. So he threw me, his trusty helper, on to the trash heap as the next best thing. Minister of Defense B. Y. Mwila, a close confidant of Chiluba and an obvious enemy of Michael, was the key to this move. My letter of dismissal hangs in the Political Education Museum in my house, otherwise known as the guest toilet.

At the end of 1996 Chiluba faced reelection. He decided to be very fancy in his maneuverings. He brought an amendment to the Zambian Constitution to parliament (of which I was still a member) that disallowed people whose parents were not themselves born Zambians from standing as presidential candidates in Zambia. There was no doubt about whom he was targeting; there in the distance, limbering up for the weigh-in, a vengeful Kenneth Kaunda waited for payback day. Although KK was born in Zambia, his parents were not, as we saw in Chapter 2. They were born in Malawi, so the amendment excluded Kaunda. This was an amazing development, logically speaking. Kaunda had been the actual president of Zambia for six five-year terms (with the last truncated to accommodate early multiparty elections). Now he was in effect a foreigner, making Zambia retroactively ungoverned for three decades. Chiluba even tried to get him deported "back" to Malawi but this twist in the tale was superfluous and the deportation never happened.

There was much collateral damage from the contrived exclusion of Kaunda. Many Zambians were incidentally covered by it. The Constitution has been recently amended and it seems I may now be eligible, but legal views are not uniform on this and a test case is awaited.

Chiluba and his government took a precipitous dive in their popularity ratings with the donors, upon whose goodwill and cash we were still utterly dependent.

The parentage clause as it is known resulted in UNIP boycotting the 1996 general elections. A number of new parties formed by the steadily growing club of disaffected leaders made very little inroad into the MMD/Chiluba victory. In this failure I am ashamed to say I was included, having been persuaded to partner with farmers' representatives to form the "Lima" party, the local equivalent of Scandinavian "Center" parties representing rural interests. This strategy has worked well historically in Scandinavian countries and some Commonwealth countries such as Australia but—psephologically speaking—it requires proportional representation in order to work. When we sent it to the graveyard to join the Constitution Party and the Liberal Party, I felt I had not learned a thing about politics, whether from my father's failures or Michael's indulgent lectures.

However, 1996 brought an unexpected boost for Michael's agenda. So far, he had been a sector person—he was chairman for local government and he was minister for local government, labor, and health in turn. Now he was presented with an opportunity. Vernon Mwaanga, an internationally famous foreign affairs expert who had been a senior minister under Kaunda and was a key eminence in the founding of MMD, decided to run for party secretary—the number three slot after the president and his vice. Michael saw his chance and stood against him. Chiluba had a problem: he liked and trusted Mwaanga and had often tried to promote his standing. However, it seemed that controversies from Mwaanga's past still hung over his head, in the eyes of some parties at least. Fred decided that he was already suffering the consequences of the tricky stuff around Kaunda's parentage, and he couldn't risk another hullabaloo, founded or unfounded. So he was forced to publicly campaign for Michael as the national secretary of the party.

Michael was duly elected and put in control of the party, as well as made minister without portfolio. He sat in his grand office dispensing all kinds of aid to party officials and members, putting public resources at the disposal of members of the public, one way or another. When the government could not oblige, he shouted down phones at businesspeople including his Greek and Indian friends, getting them to arrange jobs, or one-off funeral expenses, or whatever the need might be. It was as if the sheriff had appointed Robin Hood to be the supremo of the Nottingham welfare department and given him an office and access to the resources to do the job. Give to the poor without the bother of robbing from the rich.

From Michael's point of view it was now smooth sailing. He had only to keep his high profile high and push it higher, and get rid of any remaining likely opposition to his succeeding Chiluba.

Michael had ways of keeping his profile high, even internationally. As minister without portfolio he appointed himself in charge of the Department of Gender Affairs. He duly turned up in Addis Ababa at an otherwise all-women's conference to discuss gender equality. To render himself unforgettable he stood up on the first day and put Zambia's full support behind the equality of women provided it was done within traditional African parameters—such as the recognition of the man as having the final say. He also castigated the conveners and delegates for wasting public money going around the world. The assembly was horrified! Who is this offensive fellow? they asked. The next day Michael stood up at the start and announced he had spent the night thinking and had realized his policy position needed refining. The problem with gender relations in Africa is that they have been messed up by colonial influences. We have been trying to imitate whites, when we should have been resuscitating our own superior standards. And so forth. The delegates went wild with approval.

I heard this story from one of the women delegates. "We love your future president," she said.

While he was minister of health Michael had to deal with a number of strikes. Once he met with striking doctors in Lusaka and gave them a blasting for lack of public spiritedness. They responded by booing him.

"Who gave you the right to boo me?" he asked. "Do you have the monopoly of booing?" And he start booing the doctors. "Boo! Boo! Boo! Useless doctors!" The room eventually collapsed in tears of laughter and the doctors agreed to go back to work. To sort out the doctors on the Copperbelt, Michael hired a bus that he filled with his now compliant Lusaka doctors and sent them up with hefty allowances to enable them to lavishly host their colleagues at five star hotels and nightclubs—while they explained the need to end the strike. It worked like a dream.

B. Y. Mwila, the minister of defense, my would-be nemesis, was a big shot in the MMD government. He was a relative of Chiluba and trusted by him, at least in matters outside the succession. He was plainly and early in the running for the presidency in the 2001 elections. How to get rid of him? In Zambia every public room is required to feature a framed portrait of the president. Mwila, who had a healthy ego, did not complain when color portraits of himself started to appear in school classrooms, hung next to those of Chiluba, throughout Luapula

Province, of which he indisputably was the local boy made good—a very big shot. His sense of danger did not even alert him to the risk created by the fact that the new portraits were larger than those depicting the real president. It was only when he was expelled from the MMD government and party, on the orders of Fred, that he realized who must have put them there. I never detected so much as the faintest glimmer of reconciliation between them.

Now another problem arose. Fred was not in the mood to step down as national president when his two five-year terms expired. The Constitution was unambiguous (in reaction to the six term overdose of Kenneth Kaunda) but there were other leaders in the region who were not constrained in this way. The most notable was Robert Mugabe, who was into his fourth term. How unfair! How to fulfill his desire to rule forever?

Michael decided, certainly with Chiluba's consent, to start a process of intraparty consultation, province by province, over the "third term issue."

Province by province, the circus progressed. Province by province the party faithful endorsed the "Kaunda-ization" of Fred. If we can have KK for six terms why must Fred leave after two? Fredrick pronounced himself not-so-much a political scientist as a "political engineer." As party secretary, Michael was "just doing his job." But he also knew his history. Civil society, particularly the large chunk of it composed of the churches, has a long record of fighting against constitutional manipulation. They had lost over the question of the parentage clause because they were caught short by insufficient notice. But for the third term bid, they had more than enough notice. Anti–third term "pastoral letters" in every local language were simultaneously read out loud in every Catholic church in the country, for example. And Fred had annoyed the donor community over his mismanagement of the economy, so that a full-scale financial crisis was a distinct possibility.

Those MMD leaders with an eye on Chiluba's job were, however, worried that Fred would make it. In good order they abandoned ship and set up new parties. They did not dare adopt a wait-and-see policy since that might entail hanging on until it was too late to organize any alternative political movements. The most prominent two of these were both former vice presidents, Generals Godfrey Miyanda and Criston Tembo. Mwila's new party was already in the field. Only Michael held firm. As he saw it, he was the only viable substitute for Fredrick within the MMD. As the "stop the third term" storm grew he must have even counted a chicken or two among the vibrating eggs.

Then suddenly it was all over. Chiluba, once the wording had been deciphered, promised not to run again. MMD went for its national convention and it was widely expected that a new president of MMD—or presidential candidate—would be elected. It was almost certain that if so, the person to emerge victorious would be Michael. But it was decided that this task would be postponed and addressed by the National Executive Committee, the fifty-odd member "board" of the party rather than the thousands of shareholders. When the NEC eventually met, the outcome had been engineered by the great political engineer. Michael was out. Mwanawasa was woken in his bed and addressed as your excellency. There were another ten years ahead before State House was ours. Mwanawasa did not look too fit but he was young and nobody foresaw his early demise.

It seems likely that Chiluba was convinced that Sata had cheated him over the whole third term debate. And it seems very likely that Michael did indeed cheat him. After all, what was in it for Michael if Fredrick won his third term? But whether and how Michael assisted the anti–third term movement are questions I have not been able to find answers to. A small hint may lie in the very close relationship he had with the Catholic Church. But then again, maybe not. In those days I was reluctant to try and guess what role The System played in events.

The last laugh, however, a low cynical whoop in the bushes, was on Fred. He had engineered the succession of his long-standing friend and lawyer. But now he discovered the truth in the Zambian saying that "there are only two certainties in life: death and ingratitude." (Alas, we are useless in collecting taxes.) To please the donors, or of his own volition, Mwanawasa moved to relieve Chiluba of his presidential immunity, thus laying him open to investigation and prosecution for corruption. The donors responded with unrestrained joy and lots of private admonishment of me for not leaping into Mwanawasa's government but staying in the opposition. But before the whole episode came to fruition, Fred died as a delayed effect of acute cardiomyopathy. Some of his fellow accused are still around, and some charges are still formally in place. But the anticorruption fight, as it refers to the Chiluba era, is effectively over.

> *I can remember that night in your arms*
> *Underneath the pagan moon*
> *Beneath the light on a pillow of palms*
> *Underneath the pagan moon*
> *(Lah-lah-lah-lah-lah, lah-lah-lah-lah)*

Maybe this was a sweet maiden's prayer
To your eyes and your lips and your hair
Only the dark came a little too soon
As we watched our pagan moon
(Lah-lah-lah-lah-lah, lah-lah-lah-lah)

Who knows where Kaunda, qua singer and guitarist, acquired this song. But every Zambian with access to a TV set knows where he sang it: Mukobeko Maximum Security Prison in Kabwe. In October 1997 some young army officers launched a bizarre coup attempt that culminated in a commando unit pouring heavy fire into the National Broadcasting station while a soldier under the nom de guerre "Captain Solo" took over from the disc jockeys and played songs, including his obvious favorite "Buffalo Soldier." Some dire but confused threats were made (e.g., to the effect that all corrupt politicians were to be executed at noon). There was a crescendo of explosions before noon, however, and the coup attempt collapsed.

My own opinion was and still is that the plotters' *folie* was at least in part due to dementia, which before the days of treatment was sometimes a nasty add-on to HIV, along with a whole host of other nasty ailments. The incoherence and the subsequent physical health of the culprits, taken together with the very high seroprevalence in the army and the fact that drugs for HIV were not available at that time, all point to this.

Whatever the truth about the causes of the preposterous "coup," the event cried out to be downgraded to a meaningless distraction from Zambia's real problems. But this was not how Fred saw it! He saw another chance to fix the past. He declared a state of emergency, locking up a number of his political and personal perceived enemies. Kenneth Kaunda was outside Zambia at the time but he returned shortly before Christmas to be with his family.

I got marginally involved in subsequent events. The various political parties in Zambia, including the MMD, had come together for "interparty talks." Michael was designated chairman, and I was picked as one of two vice chairmen—the other was the utterly charming Mainza Chona, a founding member of UNIP. He phoned me at the crack of dawn on Christmas Day to inform me that he was with Kaunda in his house, and a very large number of security personnel were outside with the obvious purpose of arresting his boss. I should prepare to be questioned about the consequences of an arrest for the interparty talks.

Sure enough, Kaunda was arrested on Christmas Day, thereby guaranteeing worldwide coverage along with the limping reindeer and the weather forecast. He was sequestered in a cell in the maximum-security prison in Kabwe. He immediately went on a hunger strike and—he had remembered to bring his guitar! Fred evidently thought that seeing the high and mighty "father of the nation" locked up would damage Kaunda's standing in the eyes of Zambians. But the old man was and still is very media savvy. When the government media were brought on, he oozed humility and patriotism, and he picked up the guitar and sang for his beloved Betty.

(Old habits die hard, though. When I went to the UTH hospital to visit KK after his wife, Betty, had died and he was overcome with grief, he wouldn't say a word to me until I told him, "I have a TV crew outside in the corridor. Would you care to say a few words?" He straightened up and delivered what the nation wanted to hear, live on air.)

The "interparty talks" died when I refused to be a part of them until Kaunda was released.

Eventually former Tanzanian president Julius Nyerere came and persuaded his close buddy to resume eating, and then obliged Chiluba to end the farce by releasing Kaunda. Fred may have got some personal pleasure from an act of vengeance, but his position in the popularity charts fell dramatically.

The succession question repeatedly looms large in Zambia, and it sometimes seems that it is only by God's intervention that it has not caused more of a disaster than we have witnessed so far. In the case of the MMD there have been at least three successions: Mwanawasa succeeded Chiluba by way of "engineering" Chiluba off a narrow base. The key point to observe is the failure to convene a large group of party officials and members to give a democratic result. Rupiah Banda replaced Mwanawasa when the latter died, apparently on the somewhat feeble ground that, since Banda was the appointed vice president and therefore acting president in Mwanawasa's place, he was constitutionally allowed to use helicopters and other toys to win the forthcoming election. No national convention was held. After Banda won the MMD succession and won the 2008 presidential election, he went on to lose to Michael Sata in 2011 and bowed out of MMD leadership, leaving another former vice president, Pastor Nevers Mumba, to have himself appointed party president through what was left of the executive.

When Michael gave instructions for the creation of the PF constitution, his deep annoyance over the "dribbling" he endured in 2001 caused a very strong broad-based succession requirement to be incorporated.

There were to be no more "executive" decisions as to who should come next. A general conference of the party (equivalent to the national convention) would be the only body that could legitimately select the successor to a dead or incompetent president. It should be simple! But ambition in the realm of the government knows no bounds it seems. Following Sata's death in October 2014, the acting president (i.e., me) tried to insist that a general conference should pick the successor, but it seems that a clique in the party much smaller than the general conference had already decided who was to be president of the PF and thus, automatically, presidential candidate in the upcoming by-election to replace the deceased state president. There was rampant thuggery and threat of more and a "kangaroo" election was held in which only the "clique" candidate stood. I did not want to be the first white man to head an independent African country and, at the same time, be a failure at keeping the peace. I had to give in when the courts would not back me. It is evident that much work needs to be done on the rules underpinning good governance in Zambia.

Succession-wise, parties other than the PF have little to write home about. When Anderson Mazoka, its founding president, died, a convention was held of the UPND (then, as now, the United Party for National Development was the leading opposition party), featuring Tonga warriors with spears and friction drums galloping around the convention hall threatening anyone who would oppose the election of another Tonga to the presidency. The winner in these circumstances was the wealthy privatization expert, the Tonga Hakainde Hichilema. There was an exodus of non-Tonga leaders, most of whom joined PF (and many of whom have since attained high positions in it).

The most entertaining attempt to replace a party president occurred in 1991 when a businessman famous for keeping lions and airplanes, Enoch Kavindele, tried to stand against Kenneth Kaunda as an alternative leader for his party, UNIP. The two contestants duly traveled to the "Mulungushi Rock of Authority," an outdoor venue where UNIP always held its conventions, to vie for the thousands of votes of UNIP officials. Kavindele had launched a media campaign promising "fine tuning" in government—a bold move, given that most of UNIP was still against multiparty elections. There are small chalets at Mulungushi for the leaders to sleep in, and Kavindele was woken in his in the dead of night. A group of middle-aged women had stripped themselves from the waist down and were turned so as to expose their buttocks to the would-be president to express their contempt and disgust for him. He later described in parliament how terrified he was, and how he had instantly withdrawn his candidacy. It was only after years more of political experience in Zambia that I lost my snotty contempt for the "buttock display" as a political tool.

Unfortunately the phrase "Lady Macbeth Syndrome" has already been recruited to designate obsessive guilt and hand-washing behavior. What we really want is a word or phrase to designate the single-minded extremism, the harshness that suddenly emerges from women where issues of succession are concerned and the men are all being too wishy-washy.

> *The raven himself is hoarse*
> *That croaks the fatal entrance of Duncan*
> *Under my battlements. Come, you spirits*
> *That tend on mortal thoughts, unsex me here,*
> *And fill me from the crown to the toe, top full*
> *Of direst cruelty!*
>
> —*Macbeth*, Act 1, Scene 5

9

Elements of Fudge

THE OPERATION OF GOVERNMENT IN ZAMBIA SEEMS, OVER THE YEARS, TO have included a great deal of fudge. The outsiders, planning to help, think that we don't know what to do and give us clear policy stipulations that will—when implemented—see our smooth, elegant progression from poverty to riches. Somehow, though, there seems to be a strong propensity to fall off course, whether in respect of economics, electoral process, or government reform.

In one such formulation, ten principles taken together called the "Washington Consensus," originally stated by John Williamson in 1989, includes ten sets of relatively specific policy recommendations.

- Low government borrowing. Avoid large fiscal deficits relative to GDP;
- Redirection of public spending from subsidies (especially indiscriminate subsidies) toward broad-based provision of key pro-growth, pro-poor services such as primary education, primary health care, and infrastructure investment;
- Tax reform, broadening the tax base and adopting moderate marginal tax rates;
- Interest rates that are market determined and positive (but moderate) in real terms;
- Competitive exchange rates;
- Trade liberalization: liberalization of imports, with particular emphasis on elimination of quantitative restrictions (licensing,

etc.); any trade protection to be provided by low and relatively uniform tariffs;
• Liberalization of inward foreign direct investment;
• Privatization of state enterprises;
• Deregulation: abolition of regulations that impede market entry or restrict competition, except for those justified on safety, environmental, and consumer protection grounds, and prudential oversight of financial institutions;
• Legal security for property rights (Williamson, 1989).

This was an attempt to define what Zambia and other "failed or failing states" were required to espouse in order to catch up with the "first world."

Chiluba was the epitome of a reformist statesman. There was some loose talk of an economic cataclysm, social unrest, a return of colonialism, and allegations of burgeoning corruption; but such talk was written off by the man himself as mere froth coming from a champagne bottle that had been waiting years in the fridge (though he denied drinking any of it). Zambia was liberalizing, both politically and economically, and thus it would show the rest of Africa the way to go. True, the South Africans had not yet had their first postapartheid election; Mandela was not yet president, but he was on his way and no longer needed any help from us.

So Zambia embarked on urgent measures of economic decontrol: we started within weeks (of the election) on the staged removal of maize subsidies; we set about dismantling the exchange control machinery as if it were an unexploded bomb we had only just discovered; we compiled lists of state-owned companies to be closed or privatized within the minimum possible time; and we lifted the State of Emergency that had prevailed throughout Kaunda's reign. What could be more meaningful and committed and liberal and "open" than that?

Those of us who had done our economics and political science in the West were amazed by the transformation we had brought into being by shouting a few slogans and painting a better managed country in the future. I was particularly struck by the wholehearted tolerance, nay, encouragement, as together with the minister of finance, my close friend Emmanuel Kasonde, we started shutting down the subsidy circus. We sat side by side in parliament, staring into the television cameras, and announced new prices of maize-meal, the staple food of all urban and most of the rural population. We were cheered to the rafters. The stuffed lion and leopard that bracketed the Speaker and stared blankly like *ngulu* at all comers seemed to come half awake.

The tension was palpable . . . but there was no real tension. Just a huge sigh that signified enough was enough.

Note that Kaunda had found it impossible to run a rational maize meal pricing system. Every time he tried to reduce the subsidy, and thus increase the price, there was a riot. Now we tried, we reduced the sub-sidy—and nothing happened! We thought, we enquired, and we discov-ered. When voters put you in power—at least when the voters are Africans—they judge you against your promises, your areas of focus. Kaunda had had a social contract with the people of Zambia: you vote for me, I will keep mealie meal cheap. We had no such contract; we had even said the price would go up. We were immune. We were just doing our job!

That was a lesson—a huge lesson—and one I wish we had kept in mind. After a relatively short time Chiluba seemed to believe that the return of the riots was imminent. He basically ordered me to restore the social contract on maize—something that badly distorted agriculture, never mind government spending, and the place we were at became indistinguishable from the Square called "One." We had victory and we threw it to the winds. What was Chiluba thinking?

I was called to State House and subjected to a rant by Chiluba. It was protracted because I had a good market intelligence network and knew for a fact that there was no unrest building, either on the Copper-belt, the ground zero of urban political unrest, or anywhere else. Even-tually my guardian angel thought of a fine wheeze. Unlike some other sectors the maize milling industry was largely black-owned. I suggested that I arrange for the chairman of the millers' association, Caleb Mulenga, to be brought down to Lusaka to explain the basis of the var-ious margins that are applied to a bag of maize meal. I had him deliv-ered to State House at six in the morning.

The president and the miller fell for each other. Fred had never real-ized how much he knew about adding up costs. "What is this 6 per-cent?"; "that is wastage of empty bags." "And this?"; "Dust blown away in the cleaning process." "Let's call the bag wastage 4 percent—OK?" "Where do you buy a calculator?"

When I arrived at eight Fred had gotten what seemed like half a ream of lined paper spread out on his office table. His reading glasses were on the end of his nose. "Ba Guy! Did I ever tell you I am a cost accountant by profession? We are working to find the proper price for mealie meal." When I told Kasonde about this mutation of Fred into a cost accountant he just huffed: "Why buy a dog and bark yourself?" But we were saved, at least for the time being. The boss bought and was operating the calculator and would brook no dissent.

Alas, it did not last. The maize industry reverted and it still reeks of subsidization and its close ally, politicization. That is more than twenty years later.

A danger with the scientific socialist dispensation—or whatever you want to call it—is that it permanently affects peoples' perceptions of what should and can be done. Sanity is hard to regain; the ghost leaves footprints. Many of the most intractable problems in Zambia today can be traced back to the early days after independence. The government somewhere down the line entered into a de facto social contract with the populace that maize meal would forever be available to those who wanted it at a price well below true cost; while small farmers would receive well above cost for any bag they wanted to sell. The resulting hole is big enough to dwarf all the schooling or all the health services in the country, not to mention attract every crook within a thousand miles. But nobody can stop the nonsense—not even the IMF. Nor could I as the first "reforming" minister of agriculture in 1991 to 1993.

On the broader front it can be said that we genuine economic liberals ignored danger signals for a long time, and we proceeded with the implementation of our agenda. To our enemies or critics we just smiled and challenged them to stand for election next time. They murmured that the economic liberalization was fake; it was concocted to schmooze the "donors." And without exchange control the money would all run away to where it yearned to be (in the Cayman islands). Privatization would be largely corrupt, with public assets transferred to well-connected individuals, and indeed with capitalists and colonialists regaining their control of the productive sector. This last phrase carries with it racial connotations: the socialists are black, the private sector is white or brown. This is actually untrue—the small-scale informal sector is almost entirely black-owned—but false political myths survive exposure even to very true truths. A team of two Washington whiz kids—button-down shirts and early laptops—turned up to see the then minister of finance, Ronald Penza, and started making demands about conditionalities for an emergency loan. Penza told them to go and see the president and convince him. Arrogant in the extreme, the two "experts" found their way into Fred's office and started hectoring him. Fred voiced his complaint to the NEC: "They treated me like a child and humiliated me. I am a president, of a banana republic perhaps, but still a president." I ventured that there were no banana republics in diplomacy and that he should phone the relevant director of the World Bank immediately and demand that the two fellows get recalled to Washington. If the IMF hummed and hah-ed a bit, he could instead deport the buggers. But, though I am sure he understood what I was saying, he simply did not have the self-confidence in the face of men with an education and a measure of control over world budgets.

We laughed. But small signs began to concern those of us with even modest tracking skills and a merely reasonable amount of paranoia. Fred was a dribbler. If he found himself facing an open goal with the ball at his feet he would hold back, fearing a trap perhaps. He much preferred a situation in which he could not obviously win. He liked to pretend to be fighting a battle, in slow retreat, to minimize Zambia's losses (including a loss of independence and pride) at the hands of the Western donors. Sometimes this enabled him to get the donors to lighten the pressure ("I have tried so hard, Ladies and Gentlemen, but it was impossible"). He was also very insecure about finding himself open to the criticism that he let someone in the private sector make lots of money that rightly belonged to the people. To correct this he tended to make sure the asset was run down and nobody got a good deal whichever side of the transaction they were on.

It is a great pity that Chiluba espoused this scorched earth strategy. Logically, it caused him to resist even the things that were obviously right, because on his reasoning you resisted even what was good for all. Allowing a distinction between "good" and "bad" reform opened up a dimension of disagreement. Keep it simple; resist, resist. The result is not in question: you will lose the battle; but you will be seen to resist pressure from foreigners.

("I get it," said a Caribbean businessman to me, "the asset slowly gets destroyed and the private sector gets little of benefit when it eventually changes hands! Politically he remains clean!")

The result of this strategy? Good people tore their hair out and wondered at the reason for the shilly-shallying, especially since this reduced the apparent economic benefit to Zambia as a whole. The example of Zambia Airways (QZ) will serve to illustrate this. A small state-owned enterprise, run in partnership with reputable international airlines like Alitalia and Aer Lingus, was running at a loss of $3 million or so a month. The donors demanded that it be brought into the black or closed down. The minister of transport suggested freezing it while an investigation and replanning was carried out. The decision: we battle on. Nearly a further $100 million was frittered away, the donor gun came out: close the airline down or don't bother to attend the meeting in Paris on Monday—we won't be there. An emergency meeting was called—not just of the cabinet but of the entire party executive, the NEC. We were each asked: so, do we do what the donors want, have we arrived at the eleventh hour? We all nodded out heads; I said something otiose about it being the thirteenth hour.

But that "eleventh hour" was the giveaway. It was Fred's favorite time to capitulate, even if it was the worst time to cash in. It made it difficult for the donors to reappear and start waving the gun again without appearing brutal. And indeed it made us feel good as hardworking master negotiators all. It silenced the opposition.

Fred was no fool. He could spot and utilize an opportunity even when it emerged from nowhere. At the time he capitulated on QZ another problem barked at him: the parastatal United Bus Company, UBZ. This rather conventional state-owned long-distance transporter was going, or had gone, bust. He realized, having been a bus conductor in his long career, that if UBZ was broken up and some concessions given, he could hand the whole road transport industry over to smallish black Zambian operators. Foreign investors would not be interested whereas locals would jump at the opportunities. This would work especially well if import duty and other start-up costs were removed for a year or so. The Zambian bus sector was genuinely liberalized at the same time QZ was closed down. The two were linked in many peoples' minds and the net result was cheers from the people who were not directly hurt by the closure of the airline. Perhaps Fred really was a trained cost accountant.

But Chiluba's pièce de résistance was his reluctance over the privatization of the mining industry. To understand the detail you would have to be a chartered accountant, but I have spared the reader (and writer) the strain, I hope. The Zambian and Chilean copper mining industries used to be of very similar sizes. This was in the days of CIPEC, the attempted copper equivalent of OPEC. Both countries nationalized their copper mines but prices fell and small differences of efficiency had ramifications. Since 1970, Zambia's copper output has remained more or less unchanged, while Chile's production has expanded over fivefold.

The reasons why state-owned enterprises tend to fail are multifold, including the government's tendency to use them as cash cows. But in the 1990s nobody, and certainly no donor, wanted to look into this conundrum. Copper prices were low and the mines were hemorrhaging money. The focus was on bailing Zambia out; please come and buy our mines! Various sizes and types: underground and open cast, please buy our mines!

The state mining company ZCCM (Zambia Consolidated Copper Mines) has played a critical role in Zambia's economy. The contribution of mining to Zambia's treasury cannot be overemphasized: the country earns 90 percent of its foreign exchange from its mining industry, and before privatization, the government held 60.3 percent of ZCCM shares. All told, the sale of the majority of the company's assets (leaving the government with a modest 20 percent) was expected to raise upward of US$2.5 billion for the Zambian government in up-front and committed investment—a figure that in those days approached the country's annual gross domestic product.

After much debate, in 1997 it was agreed that the mining complex be "unbundled" into lumps that were then auctioned off to different buyers. The story of the Kafue Consortium bid, from high hopes to dejection, serves as a taster for the larger process. The consortium comprised a powerhouse of international mining companies—Avmin, Phelps Dodge, and Noranda, plus the UK Commonwealth Development Corporation. After a year of negotiations, the government dismissed the negotiating team as mandated by the Privatization Act, replacing it with a team headed by the old-guard of parastatal mining executives. Repeatedly, the protracted negotiations hit roadblocks, as the government excised assets and disposed of them on the side, backed out of other deals, and rejected some very decent offers. At the same time, the government was reportedly losing millions of dollars a week subsidizing mines that needed investment and refinancing. Eventually, the consortium backed out, the IMF withdrew the balance of payments support subject to finalizing the privatization, and the mines were sold off quickly to Anglo American Company for about half of what they had offered just months before.

There seems to be no good reason why the negotiation team would flatly reject a fair offer and then sell the mine off in a hurry at half price. Chiluba then got it into his head that the presence of CDC in the Kafue Consortium was a threat or an impropriety. CDC was, or had been, a creature of the British and it was given control of a tranche of British aid as its contribution to the consortium. This to Chiluba was tantamount to the British taking over a chunk of Zambia, an insult to Zambia's independence. I am not sure that he was wrong.

Anglo American Company had picked up the whole Kafue package at just $90 million, including a bundle of mines such as Nkana, Nchanga, and the "jewel in the crown" Konkola Copper Mine (KCM), together producing over 50 percent of Zambia's copper. But two years after acquiring the companies at a giveaway price, Anglo decided that its heart was no longer in Zambian copper mining and announced it was pulling out.

The privatization of the mines had been a messy process and was bound to be to some extent. But Chiluba's changes of position, driven by his lack of political confidence (or lack of belief in his advisers) made it all the messier. (The Anglo pull-out was now, in January 2002, within weeks of Chiluba's departure, and one of the first things to keep Mwanawasa awake at night. But it is all part of the same story, so I will continue.)

Invitations to bid for the KCM complex were published throughout the world and even reached the eye of Anil Agarwal, a metals trader and self-made millionaire who had no mining assets but apparently was looking for a chance to enter the industry.

Agarwal arranged to visit Zambia with his accountant. It was announced he had acquired the mine. Later he described what happened in a "motivational" speech at a convocation of young business professionals in India. The video took a while to work its way into the public domain, but here it is, transcribed and translated:

> Seven or eight years back, I was still hungry [for some] big work, and pondering what to do. How can we let life go in vain? [Then] I saw it in the paper FT (*Financial Times*). There was largest copper mine in Africa, and [it] was up for sale. The government was privatizing it [and]I got quite interested in it. I asked few people, and they replied, "Aren't you ashamed? What ridiculousness you are talking of?" I told them, "Where is the problem in talking? Let's speak to them . . ."
>
> I have a friend in McKinsey—Ranjit Pandit. I went to him, asked him to make papers. "Make the papers beautiful, professional." Papers were prepared. We kept it at 400 million. In pocket we did not have 4 million! . . . [but we] bidded for 400 million!
>
> Take chance in life definitely! All [you] people sitting there . . . Take chance! If you won't take chance, nothing will happen
>
> (*Clapping, whistling . . .*)
>
> Then we said, "Twenty-five million we will give you cash, and 325 million we have to invest in making the machines running."
>
> We forgot the matter, but suddenly in about a month or so, we received calls. They invited us [to Zambia]. We called up and inquired [about our bid]. They confirmed, "This company is yours!" Really!
>
> I took one of our engineers and went to Johannesburg and farther, changing flight there to Lusaka. When we arrived there, [we] were surprised to receive VVIP treatment there, with red carpet. The entire government machinery has arrived at airport to receive us. Surprised seeing such arrangement we asked someone [what it was for].
>
> "It's all for you sir. How many people you have in the delegation team?" We were told, "You will be going to the parliament today; and President's place as well. Where are your people? It's necessary to meet the President." Repeatedly we were asked "where is your delegation?" I asked "what delegation? We are the delegation only!" (*Laughs*)
>
> We were taken to the President. I said "Your excellency, we are 30 people in our delegation. But we missed the flight at Johannesberg." (*Audience laughs*) "Can you wait till tomorrow? They all will

come." The President said "No no no! The Parliament is tomorrow, we have to decide today. The key is ready—are you ready?"

I said, "I am ready, I am always ready. I will handle it." (*Laughing*)

And they came, what a Parliament House! (*chuckling*) I had held a bead necklace (in name of God RAM) and kept chanting, moving ahead with my smiling face. When I seated there with my [engineer], the President came and sat by our side. He told the entire parliament that what great people we are, [with a] great empire, and that we will make their lives gorgeous. And we will make schools, make hospitals and blah blah . . .We just kept watching chanting God's name there. Ahhh ha ha ha ha ha ha! (*Clapping*)

We took over the company. It's been 9 years, and since then every year it is giving us a minimum of 500 million dollar or 1 billion dollar every year. It has been continuously giving back. It's a matter of taking a chance. (*Lusaka Times* 2014)

It seems he was boasting, deliberately overstating his profits to attract adulation, and as a government we accepted his apology. Levy appeared as a sucker and Agarwal looked about as charming as a snake in your slippers. The bad feeling among ordinary Zambians toward foreign investors, resulting from this incident particularly, but of all types, still stays strong.

To say that the donors were annoyed by Chiluba's conjuring tricks is an understatement. His subsequent move to change the constitution of Zambia so that an individual should be allowed more than two five-year terms made them particularly angry (Chiluba was the only possible beneficiary in sight so there was no doubt as to the aim of the maneuver).

From the 2001 election—the one that ended with Michael and me suffering a shameful defeat, jail, and the intensive care unit—an interesting situation had arisen for political jugglers. Yes, Levy won, he was the new president, but MMD no longer had the parliamentary majority. Even with eight nominated MPs the president's loyal voters totaled seventy-seven, leaving eighty-one to potentially vote against him. Also, the two-thirds minimum chunk of votes needed for constitutional legislation was very far from sight. To add further to his worries, the UPND, the follow-up party, showed no sign of compromise (such as a government of national unity) and had triggered a petition in court against the election result.[1] The particular aggravation I believe was the vocal allegation of electoral fraud from former British MP Michael Meadowcroft, the leader of the EU observer team. He was no adherent to the more modern international observer attitude, which is to produce some motherhood statement (e.g., about progress to democracy) and then to disappear on a night flight. Meadowcroft openly declared his belief that the ruling party or system had rigged the result. He duly appeared back in Zambia some weeks later to give evidence to that effect.

In the end there was no interference by the judiciary either in the short or the long term. I slowly came to realize that even a parallel count of *all* votes will not necessarily change the judicial view of reality. A count based upon haphazard collection of vote tallies in 6,000 polling stations is dubious enough. But a perfect count does not work either. Truth is not the issue. I believe that Zambian judges, whatever the wording of their oaths, tend to regard themselves as some sort of keepers of the peace—of the stability of the government and the nation. Truth in some positivistic sense, as opposed to fiction, falsity, or indeterminacy, does not rule supreme. Peace—the status quo—is the ultimate good and goal. As a nation we have always understood post-truth.

(The "peace" interpretation may be too generous, say some of my friends. Judges just tend to want to stay in office since they are extremely well paid even compared to judges in much richer countries.)

When I had originally joined hands with Michael to take over the country I assumed he would teach me about some aspects of African electoral "science" whereas I would hold the more educated ground. I was very quickly disabused in this regard. I made some comment apropos of Meadowcroft that an independent MP has complete freedom to speak his mind, unlike the foot soldiers of the major parties to whose policies they are bound. "Do you know Dick Taverne?" he asked.

"Wasn't he a highwayman?" I responded.

"No, he resigned from his party and stood against it in the following by-election. And he won with a landslide . . . "

"You see!" I interjected.

"And that, my friend, was the end of Dick Taverne."

"Where is he now?"

"I have no idea whether he is still even an MP."

So he hadn't just been pushing luggage around Victoria station.

The EU, though they were in some respects unhappy at the prospect of the petition failing, could not leave things as they were. Meadowcroft or no Meadowcroft, the problem became one of how to clean up Mwanawasa's government without becoming too complicit. He of course wanted to turn his attention to restructuring parliament so that he could pass his laws (he said he wanted a government of laws not men) and sleep securely at night. He had to somehow accommodate the following situation:

In Chiluba's last two years donor aid fell away, since Zambia did not meet "conditionalities" of good governance either political or economic. Mwanawasa was already worsening the situation by preparing to award public servants with an unaffordable pay hike. Meanwhile, with the shattering and scattering of MMD, previous ministers of the highest rank found themselves publicly accusing Chiluba of being a thief, while he threatened action against them for libel and lèse-majesté. Matters came to a head as documents fished up from the dark waters of The System seemed to prove that Chiluba and many close to him were spending government money without proper authority or audit (the main document was the ZAMTROP bank account, held at a London bank).

The donors, Mwanawasa, and the anti–third term rebels saw the opportunity of pasting together a government consisting largely of opposition members as cabinet ministers. These included the persuasive Dipak Patel, an MMD founder turned articulate campaigner against the third term (appointed as minister of trade), and the equally charismatic Sylvia Masebo appointed as minister of local government. Some backbenchers were persuaded to resign and, in effect, to surrender their seats to the MMD.

Of special interest was the "hit" made against General Miyanda's party, of which all four MPs resigned. There was and is no doubt about Mwanawasa's motivation in removing all of Miyanda's support. Mwanawasa still blamed Miyanda for being behind his "accident" on the airport road ten years previously. The fact of the matter was that the veep's security detail should never have taken the road with only one support vehicle, let alone with it trailing the VIP vehicle. When a drunk driving a Land Rover left the airport, he fell asleep and hit the veep's car head on. An inquiry revealed that the approaching driver had so much alcohol in his blood that he should have been dead.

Mwanawasa's display of superstition was the major reason for my refusal to join his government. I had been offered a return to the job of minister of agriculture. I cannot abide juju.

Donors felt that they had a chance of working with the "New Deal" government and some of them started using their strength and helping it along. Chiluba and many of his perceived sidekicks in the civil service were targeted for legal action. The UPND was neglected. The warmongering spirits of northwestern Europe roamed through the savannah in broad daylight. The Danish ambassador Mads Sandau-Jensen was inspired to criss-cross the country, stopping at predetermined hours, shouting into his shortwave radio, "Wiking! Wiking!" I know—I was one of his passengers because he had hired me as a consultant (as a sort of Wiking who knew which way was north) in order to keep me from sabotaging what was happening in town. Baroness Lynda Chalker did an impersonation of Boadicea. Very impressive; one hardly needed to hallucinate the rotating axle-knives (or whatever they are called). Words of hope passed sotto voce around the donor community.

"Michael, where is that elections monitoring fellow who is supposed to come back and give evidence that our democracy is a fraud?" I asked.

"No idea."

"You know, the English independent MP, Meadow something."

"Never heard of him."

Note

1. A historical footnote since nobody else seems to have printed it: the messengers of the first UPND petition against the poll result were Michael Sata and myself. The petition had been drawn up by lawyers and other in-house experts with the aim of blocking Mwanawasa's inauguration, but it was a public holiday. By the next day Mwanawasa would be sworn in; is there no way of stopping this, I wondered? I heard about the problem and talked to Michael who was initially reluctant to help—though as a professional gatherer of goodwill for future use he nearly always came round in the end. He changed out of his pajamas and we wandered off in search of Chief Justice Matthew Ngulube who likewise had to change out of his pajamas, and we served up the letter. The CJ was friendly to the point where we thought he might actually concur with the petitioners. Fat chance! Mwanawasa was sworn in the next day. He swore before God, and the CJ, but he swore like the devil at Meadowcroft and—guess who?—"those who visit the Law in its home will themselves be visited in their turn in their homes." That is the origin of what has become a common saying in Zambia.

10

X Years in the Wilderness, *Y* Days in Jail

WE HAD REACHED A POINT WHERE MWANAWASA HAD ALL HE NEEDED TO garner the sympathy of the donors save for one thing: the prosecution of Chiluba for corruption. Dominant donor theory (supported by some Zambians) was that "structural adjustment" or "neoliberalism" were failing to make the beneficial changes expected, on account of the habit of corruption. It does not seem to have occurred to them—the donors—that the Zambians were just telling them what they wanted them to hear; the real problem was that their theory was faulty. Anyway, when Dipak Patel and others pointed a finger at Chiluba, the donors jumped at the idea of dragging him through the Zambian and international courts, thereby setting an example to other would-be enemies of the Washington Consensus. Mwanawasa happily initiated the prosecution of his former friend and client and the maker of his kingship. With Fred in irons in the bilges of his trireme (and the improbable involvement of British Conservative politician Baroness Lynda Chalker as figurehead and an unofficial spokesperson), Admiral Levy's little navy set off for the promised shore.

And at the time, there was indeed a promised shore—debt relief. In IMF-speak, Zambia was a HIPC, a Highly Indebted Poor Country, verging on becoming an even lower species, a LICUS, a Low Income Country Under Stress. A relief program was under way, but Zambia would only qualify if it met various benchmarks. Chiluba (now rattling his chains) had run the Zambian economy into the ground—or perhaps had simply failed to run it out of the ground into which Kaunda had driven it in the first place, or maybe indeed it was all the colonialists' fault from the beginning. In any event a good number of third world countries were

123

in the same basket, and the popular Jubilee movement had been set up worldwide as a campaign for debt forgiveness. The idea, of course, was that these debt-stricken countries would be able to start with a clean slate and actually achieve some economic reform, some care for the disadvantaged, and so forth.

The story should be that Zambia did the needful, HIPC day duly arrived, and the economy strengthened. Actually, it did the opposite. We Zambians believe that a healthy economy is virtually the same thing as a strong currency (which it may be from the perspective of permanently employed consumers but not of the army of unemployed and the producers). HIPC, the well-intentioned big freebie from the West, aimed ultimately at lifting the poor from their destitution, had a negative effect on the growth and distribution of incomes in Zambia that still haunts us. It caused a dollar glut on the currency markets and a corresponding kwacha appreciation from just 4,800 per dollar to 3,000. It seems neither Levy nor his bankers understood the danger of a foreign exchange windfall. Nor did many diplomats. (Nor, amazingly, did the IMF or many donor theorists.) HIPC more-or-less directly, by its action on the exchange rate, put the health of agricultural production, local input support for the mines, tourism, and non-mining export initiatives into instant jeopardy.

It might not have been so destructive if the whole negative process had not been reinforced by yet another free gift—a sharp upward movement in copper prices caused by the awakening of the Chinese dragon. It would have taken a strong bank governor or minister of finance to prevent the kwacha from appreciating under the twin attacks of two streams of unearned income, but they could have done more to ameliorate the damage. They could have taken a leaf from the Norwegians, just for starters.

This tale of unintended consequences is terribly important to Zambia's future, and it needs to be understood by all politicians and well-intentioned activists. I do not believe there was any malign intent to harm Zambia involved among the Jubilee campaigners and the donors. But we shall return to the destructive Zambian proclivity for "strong money" when we have first narrated ourselves into power.

We in Michael's university (surely by this time we were graduating away from merely being his academy) had plenty to learn during the ten long years that we waited for a sufficient number of Zambian voters to take a punt on us. Michael's constant keeping in front of all the other party leaders, as well as the incumbent Mwanawasa, was an exercise in courage and ingenuity, as well as emotionally exhausting for all of us.

At one point, in July 2005, he judged it desirable to go to jail for a few weeks. It only remained for him to say something that would land him in sufficient trouble (but hopefully not too much).

The opportunity presented itself with industrial unrest on the Copperbelt. The mineworkers unions seemed to have lost control of its members and a number had actually laid and detonated some explosive charges underground. The mines minister Lembalemba mentioned the PF . . . Michael joined the fray; bring on the soup; a stream of *Post* headlines captures events as follows.

I INCITED MINERS—SATA

SATA IS A TERRORIST, CHARGES LEMBALEMBA

LEVY ORDERS SATA'S ARREST

SATA GOES ON HUNGER STRIKE

COP THREATENS TO SHOOT SATA'S WIFE

LEVY FIRES IG SIAKALIMA

[JUDGE] DENIES SATA BAIL

PROVE THAT I'M A THREAT TO SECURITY

I AM TREATED WORSE THAN SADDAM—SATA I'LL DEFEAT
    LEVY'S PLANS TO DESTROY MY CAREER

I WAS BORN UNDER A TREE, REVEALS SATA
    (and therefore understand your suffering)

It is of course illegal for a president to order the police to lock up a particular person, though in Zambia as in most countries there's quite a lot of flexibility in practice. But Levy's first attempts to have Michael incarcerated came to naught because Inspector-General Siakalima was too professional to comply with the order. This left Levy with egg on his face, since he was playing to the gallery by boasting that Michael was already in prison, while in point of fact he was home in bed. The IG was unsurprisingly fired and replaced with a more malleable person. The police surrounded the house that night, bringing with them a waterless fire engine from the fire station. They started to throw up its ladders against the garden wall, aiming to storm the place. Solicitous of their safety, Michael, wearing pajamas, locked up the dogs and unlocked the front gate. Then he offered them tea and led them out to their vehicles in good order. He was, after all, a police officer himself.

They first locked him up in an obscure police post in the cement manufacturing town of Chilanga, south of Lusaka, where I found him chatting to the copper in charge (who would have soon joined the PF if he had not already).

I kept the public informed: "Levy akaka eliyo a tontonkanya" (Levy has already arrested him, now he is thinking). (Actually I spoke in execrable Bemba but the media translated into perfect Bemba to make me look a brilliant linguist and orator—that was part of our campaign machine.) Eventually they maneuvered Michael into court and thence into the Chimbokaila prison. As news of his arrival quickly went round an enormous roar like a passing jet went up from the crowded prison. Our next president! Our savior!

I missed going with Charlotte, her sister Stephanie, and our families to the South Luangwa (seriously the best game park in Africa, and the best company for a holiday too), staying in Lusaka to see Michael daily and run errands. He was a magnet for the stirrers and the discontented— other opposition leaders, church leaders, international journalists, and just simple poor Zambians in search of the man they were coming to believe was their Gandhi. There were sometimes problems with the younger prison officers, who tended to be defensively officious. The most memorable exchange occurred between a prison officer and two Catholic priests. The priests, one of them a cardinal, were originally from Poland. The invading Germans had first locked them up for some years and then the rescuing Russians had closed down their church. So Cardinal Adam and Father Klaus had ended up in Zambia.

"Fathers, you cannot come in. This is not a church; it is a prison. Do you know what a prison is?"

"Er, does Auschwitz qualify?"

The system was trying to get Michael for "espionage," meaning something more like "sabotage" but, either way, the charge was brought because Michael had contrived to make Levy Mwanawasa as incandescent as a re-entering space capsule, temporarily overwhelming his lawyerly self-discipline. After some weeks of legal footling—ending in production of something called a *nolle prosequii*, which is a kind of indefinite stay of prosecution but not a formal quashing of the charge— he was released and I went to fetch him. We drove the longest way possible through the center of Lusaka with the whole town cheering its lungs out. He should have been a gladiator.

One side effect of the espionage affair was that Michael did not dare go near the Copperbelt lest he should be arrested there and the court action restarted. I did not quite follow his reasoning but eventually figured he knew something I did not and stopped talking about it. He must have learned a lot of police tricks in his time. Instead I used to drive up to the Copperbelt to organize meetings carrying a mobile phone strapped to a microphone on a PA system. At the appropriate juncture I would phone Michael and put him on air. "I cannot be with you because Levy has tied my ankle like a chicken." He did not have to say very much since his harsh voice served as proof of identity and everyone started cheering. It was hardly high tech IT but we became fond of it and used to "visit" each other's rallies when we were in different places—even in different countries. I have wooed voters in Zambia from a train in South London and had to answer questions from friendly policemen outside my mother's flat in the Cotswolds. They were curious rather than suspicious: "What language were you singing in, sir?" A few years later one must suppose that one would be more likely to take a hit from an antiterror team. I am sure there are no exceptions for Bembas.

Soon the pro-PF technicians in the FM radio stations learned how to hack in to my *shaupwa bwino* old Nokia and they used to broadcast live whatever we were feeding into our rallies.

The 2006 elections were held in a gala atmosphere of roughly 0 percent inflation and unequalled personal prosperity for those in public service. The HIPC boom was ending but not quite yet. The noncopper exporters were going out of business but did not constitute a large enough base for effective opposition. Would HIPC and China's hunger for copper wipe us, the opposition, out?

Life is not as rational as Oxford. Since when did economic prosperity interfere with the political magnetism of Michael Sata already up to speed? He quickly found ways of taking the credit.

UPND got together with other opposition parties (FDD and UNIP) to form a united front called UDA. Despite this gambit they slid down the scale in the 2006 elections. PF, which had managed only 2 members of parliament so far, zoomed up 43 seats out of 150 in parliament. UPND/UDA managed only 23.

What had happened?

So far as rural votes go we had established ourselves as the Bemba party. Our share of the rural action was about the same as UPND, the Tonga party. But in the urban areas—particularly the Copperbelt and Lusaka—we had established ourselves as the party of choice, virtually ejecting UPND as well as the MMD from the towns. In the urban areas people share the same schools, hospitals, unemployment queues, and the rest, and tribalism is far less of a factor. We had managed to market ourselves as the tribe-less, pro-poor, intolerant-of-low-standards party for the cosmopolitan voter.

© Charlotte Scott

At the last Lusaka rally before the 2006 elections. The crush of the crowd as we arrived was so great that the platform collapsed and sound system was destroyed. Michael is standing on a roof rack, waving at the crowd, with the ever-vigilant Judge Ngoma behind him, and Guy perched on the edge of the sunroof.

I was one of the PF MPs elected (representing Lusaka Central, which I won easily with more than 50 percent). I also became, if unofficially, Leader of the Opposition for the period 2006–2011. The tide of feeling was with us. Michael and I and others had presented ourselves to work for the people of Zambia repeatedly. Yes, we had the best printed manifesto and the most complete radio and newspaper coverage. But we had been kept on probation; surely we should have been brought into the front line before time ran out?

With the enormous jump in our performance and perceived credibility we started recruiting candidates for the next election, which of course we envisioned as taking place in 2011. We had in mind potential cabinet ministers and as much tribal variation as we could attain. I persuaded Michael's colleagues from the days of local government under UNIP to come on board. Wynter Kabimba, a lawyer and a close friend of mine, had been head-hunted by Michael to be town clerk for Lusaka in the 1980s. Emmanuel Chenda had likewise been town clerk for

Ndola. Both were de facto members of the Academy—in fact they were senior to me. They were most welcome.

In 2006 Mwanawasa brought an old UNIP warhorse called Rupiah Banda, at that point retired, to his team. Banda exerted his influence to bring the support of the Eastern Province to the incumbent president with him as insurance against PF doing better than expected. He was duly appointed VP when the election result was announced and life continued smoothly for MMD for a while.

The next flirtation with prison started with a demonstration by PF cadres along the route of the presidential motorcade on the day of the opening of parliament. The police smashed it, or at least dragged a few people off to a shipping container labeled Police. I went and bought the prisoners, and of course the police, chicken and chips. I put someone on duty to feed them all in the evening and went home, where a furious phone call from the boss ordered me to make a severe statement about police brutality and Levy's totalitarian tendencies in ordering such brutality. Long since inured to unjustified exaggeration, I complied; with Charlotte's unofficial help I plundered the stock phrases like "tin pot dictator" and the rest and sat back and wondered what was next. Miraculous to narrate, the next thing was a leaked copy of a letter from the president to the inspector general of police praising him for his violent modus operandi!

But my heart suddenly filled with dread as I realized we had probably been set up. "Hold it!" I shouted down the phone and rushed round to Michael's house. My worst fears were confirmed: it was a forgery and a very clumsy one at that. It was signed by the "Persident [*sic!*] of Zambia" and had been photocopied so that the print was at an angle to the edges of the paper. "This is a forgery," I exclaimed, "thank God I got here in time."

"You didn't," he answered, "I gave it to *The Post* half an hour ago."

Insulting the president and circulating forgeries of his words and signature are all serious offenses in Zambia, and we got the book thrown at us. A tin pot dictator carries all the same connotations in Zambian English as in any other version. Defaming the president—lèse-majesté—alone could get us three years. Sure, being put behind bars was excellent free publicity—the only kind we could really afford—but what would it all be worth once we were locked up forever?

But I was becoming attuned to the Sata way. He liked to say he was guilty of misjudgment in releasing the forged letter, but I suspect he wanted the publicity that would be (and was) generated. He was a believer in the adage that all news is good news in politics.

And besides . . . miracles kept happening. Prosecution witnesses kept mysteriously failing to turn up and the irate magistrate would be forced to adjourn. This carried on until after Levy's death. I was at last learning the game and asked Michael: "What does it cost to keep those prosecution witnesses away?"

"Too much."

When, still in Levy's time, Michael had a heart attack that the doctors proclaimed was dangerous, he hammed it up shamelessly, hemmed in as he was with nurses and technicians. He was lying in the dark night strapped to a stretcher on the tarmac at the international airport when the sharper press photographers found him. He was waiting to be loaded on to the emergency evacuation plane destined for South Africa. He sat up for the journalists, removed his oxygen mask, and declared, "Go away, this is not my time to die." He then struck up various poses to be sure of making the front page in the morning.

Levy had apparently ordered an air-evacuation without any delay—he was filled with dread at the prospect of explaining Michael's death in Zambia, on his watch. But, cynical as that action may be, Levy had a change of heart with respect to Michael. "I suddenly found that I did not wish him to die." When Michael returned home it marked the start of a quite remarkable political love affair. "LEVY AND SATA RECONCILE!" the headlines shouted. I accompanied Michael to State House for an official love-in. Michael first apologized for me getting the wrong end of the stick by saying publicly that we (PF) did not need Mwanawasa's help. He used the Bemba saying that says to pay no note to what people say when their faces are distorted in their grief. Then they said nice things about each other and about God. I do not think Maureen Mwanawasa, the first lady, was a true believer in the reconciliation, but she could not deny Michael and her husband the opportunity to hug and laugh together.

The news media blazed positive headlines:

SATA WANTS TALKS WITH LEVY ON NATIONAL ISSUES

LEVY IS A VERY NICE AND FRIENDLY PERSON—SATA

SATA IS A GOOD FELLOW TO HAVE AROUND—LEVY

SATA SEEMS TO BE AHEAD, SAYS SIKOTA . . . AND ADVISES LEVY TO BE CAREFUL IN HIS DEALINGS WITH HIM BECAUSE HE U-TURNS

NO U TURN ON OUR DEAL WITH LEVY, ASSURES SATA

LEVY, SATA DEAL IS UNIQUE IN AFRICA, SAYS ZUKAS

MIYANDA BACKS LEVY, SATA DEAL

SATA ACCUSES MMD MEMBERS OF LACKING ALLEGIANCE TO LEVY

I'M NOT SEEKING A JOB FROM LEVY, SAYS SATA

"PEOPLE ARE USING MY DIFFERENCES WITH LEVY TO ENRICH THEMSELVES" KING COBRA SPITS AT HIS RECONCILIATION CRITICS

SOME CHURCH LEADERS ARE UPSET BY MY RECONCILIATION WITH LEVY—SATA

THERE IS NO NEED FOR AGE LIMIT CLAUSE . . . WE HAVE NO INTENTION OF BLOCKING SATA—LEVY

GIVE OUR RECONCILIATION TIME TO BEAR FRUITS—LEVY

This last headline on this subject was on 29 May 2008. Then a sequence of events took place that ended with Mwanawasa's death. First he decided to take it upon himself to criticize Mugabe's management of the Zimbabwean economy, which he described as a "sinking Titanic" (Hoas, 2007). A few days later, in Sharm el Sheik at a meeting of the African Union, Levy suffered a stroke and was airlifted to Paris, from whence bulletins of some credibility were regularly issued. The word *critical* started to appear with ominous frequency, and eventually death was announced. The French flew his body back to Zambia in their presidential jet with fighter escorts.

The powers that still remained in charge—be they The System or merely some lowercase systems—decreed that Levy's body should be preserved and hauled around every province in Zambia so that everyone would get a chance to view him. It was the hottest time of year when the Zambia Air Force painstakingly hauled his corpse in its coffin—attended by a mortician armed with cotton wool and formaldehyde—around the country. At the end of the airborne funeral procession came a rented Cessna, bouncing around in the spring thermals, carrying Michael.

So far as Michael, the ultimate opportunist, was concerned, Levy's posthumous "campaign" throughout the country was also a campaign for whomever would be his successor in the MMD. So Michael did his best to turn it into his own campaign. Claiming reconciliation and friendship, Michael duly turned up at the first body viewing and took center stage. Maureen was incensed and banned him from future attendance at repeat performances (is it unfair to point out that she was herself harboring presidential ambitions at this juncture?) Eventually the body completed its three-week marathon, the mortician gave an interview in which he described his task as "the job of a lifetime," and we set about burying Levy in a Stalinesque sarcophagus provided by the Chinese. Vice President Rupiah Banda was selected as MMD candidate, Michael got the money from somewhere to hire a helicopter, and off we went to war in a presidential by-election (parliamentary membership remained untouched). Michael stood against Rupiah. He narrowly lost—by only 2 percent—and we knew that next time we would bag it.

Our supporters had been threatening not to accept a defeat and a story was going round that buses were on their way from the Copper-belt with armed pro-PF thugs on board. Despite Michael's prompt appeal on the media to accept the results peacefully, careful citizens were staying home. I drove into town after the announcement of results. Cairo Road (which does lead to Cairo if you turn the right way at the Post Office) was deserted in what should have been rush hour. Michael and I stood with our hands in our pockets in the street staring in wonderment at all the traffic lights blinking out instructions to non-existent traffic—North Korean style.

"See what you have done," he said.

"Who? Me? I thought you had caused this."

"Oh, and there was I thinking it was you."

We walked up to his office, which contained one woman organizer, prostrate on the floor. She was wailing like any recently widowed lady is obliged to do in Zambia.

"Shut up," Michael shouted, "we do not allow funerals in this office." And he pushed her across the floor and out of the door with the point of his shoe. "Where are we campaigning tomorrow?"

"Parliament is sitting," I told him.

The relevance of parliament turned out to be significant. MMD was trying the crush us in parliament by buying our members with generous allowances if they attended the "National Constitutional Convention," a body charged with drawing up a new constitution and bringing it to parliament to be passed by two-thirds of its members. We had announced that PF was boycotting the NCC, which was highly biased in favor of the ruling MMD. The prospective new constitution became worrisome for three reasons. First, we suspected many traps aimed at Michael—age limits, education requirements. Second, our credibility was going to take a dive if we lost the battle to defeat a new constitution thanks to betrayal by our own MPs. Moreover, the new constitution was going to deliver a host of new parliamentary seats—all of them in pro-MMD areas. We might have won the presidency, but we'd have been unlikely to deliver a parliamentary majority.

About half our members had rebelled against our boycott and followed the money. This left only twenty or so "loyalists" with which to fight when it came to voting in the House. The government had the numbers to drive through their constitution. I suffered in silence as the

vice president, George Kunda, maneuvered toward the start of the constitution process. Then suddenly, "the Lord delivered him into my
hands," to paraphrase the reported words of Thomas Huxley in the 1860
debate with William Wilberforce on Darwin's theory of natural selec-
tion (which is the kind of thing I sometimes think about when the political process is too depressing).

A new constitution act, or amendments to the existing act, must be
preceded by the passage of a housekeeping act that enables government's
business throughout the land to continue while the substantive bill is discussed and voted upon over the period it takes to pass it. It essentially
maintains the offices and functions of state through the procedural interregnum. Like the main bill, the housekeeping act requires a two-thirds
majority of the 158 members of parliament to pass. Without the 106
votes, the bill fails and cannot be reintroduced for six months. With all
attention focused ahead to the actual constitutional amendments, vice
president Kunda had somehow forgotten to consider how narrow his
margin of error was for the housekeeping bill. With the possibility of the
opposition UPND and the loyal PF voting against it, and of a possible
shortfall of MPs in the house (an abstention counting as a "no" in effect),
the housekeeping stage was every bit as important as the main event.

In fact, it's only fair to admit that none of us had really considered
the opportunity presented by the housekeeping bill at all until that afternoon. To prepare their troops (and our rebels too) for victory, Banda had
hosted a caucus meeting followed by a heavy lunch at State House.
When the parliamentary session opened at 2:30 P.M., most of them were
still digesting their dessert. The housekeeping bill was called for a vote
almost immediately. In normal circumstances, it would be childish to
vote against a procedural bill. But the Lord really did deliver that
moment. I realized the situation with the numbers and signaled my own
MPs to vote against, and sent a message to the UPND suggesting they
oppose or abstain. Those of us who had had no lunch abstained— and
there were no 106 votes on George's side. The speaker decided the vote
should be run again, which gave our opponents a chance to summon
their colleagues. But too late. Still no 106 votes appeared. The constitutional changes that would have destroyed our chances of success were
over and done with, before 3:00 P.M.

IN ANTICIPATION OF A GOOD FIGHT, Banda and his businessmen children
organized heavy funding for the MMD campaign in 2011. Sufficient
funds were available to Banda and his parliamentary candidates to buy

almost anything that they thought might be useful. One candidate had his name printed as the brand on soft drink cans. Lollipops the shape of Rupiah were dished out to children, slowly losing their smiles and identity as they were eroded by little (non-voting) tongues. The buy-two-get-one-free helicopters from China might have helped but they were late. Women vied with each other for the number of chitenges (printed wraps) they could grab. Some would have twenty or thirty in their possession by the end. Bicycles appeared—and disappeared—by the thousand. *Don't kubeba* (pronounced kuveva), we told people. Don't tell them. Keep mum about your intentions in the polling booth; just take anything they give you. This slogan was accidentally invented by me. I tried to shout "don't tell them" in Bemba but forgot the word for "don't" (*mwila*) and stuck to the English. For reasons that have to do with the mysteries of linguistic chemistry—even with poetics perhaps—the slogan stuck. It was modified to "*donchi kubeba,*" ostensibly a more easy-to-pronounce neologism, and went on to provide the basis for a long-running top of the pops hit song.

The 2011 election was a nail biter. I had spent time on the computer estimating expected outcomes, constituency by constituency, and correspondingly directing our efforts and limited resources. It was clear we would not have a landslide in terms of parliamentary seats—in fact we figured we would maybe not even lead in the parliamentary stakes. The anomaly of a presidential win and a parliamentary loss was feasible because we had overwhelming support in the main cities and towns, but the urban constituencies were much more populous than the rural ones. Accordingly they "punched below their weight" in parliamentary terms.

But a hung parliament would be tolerable so long as we won the presidential contest. Put bluntly, there would be many non-PF MPs who could be bought with jobs in the executive, and the president could also nominate eight MPs at a whim. That after all was exactly what Mwanawasa had done and continued with. So the presidency was our target.

In the Eastern Province a fat majority for Rupiah was a foregone conclusion. But if we could trim some of that fat we could undermine him. That was the purpose of me abandoning my own constituency so often and heading east—and also heading for other areas in which the MMD had dangerous reservoirs of friendly voters, despite their being theoretically "Bemba." These tended to be in the center of the country where we knew the MMD campaign was strongly focused.

We had a number of things working in our favor. First, so far as the electorate was concerned, we were no longer new boys who could not be trusted to run away at the first sniff of danger. We had been beaten, pos-

Presidential nominations in 2011

sibly unfairly beaten, and we had stood up after each defeat and organized ourselves for the next big clash. We were instantly recognizable by almost anyone above the age of two (though in my case any white man over a certain age stood a chance of being "recognized" as me). People were by this time curious to see how we would perform in power. MMD meanwhile, three presidents and twenty years in, was suffering from an excess of time in control. The deep psychology of African electoral politics seems to be that of serial, or perhaps cyclical, adultery. Yes, there were other opposition parties but their leaders had enjoyed too much and were taking folks for granted. And they had not done the heroic thing and spent time in jail; nor were they sending out a new message. Nor did they have a white man on the front bench to show they were part of the new world order. Obama! Obama! The crowds sometimes called when I appeared. If you have a grasp for the logic of that, you are making good progress with central African thought patterns!

Second, Rupiah was helpfully untalented on the stump. He lacked charisma, even the charisma of being incomprehensible and thus seen to be "deep," or the charisma of painting the wonderful things to come, the poetic talent. By contrast Michael and I were star performers. He with his "deep" Bemba, gravelly voice, and evident courage. What they saw in a *mzungu* pretending to sing and dance like an African, making up slogans on the hoof, I am not quite sure, but I think it tends to make voters feel connected to the rest of the world, not just Zambia or Africa. Perhaps the medium was the message.

Third and above all, we had the country's best newspaper, and quite a few FM stations, on our side. *The Post* was a nongovernmental tabloid set up by private subscription in 1991, in the "glasnost" period preceding the 1991 election that brought the MMD into power. Its support or hostility in an election was capable of making a difference on the order of hundreds of thousands of votes between MMD and ourselves.

Fred M'membe, the editor of *The Post*, had a fairly volatile temperament feeding on religious and socialist fervor, the latter acquired apparently in Cuba and the former who knows where. Sometimes he fell out with us, but these fits apart, Michael and I both got on well with him; Wynter and Fred particularly became close political allies. I suspected Fred of aiming at pushing Wynter to the presidency. At times *The Post* looked like our own newspaper, publishing everything we said (including a full page article by me every week) and photo spreads of our activities. This opened up opportunities that we were not slow to seize. We became very image aware. Michael was called to the Drug Enforcement Agency to answer accusations about money laundering. (Never mind the non sequiturs in Zambian law enforcement.) At the gate he had an argument with the police who he deliberately provoked into teargassing him and his entourage. Instead of running away— which is the response prescribed by doctors and desired by policemen— he stayed put in the car and told the driver to proceed. He did not wipe away the tears and he seemed to ignore the pain—providing iconic shots for the front page of *The Post*.

My method of campaigning also became photojournalism centered. On every bush trip I would take Eddie Mwanaleza of *The Post* and his trusty camera and sense of the symbolic moment. He caught me whooping on the back of a bicycle taxi in Chipata, Rupiah's own "bedroom." He caught me en route to the village of Sitwe, crossing a crocodile infested river, supported by comrades against falling in the current, to all appearances the bearer of good news: perhaps some modern day version of Livingstone's civilization, Christianity, and commerce. Eddie was every bit as up to the task of capturing the moment as his fellow journalist Stanley.

Look at the picture of us in the river on the back cover. You might think we were clustered together in solidarity and against the force of the current. But, look again—the reason I needed to be supported against the

Campaigning in Chipata, provincial capital of Eastern Province, on a local bicycle taxi

One of very many stops at a local radio station

© Eddie Mwanaleza, 2011

Walking between villages to drum up support

© Eddie Mwanaleza, 2011

Taking a rest, waiting for a rural meeting to begin

current in the Sitwe River was that I had minor symptoms of Parkinson's disease, of which I was not yet aware but which certainly affected my more delicate attempts to maintain balance. You can tell from the weak muscle tone.

Money became progressively easier to obtain—you didn't need to be Einstein to know where a lot of the electoral support was flowing. Business leaders generally did not shift all their resources to us, but they started splitting their bets to ensure goodwill in the event. It still wasn't much but we got enough to be permanently on the road, on the community radios, and altogether in the public eye.

We were not of course concerned about the UPND winning overall. So a voter switching from UPND to PF added only one extra vote to the PF majority over MMD. Getting an MMD voter to come over to the PF on the other hand made a difference of two extra votes to the PF majority—one more for the PF in total and one less for the MMD in total. But if we hammered the UPND and unintentionally drove some of its voters to MMD, we were creating votes against ourselves. So we were quite gently disposed to UPND.

It takes about three and a half days to cast, count, and collate the votes in a national election in Zambia. If it is close it can take longer since increasingly isolated polling stations have to be included in the tally to make the presidential result certain. The period is long enough to allow rigging allegations, theories, and bogus eyewitness stories to abound. My opinion is that if there is real rigging going on it is not captured by all this conspiracy hysteria—it is quietly going on offstage. In fact the real riggers may even be the source of a lot of this distracting foil. On the positive side, however clever a rigging scheme may be, it can only make a difference of a few percent—say 5—without becoming patent. It is much more productive for a competitor in the election to campaign for a few extra percent for his candidate than to try and uncover a systematic electoral fraud and prove it in court.

However, to make sure we knew exactly what was happening, Wynter set up what we wrongly called a PVT (parallel voter tabulation) process. We phoned anyone in the know about results as they were announced by the local presiding and returning officers. The swing-o-meter swung from us to them and back again. Then suddenly it was a done deal and we pleaded with the appropriate players to announce Michael's victory as the crowds grew restless and the sounds of rioting became louder and more ubiquitous. At 1:40 A.M. they did their stuff. Michael was announced as the winner. Stories abound of a last-minute attempt by Rupiah to negate the electoral result, but nothing like that happened.

"How did you lose?" I asked my former colleague in the 1991 MMD front line, Dr. Boniface Kawimbe, the election manager for MMD. He told me a story about his medical training in London. A patient lay wired up to an ECG machine; his heartbeat was very unsatisfactory. The teaching cardiologist invited Kawimbe to defibrillate the patient by applying the electrodes to the chest. He did so, pressed the button, and beautiful regular spikes appeared on the ECG trace. However, after a short while they started fading and missing. Do it again! The same thing happened. Kawimbe needed no urging. He did it again. And again. Eventually the cardiologist interceded. "Dr. Kawimbe," he said, "This is a resuscitation machine; it is not a resurrection machine. The poor chap is dead."

11

Inside Looking Out

THE OFFICE OF THE SECRETARY TO THE CABINET HAD PLANNED FOR Rupiah's inauguration a low-key, small, high security ceremony at the parliamentary grounds. Michael was having none of it. A stage was hastily attached to the front of the Supreme Court and public notice was given that the inauguration would be late in the afternoon. A crowd immediately started to congregate, many walking miles, others transported by taxis and buses without charge. It was surely the largest mass of people that ever assembled itself in Zambia—bigger than the Pope's Square rally at which I tried to measure the crowd using the speed of sound. I tried to walk to the venue from a nearby hotel, together with my long-suffering wife, but we got ourselves mobbed very quickly. Luckily we were rescued by a foreign diplomat who was sensibly driving his Mercedes to the venue, and who even more sensibly had been a rugby player for his country.

Rupiah was there to hand over the instruments of power. The Chief Justice was there to make it all legal. Michael was in charge; Rupiah was booed; Rupiah wept (but credit to him for turning up).

We went to bed, only to awaken now and then in disbelief. What hath God wrought? What have we wrought? Have we any clue what we are supposed to do now?

For a few days I stayed at home and read my mail and phoned my friends. I knew Michael would take a few days to settle his cabinet and he would not appoint us until he had most of the balancing acts set up. The election had been on 20 September, and the result, the swearing in, and the crowd on 23 September. I guessed it would be some days until the cabinet was announced. I knew him too well to get under his feet while he worked on it. One or two of my colleagues couldn't stay away from him—lest he forget about them—and got themselves frog-marched out of State House.

We had a few MPs who had a background in government as high as cabinet minister, and Michael accommodated all of them. But he had other challenges in placement. Many organizations—churches, trade unions, and NGOs—had "booked a seat" in our cabinet, seeking influence on government through us in return for electoral support. Then there were relatives and financial supporters. I did not know half of Michael's commitments and was content to lie by the pool (at the hottest time of year) and take on board the media coverage while Michael pondered his options. On the evening of 28 September I received a text to be there the next day. I duly presented myself at the Big Man's office and we took a stroll through the old colonial classical building. It was in terrible shape, giving off an air of impending collapse, and, as it was raining, water was running down the walls. As if to stay in keeping with the atmosphere of decrepitude, the kitchen was a health hazard (the chef lost his job instantly). Inside Zambia, State House (formerly the Northern Rhodesian Government House) is famous for its network of Yugoslav built tunnels. These connect State House itself with a number of houses outside the grounds; we had a look into one portal and found it flooded. Perhaps the whole building was settling into the tunnels.

I remember we chatted about how Frederick Chiluba was persuaded to feature the tunnels on TV in order to embarrass his long-defeated foe Kenneth Kaunda for wasting state money ("no light at the end of his tunnel, ho, ho"). But he conveniently forgot that a strong ally of Zambia had his life, or at least his dignity, saved by the tunnels. According to information that ought to be reliable, Joshua Nkomo escaped by using a secret door to the tunnels when the Rhodesian special forces covertly entered Zambia one night and attacked a house near State House that Nkomo was using as his ZAPU/ZIPRA headquarters (rechristened promptly when sunrise revealed the result by Zambian wags as the Zimbabwe Ruins). Publicly he did not confess to the existence of the tunnels, instead concocting the story that he had escaped through the toilet window as the attack began. Since Nkomo was famously big around the belly this story was not taken seriously, except perhaps by General Peter Walls, the commander of the Rhodesian army. When a journalist asked him about the bathroom escape in

Lusaka, Walls appeared to think for a few seconds and then declared: "That would explain why the house fell down!"

Jokes: Zambia 1, Rhodesia 1.

"Go and have lunch somewhere hygienic and come back and I'll swear you in."

"As what?"

No answer.

As one of my first acts as VP, I extracted approval from parliament to make State House safe and workable. Then I went to find my own office on the top floor of the Cabinet Office building. Naturally this was leaking enthusiastically and I went back to parliament again.

Normally, it is standard security practice that president and vice president do not spend much time in the same building or the same vehicle. This rule reduces the chance of the two being involved in the same accident or deliberate attack. Michael did not have much respect for this rule, so I saw more of him than the average VP in this nervous world sees of his or her boss.

Let me try and understand and describe some of the conundrums Michael had to solve, as well as some of his acts that baffled me.

Most English-speaking African countries have constitutions that are a hybrid of the British and the US model, with some traditional African elements thrown in. The president is elected American style by means of a popular vote. He appoints his cabinet mostly from parliament, British style. What about his advisers? Are they professionals with no political coloring, inherited from the previous government (as ideally in Britain)? Or are they politically tainted people who are loyal to yesterday's government and who need to be replaced by other (differently) tainted people?

And what about tribe and family? If you are looking for loyalists how are you more likely to find them than through nepotism of some degree or other? If on the other hand you refuse to practice nepotism, can you withstand the family pressures that will come back at you? These kinds of question may not trouble advanced countries too much—though they are not evaded entirely—but they are bound to trouble a newly elected supreme leader in most African contexts.

And Zambia, whatever the legislation says, is a country in which polygamy is not unusual, especially for men who are "big shots." This doesn't mean that the state registrar will solemnize more than one wife at a time. Michael, so far as I am aware, was married under English common law three times. In his last marriage from my own observation, and according to others in his earlier marriages, he was a doting husband and father to his numerous sons and daughters.

So Michael is in State House. Who can be relied upon to do his typing? Who is going to advise him on whom to meet and what to say? Who can he trust to understand and believe in the Party Manifesto? PF is a party of the poor, for the poor. The people who run the organs of state as civil servants are not poor. Can they bridge the divide, even in their own heads? What are you, the president, going to do for your poverty-stricken auntie who fell upon hard times in the business of importing women's lingerie on the weekly state-subsidized flight from Mauritius? Doesn't she deserve or at least need to be accredited as ambassador to Timbuktu and remunerated by the taxpayer?

Is the West truly more rule-based and objective? If so, then how does it come about that US administrations in my time have replaced as president a father with a son, or appointed a brother of the president as attorney general? Hillary didn't make it into Bill's shoes but the very fact they tried . . . well, it was intended as a rhetorical question but we now know that the correct answer was "no." The White House and its knights seem to have many of the hallmarks of a medieval court. You expect us in Africa to turn things round and "modernize," just like that?

And we should not forget Michael "Robin Hood" Sata's office responsibilities, which followed him to the highest post in the land, gathering IOUs in transit as it were. You did not have to be a member of his extended family, even in the most all-encompassing sense, to be able to place demands on him in regard to your personal needs. You merely needed to be a Zambian. In fact, Michael now had access to more business leaders and government departments than he ever had before and was addressed by nearly everybody as "father." And it turned out that many were not using the noun out of mere politeness.

It is easy for someone who hasn't been there, and who hasn't taken the time to imagine being there, to lament all the "old-fashioned" aspects of African governance—the demands of the extended family, the pay-offs, the search for personal loyalty. But you cannot simply plonk yourself down in the presidential armchair and decide to operate in a "modern," meritocratic way without reference to kinship ties and recognition of services rendered (even if we onlookers don't know what they are).

Nor is it child's play setting up a system to deliver goods and services in line with the task you were elected to perform. The Cabinet Office may be able to deliver a bunch of potential troops to follow the president into bureaucratic battle, but it is far from certain they will be any good. Within days of Michael taking up business within the water-logged confines of State House I had one "special adviser" nailed for taking money to fix appointments with the big boss. It seems this was routine behavior in previous administrations, and I am sure just busting the odd bent staff member was not going to change it.

There are several hundred traditional chiefs in Zambia, many of them with issues of which the only one in the world who could solve them was "Our Father." There is constant friction between chiefs and other land users, a category that includes many people who are not honest. Some issues, such as the question of East Bembaland, have festered for nearly two centuries. Different African countries have found different "solutions" to the problem of how chiefs fit into a modern governance structure. Tanzania abolished the institution; the Southern Rhodesians retained it but took almost all responsibilities away, notably in the area of land.

In our large country the colonial administration introduced a form of indirect rule, investing chiefs to carry out functions relating to the land, wild animals, some public works, and resolution of legal disputes. Chiefs who were suspended by the colonial authorities for serious offenses were deregistered and they remain so still today. The question of chiefs' and subjects' rights to land is very unclear, in no small measure due to ideological positions imported by donors. For example, in Scandinavia it would seem the institution of the chieftainship was abandoned some years back. Consequently, our chiefs are on the receiving end of a strange mix of respect and scorn from emissaries of Northern Europe.

The refusal of donors to formulate a common position on rural governance has been most unfortunate for the wildlife sector. When responsibility for wildlife was taken away by Kaunda's government, the traditional system of the chiefs selling hunting rights to "poachers" on their territory simply went underground. When the chiefs' authority and rights to some of the hunting revenues was restored, matters improved enormously. However, the pressure to cut the chiefs out of the loop continues, and the current arrangements are half above and half beneath the ground.

Shortly after taking office, Michael created a new tenth province of Zambia that he called Muchinga. This contains East Bembaland—Mpika and Chinsali—and some non-Bemba districts. In 2013 he deregistered the sitting Chitimukulu and a long bitter political fight for control of the Bemba followed. This was eventually won by a Western chief, but probably only because Michael's illness was getting him down. President Lungu, upon taking office in January 2015, recognized the Western chief, and that should have been the end of the story (for another century or two perhaps). However, there were credible reports of ongoing unrest in the east, a year after Michael's death. Who was behind it? I do not know.

For THE MAN OR woman in State House, there is a cognitive problem that is certainly severe in Zambia, though it is probably widespread in the world: The problem of determining the truth when most of your informants appear to have MAs, even PhDs, in creative fiction. Many who make it to the presidency complain that the view from the top of the tree can be very confusing. Accordingly you are prone to believe things you would not normally believe, and this distorting effect is made worse by the people who surround you and take advantage of the unfamiliar perspective. I have experienced it to a limited extent and, yes, it is a very different world—not in the sense that the inside is new but in the sense that the outside looks different when you observe it from inside. On some days there are so many dubious "facts" in the air that you suspect not just that you have some liars among your entourage but there must be a whole university Department of Fibbing somewhere that churns graduates and postgraduates out in numbers, the flagship department in the University of Whopping.

The ability to pick the true story from the inbox full of false ones varies with individuals. It also varies with time, as old age engenders gullibility. I do not know of many presidents who would swallow the story of "Heaven on Earth"—originating from California's Maharishi Yogi transcendental meditation movement—where the practices of a bogus guru, including levitation, would magically transform a whole country to a paradise that would never have problems with droughts, IMF conditions, HIV/AIDS epidemics, or anything else nasty. However long you live, you might think, you would not fail to see through such an outrageous confidence trick. But Kaunda fell for it. He ordered the transfer of huge chunks of land to the conmen. The civil service was for once able to represent its notorious inefficiency and tardiness in carrying out orders as a feature and not as a bug.

I am quite sure that Kaunda would not have fallen for Heaven on Earth in his first ten years or so in office. I believe anyone's grip on reality loosens with the time spent in the "unreality" of high office. After twenty-seven years in power, the urban myth goes, Kaunda did not know what a traffic light was, for example ("Why have you stopped, driver?"). This is my justification for the belief that leaders should not stay too long, irrespective of who they are or how good they were in earlier days.

Michael was less gullible and less credulous than Kaunda and many of his fellow African leaders. But he had only just arrived in the seat of power. Michael was never prone to act on insufficient information, or at least not until he was weak and close to the end of his life. In this last regard it seems he gave up trying to defend Wynter Kabimba and some other targeted individuals on the strength of a number of emails ostensibly sent between them, confirming a scheme to remove Michael from office on the grounds of health. The mail service provider assured me the day I became acting president that the email traffic in question was fraudulent.

Michael fit and at full throttle was as full of tricks as that "amateur" upstart Nicolo Machiavelli. But he was vulnerable. Slowly dying he was as painful to observe as a beast of prey mortally wounded by a tourist.

The president of Zambia gets to appoint eight nominated (i.e., unelected) members of parliament. These positions were earmarked for a few technocrats and faithful senior members of the party who had been told to pull out of the parliamentary race in their constituencies in order to spend time beefing up Michael's campaign team countrywide. Once we were in the hot seat he realized that one of the national campaigners—call him Mr. X—to whom he had promised a nominated seat would bring embarrassment. He had been involved in some ugly violence in his own household that would not sit well with the party's image. How to resolve this?

Michael appointed *nine* nominated members including Mr. X and sat back. The press and social media were quickly on to it. "The president cannot count!" they all screamed. Michael had no problem confessing he was innumerate of course. And he had no problem asking for volunteers from the nine to back off and accept another appointment. All nine volunteered and Michael "reluctantly" and "thankfully" accepted the offer from X—who felt really cool, even honored, about the whole affair. And there are still people who think he could not count!

Every morning the president started by admitting to his office the usual suspects. These included the Chief Spook, the Acceptable Face of The System, with his intelligence report, which Michael read without missing a trick. One or two special assistants would be there too. I was there if I had an issue I wanted to raise or we were going into cabinet afterward. The secretary to the cabinet, being the senior civil servant, was there. A minister or two may be there, as is a security chief or two, to explain something in the intelligence report perhaps.

If he read something in the intelligence reports that intrigued him, or if he figured a spot of intimidation would be appropriate, he would pick up the phone and direct dial the person concerned.

"So, I am losing popularity, am I?"

"Who is calling?"

"The name is Sata, Michael Sata."

I appreciate that this is more vague than some readers would like but the whole area is Top Secret and specifics from which any hard facts may be deduced are forbidden to the outside world. (This is not to say that the secrets are all worth knowing.)

Some days started ferociously with Michael attacking us left, right, and center for a range of sins. On these occasions the targets liked to position themselves so that my body would block out Michael's view of them. "Please come to the meeting tomorrow morning," they pleaded with me. "You can protect me from the president!"

"What makes you think I enjoy being blasted?" *"Kolwe angala pa musamba anashya"* (The monkey plays on the branch that is familiar with him.)

Then it would all suddenly calm down, with no permanent injuries inflicted, and all turned to jokes and mockery directed at our real enemies.

Sometimes however, someone really was for the high jump and we got to witness Michael's "rotating turret" trick. Since he once invited the press to a cabinet meeting at which he employed this, it is in the public domain and I can use it as an example.

He let the press get comfortable and welcomed them. Then he said something along the lines of "we must get this government sorted out." Then he attacked me: "Even my vice president is useless—he wants to import used Japanese cars. Why does he want Zambians to be driving secondhand cars? Is that all we are fit for?" He was looking straight at me, talking nonsense as he knew and I knew, but he had his motives—he was getting his dander up, using me as the *musamba anashya* (the familiar branch.) Then he rotated his head to another minister—I think it was the minister of finance—and gave him the same treatment over some pointless issue. By now, he was looking very cross.

He rotated his head one last time and faced the permanent secretary, his real target. "If you want to play politics, form your own party; don't you use my bloody party. Get out! Get out!" Collapse of Perm Sec, end of episode. The rest of the meeting was quite jolly and even featured a couple of used car jokes.

NOBODY LIVES IN STATE HOUSE so far as I am aware—it is a place full of offices and meeting rooms. Michael and Christine lived in Nkwazi (Fish

Eagle) House, a gloomy residence on the State House grounds, built by the Yugoslavs. It is a good place to get away from, if you have an excuse.

Some days were scheduled for flitting across the country. Oh, there's the big chopper warming up! An outing!

On one occasion, I was sent to open a new bridge in the Zambezi Valley. I flew in but others had to drive; they told me it was an unforgiving road, featuring potholes that might have been dug by a consortium of anteaters in revenge for an assault on their environment. But they came just the same: earnest Dutch conservationists, the Chinese ambassador, and regiments of young men and women who had at last "seen the light" and decided PF was the way to go even if they had not voted for us. They wore clean PF T-shirts.

Some people of a certain age might think that I am describing a famous scene in *Call Me Bwana*, a film made in 1963 featuring Bob Hope as a white, fraudulent professional hunter who is hired by the US government to recover a space satellite that has landed in an African country. The film is a funny juxtaposition of visual clichés about Africa and the West. Here is reality: after a grueling few miles of pot-holed dirt road, you find yourself on a wide strip of new tarmac. A few hundred yards on, you reach a four-lane steel bridge and you proceed to cross the Kafue River near the end of its long run from the Congo border to the Zambezi. No need to stop or even slow down—this is a modern bridge, designed for heavy loads and built by a high-speed Chinese work team with the enthusiasm of termites building their towers and tunnels.

At night, there are twenty-odd streetlights (solar powered) to keep the bridge visible and safe for pedestrians in the overlapping circles of illumination. Around the last one, somebody has invested in a pub and fish-and-cassava joint. If you keep going you will traverse another brief stretch of tar and then plunge back into aardvark territory.

A group of expatriates were cooking Boer sausages and T-bone steaks the other day at a party and they started teasing me: this thing emerges from the dark suddenly and you find yourself in the middle of civilization. Streetlights! Have you got anything to tell us about it, Dr. Scott?

It was no use pleading ignorance. They had almost certainly read the plaque, which goes:

THE MICHAEL CHILUFYA SATA BRIDGE
WAS OFFICIALLY COMMISSIONED
BY
HIS HONOUR THE VICE PRESIDENT OF
THE REPUBLIC OF ZAMBIA

Dr Guy Scott
On 22 August 2014.

Michael's pure belief in physical infrastructure was perhaps in part derived from the UNIP era, when there was (a) plenty of money for capital expenditure, and (b) the theory held that physical infrastructure was the main constraint to economic development. Naturally the "bringing of development" acquired strong political resonance among the many regions and tribes. Give them roads and bridges and they will give you the vote!

Fewer than ten years after independence, as the money ran out and a lack of maintenance took its toll, large parts of Zambia became decrepit and impassable to heavy traffic. Ironically, it was the roads that were used that rapidly became unusable in the absence of load control and other basic measures. If you came across a road in good condition the mostly correct assumption was that there was no economic activity wearing it down. Some donor countries took up the task of replacing inter-provincial roads as they became unbearable to travel on—even they appreciated that some infrastructure was needed, though the theory that lack of infrastructure was *the* brake on economic and social development became pretty obviously wrong. A road does not generate its own traffic (except during construction). Nonetheless there is a case that some infrastructure is a necessary, if not a sufficient condition for development.

Michael's belief in roads and bridges never wavered, so far as I can see. His proudest achievement as governor of Lusaka was to relieve the pressure of rush hour traffic by persuading Zambia Railways to meet the costs of a flyover bridge over their track. How he achieved this we may never know but it was and remains a great boon to car-owning denizens of the city. When he took over from me as the MP for Mpika—while at the same time being Minister Without Portfolio in Chiluba's government—he virtually covered the commercial and administration areas of the town with tarmac and concrete. If Mpika ever develops to the point there is such a thing as a rush hour, drivers will certainly appreciate it!

Almost as soon as we had won the 2011 election, the building of roads began, with Michael as the chief whip-wielder. But it's hard to overstate the inefficiencies and quirks of the machinery of government, which seem to obstruct progress on an almost continuous basis.

The British comedy TV series *Yes, Minister* is popular in Zambia; it resonates very strongly with the day-to-day running of our version of government. There is even a saying in all vernaculars that "You found

us here, and we will wave you goodbye when you depart"; it purportedly represents the attitude of civil servants to the political leadership.
The problem is exacerbated by quangos (quasi-autonomous nongovernmental organizations) of every shape and size. Decisions the elected
government ever gets around to making can be wrapped in red tape,
shoved into workshop-mode, and buried forever in strategic plans. The
response from most people is to talk about the need for reform, consensus building, and such, like mostly sedentary "activities."

With Michael in charge, however, you might as well try and play
Yes, Minister in a squall. When someone would gently point out that we
were paying too much for the new roads he would just become irascible
and ask, "So what can I do?" He believed in speed and force in public
affairs; they were his weapons against bureaucracy. He had the quango
responsible for roads, the Road Development Agency, moved directly
under his office for ease of shouting.

The Chinese, it can be said, understood him. He wanted physical
output; he did not believe in "soft" development—wishy-washy awareness raising, anything with the word social or its offshoots—and he was
in a hurry, like China itself. He was making up for lost time, fighting
decades of decay. It is conceivable that from the beginning of his reign
he knew he had only a few years to live. If it were not for the Chinese—
albeit they were expensive—there would be no bridge with streetlights
across the Kafue River. It would have been waiting for the road to be
embarked upon first, and the road would have been waiting for finance,
which would have been waiting for a thorough evaluation and competitive tendering, during which money changed hands illegally and the
interests of the Zambian people were in no way served.

One day I took a media army and went to inspect all the wonders
we had wrought in a country three times bigger than Great Britain and
at least fifty times poorer. We started at a new tar road running almost
100 km along the west bank of the Luangwa River. I had been with
Michael when he launched the project two years earlier and been
ordered by him to sing.

"Sing what?" I asked.

"Just sing!"

My spirits came to my rescue by causing me to remember for the
first time in nearly fifty years a song composed in honor of Kaunda's
achievements as the Father of the Nation. It says in English: *Whenever
I try to think about all the development going on, my thoughts are not
up to the job!* I sang in Nyanja, the local lingua franca. *Ngati niganize
za chitukuko, maganizo yanga yonse a pelewela.*

"Where the hell did you get that?" Michael asked.

"When development died, the song died too; now it is back!"

And the women joined in and drowned me out.

Moving on two years, they were singing the same song. "Now what will you get out of this road?" I asked them when they had stopped.

"We thought you had forgotten us! It shows us you have not. We are so happy!"

"Yes, but it has cost more than a jet airliner. How is that justified?"

We had set down the choppers and parked the ground detail on the road itself, and we had been more than half an hour chatting with the locals without a single independent vehicle trying to use the road for its proper purpose—at nine in the morning.

"Ah," said the chief, "I am going to town this afternoon and it will be very comfortable and my vehicle will not get damaged."

The road is perhaps a sort of wedding ring—testimony that government and people are together, but of no material use in an economic sense. It is also conceivable that the road is more rationally seen as something that will lead to income-earning development in time, but there is not much indication that people are thinking about actual self-sustaining economic activity. Either way the psephology is magic! We lost this constituency in 2011 and won it, by a landslide, in a subsequent by-election. Indeed, if we had been able to keep up the pace Michael had set, it looked as if there would be no need to say a word during the campaign for the elections in 2016. It would take nothing more than, perhaps, a few photographs to remind voters how the whole country—three times the size of Great Britain, equal in size to Texas—would have taken on the unmistakable signs of a work in progress, not to be disturbed by a new government.

While unlikely to name a child or an airport "John Maynard," it might be argued that my friend had some identifiable Keynesian affinities. Keynes believed in solid, directly funded undertakings that would add productive capacity to the economy, while at the same time creating more jobs and putting more money in your pocket (two Sata slogans), thus causing growth in aggregate consumer demand and thence growth in aggregate supply. Keynes was keen to evade the conservative monetarist criticism that money would just lose value if pumped into the economy any old how, while at the same time he was keen to combat the march of socialism, which he abhorred. Keynes used to promote his ideas among associates in the "Other Club," a predominately conservative institution. "It is notable that Steel-Maitland was the foremost advocate in Baldwin's cabinet in 1928–9 of road-building and public works programmes to revive business confidence, to create jobs and thus to resist socialism: perhaps Keynes murmured to him at the Other Club more effectively" (Davenport-Hines).

Infrastructure programs have quite a reputable worldwide history in years of recession and unemployment and other disaster. The Irish who had not died or fled in the time of the Potato Famine (late 1840s) built canals and roads in exchange for emergency food relief. Employment was created in the United States during the Great Depression by similar New Deal–infrastructure projects. In Zambia some people have tried to justify the accelerated physical development in terms of employment creation, but the extent of this can be questioned. The Chinese seem to employ as many Chinese workers as they do Zambians. Who or what they all are we do not know. Once, while traveling the Western Province in 2008, I was flagged down by a road construction gang whose spokesman was a Zambian. "Have you got anything to show we are supporting Michael Sata?" he asked. We had a sack full of badges with Michael's face on each; we handed out dozens, one to each Zambian. The Chinese workers who were in the background saw the badges and asked, "Who is this one?" "It is our leader, Mr. Michael Sata, who is going to liberate us from slavery." I had to shell out another sack of badges to the Chinese. They also wanted to be freed by Michael.

We knew from our experiences in 1992 with the "food for work" relief effort we had to mount in response to the "drought of the Century" in our region that it is actually very difficult to kill more than one bird with one stone; in fact you must count yourself lucky if you assuredly have the one in the bag. The result of Michael's three-year spell of constructing universities and roads where none would have appeared otherwise is controversial, especially to unemotional cost-benefit analysts. The levels of corruption in the construction sector are alleged to be phenomenal; certainly there are impediments to competitive tendering and supervision of works.

Michael could not abide any public-private arrangements in which he felt the Zambian people were losing out. As opposition we had participated in protest marches to give vent to our fury that Colonel Gaddafi had apparently got his hands on the Zambia Telecommunications Co. in the course of some (allegedly nontransparent) privatization exercise. There were other instances of the same kind of thing (though not with such colorful personalities involved). A management deal between an Israeli–South African consortium and our state-owned Zambia Railways was annulled by us unilaterally. Michael pushed very hard in these areas, causing the minister of finance (his "uncle" Alexander Chikwanda) to appear in the office each day before dawn to get all the work done.

A Lusaka businessman came to my house the other day and said, "Come and look at this." He put me in the passenger seat and drove me to the Lusaka South Multi-Facility Economic Zone. This is an area carved out of the bush and adorned with power lines and wide tar roads. It cost millions and is supposed to attract investment from all over the world. It can contain more than 200 factories. Right now it houses one office block, one pharmaceutical warehouse, and one malting plant for a brewery. No other licenses have been issued, and there is a stand-off regarding tariffs between the zone management and the power utility (with silence and darkness the results).

What was the name of that movie? We flailed around a bit and found it: *Paris, Texas*. Scrubland, power lines, roads, and amnesia, with Ry Cooder on an impossibly deep, slow, and soulful guitar. Not much chance of finding Nastassja Kinski around here however, I reckon.

12

Daily Business

APART FROM HELPING TO FIND THE MONEY TO STOP THE LEAKING, I HAD
nothing to do with the presidential real estate. As vice president I was
given an office opposite the embassies and back-to-back with the main
ministries; I was also given a house in town opposite the golf course—
Government House, at which it was assumed we would reside.

However, Charlotte and I opted to stay at our farm (just outside
Lusaka) for the privacy, the hot running water, the post-Soviet era fur-
niture, and the feeling of reality regained each evening. Besides, who
wants to stay in a master bedroom that was once inhabited by Colonel
Gaddafi, who came to Zambia to try and seal his bid to be the head of
the African Union—the King of Africa?

"I thought Gaddafi used to sleep in a Bedouin tent on the lawn?"

"No your Honor, maybe in Libya. In Zambia he used the tent in the
day but rushed indoors as soon as night fell."

No guarantees about the whereabouts of his ghost then.

As I indicated in the introduction, the vice president of the Republic
of Zambia has very heterogeneous terms of reference. Among them is
the responsibility of dealing with internally displaced people—Zambian
refugees within Zambia, vulnerable individuals or groups who have lost
their land or livelihoods to droughts, floods, carpet-baggers, or other
species of predators including witchdoctors and home-grown fundamentalist churches.

My first substantial act as VP was to order the resettlement of several thousand village farmers. They had been evicted, by the traditional
chief in whose domain they lived, from a valley endowed with sparkling

155

pure water and nutritious soils. The UPND had brought the matter as a petition to the House, before we took over the government, and I had put PF behind it. The government (Banda's MMD) had ducked the issue since the chief had some clout in the electoral game—he still had many subjects whom he had not displaced.

Quite what the chief's motivation was could not be determined, but a likely answer would be that there was a foreign investor, almost certainly with interests in the wildlife sector, who was willing to pay the chief for the land. Indeed, it turned out that money had changed hands and some had already been "eaten." Such a transaction overlooks the provision of the Lands Act, but it had worked so many times that the law was virtually paralyzed. Foreign and local carpet-baggers are wont to sell land from under the feet of rural people, who are then forced to settle or squat in places that are inferior from their point of view.

But I wanted to send a message that in the new Sata government we did not chicken out of doing the right thing. That was the point; that was the precedent we wanted to engrave in the minds of would-be land speculators. We also wanted to signal that customary use of land would not be ridden over roughshod. Furthermore I wanted to show that the usual escape route from justice—endless adjournments and implementation delays—was no longer open. We were something new: the A-team. Here today, still here tomorrow.

And so it came to pass that on my solitary signature a task force consisting of police, army, intelligence, the department of agriculture, as well as IDP (internally displaced people) specialist staff from my office drove off in a convoy to the hidden valley and planned and repopulated it, while the chief sat in my office hoping his lamentations would soften my heart. When the word came that the job was done, I took him back to his home in a helicopter and left him there, with a quote from Arnold Schwarzenegger, translated into Tonga, ringing in his ears.

The impact of my restoring part of Sichifulo Game Management Area to the customary inhabitants has been considerable and in some part problematical for politicians. We demonstrated that we would not tolerate, less be an active party in, the dispossession of small farmers. This is an important message for the farmers but also it must keep the chiefs awake at night, since it means they do not have get rich quick options in the form of land sales.

Sichifulo, adjacent to the Kafue National Park, is deep in the Southern Province, where the people are loyal to the UPND. They would never cheer a PF leader, though that is what they did to me. If a confrontation develops between the customary residents and the chiefs across a wider area, the UPND is going to have to play its cards very carefully, since both sides will threaten to abandon it politically if it comes down on the wrong side.

As the speed and lack of blockages attested in the Sichifulo case, the public service was shocked into acquiescence by the election results. Sooner-the-better was plainly the ideal moment to do what needed doing, since the system was incapable of saying either Yes or No with any conviction or force. I embarked upon a hunt for what some people call "low hanging fruit." Easy pickings. Michael was not going to interfere with me, I knew, and the secretary to the cabinet we found in post was already in the wilderness so far as Michael was concerned. So what to do next?

By chance a doctor dropped by to congratulate me, and alerted me to the results of an important HIV/AIDS trial that were published just as we were winning the election. The trial had established (or more accurately confirmed) that HIV+ people who are on antiretroviral (ARV) drugs had very little of the virus in their blood stream and were effectively noninfectious. This had the implication that if you identified all the HIV+ people and put them immediately on ARVs, you would stop the epidemic dead in its tracks. So let's do it! This new recommendation flew in the face of existing practice—up until 2011, worldwide policy on ARVs had been to withhold treatment from HIV+ people until they were quite seriously sick (as measured by the CD4 count, an indication of the strength of the immune system). But during that nontreated period they were infectious, and their own health was being compromised.

I have some experience in third world humanitarian funding. I knew that the faster Zambia came to the fore in championing a new "test and treat" policy (meaning the practice of putting people who test positive for HIV on antiretroviral therapy immediately), the easier it would be to get funding. I convened the Ministry of Health and others to review our policy. There are two sides to this argument, believe it or not. One says that Yes, immediate treatment removes the virus from the blood stream and thereby prevents transmission to HIV negative people. However, it goes on to say, such early treatment may cause resistance and other complications, and anyway wouldn't it cost too much money?! (I actually got this latter response from Bill Gates.) I got the permanent secretary at the health ministry, Dr. Peter Mwaba, to analyze the issue for us. He was brilliant and almost as good at guilt-tripping donors as I was.

Now reader . . . just think for a nanosecond. Which side of this argument would you want to wake up on? The one where rich people in rich countries withhold treatment of a killer disease afflicting or threatening to afflict poor people and poor countries? Or would you prefer to be on the other side? It is a no-brainer. Zambia is currently credited, in such localities as Washington and Geneva, with being ahead of the game in HIV policy. Why? It's just that we have better psychologists and politicians than some others. Even if all the money is not going to be forthcoming, the donors cannot say it won't, and they will back that with something extra.

I confess I like exercising power, even and perhaps more when it involves convening people who don't normally come together. Too many organizations and departments tend to be involved in solving any given problem and the only way to make progress is if they consult each other in a structured way. But this is likely to happen only if there is someone senior enough to order a meeting and to draw up the agenda. (Then you can get them in the room and lock the door, so to speak.)

Power is particularly gratifying when it is deployed on behalf of the disadvantaged; that is to my taste and was also to Michael Sata's taste. It is also to the taste of the disadvantaged people, who had accordingly voted us into office in anticipation. If that is populism let there be more populism. And let them vote for us again when the time comes.

While we had one health problem on the convened table, we lined up another and passed it around. One of the reasons that our tourism was suffering from a shortage of customers was the insistence of the South African government on enforcing yellow fever immunization requirements on travelers who passed through Johannesburg en route to Zambia. South African officialdom had the temerity to block passengers from traveling on to Lusaka, for example, for not having a yellow fever certificate even though they had no legal powers to do so.

The South African government has always been high-handed with its smaller neighbors—all the way from the days of apartheid and sanctions. Unfortunately for us the transition to a more democratic and easy-going relationship between us has at times been impeded by "sunset contracts" given to long-standing white public servants in that country. So we find ourselves dealing with people who—although they may have forgotten—once blamed us for the loss of a civil war in their country. The retention of many of the same civil servants who ran government in the bad old days has resulted in the deployment of a variety of non-tariff barriers to the disadvantage of competitors.

The fact that so few countries were worrying about yellow fever vaccination for travelers made travel to those destinations with restrictions very inconvenient. My daughter Thandi spent nearly a week wandering around London looking for a clinic that had both the vaccine and the yellow books in stock. In the United States, clinics were charging US$400 for a "consultation" involving yellow fever. Arriving for Nelson Mandela's funeral, we were held in a Zambia Air Force plane at Pretoria's infamous Waterkloof Airbase, waiting to park next to Republique de France Numéro Un. Unknown chemicals were sprayed into our plane and on us, and the door held shut for ten minutes to ensure that any *aedis* mosquitoes would die and not carry the dreaded disease into the *aedis* population already resident in the country (and mysteriously YF negative).

We asked the World Health Organization (WHO) to reclassify Zambia from a high-risk to a low-risk country. WHO asked in return for us to conduct a sampling of the blood of residents in the supposedly infected area of Zambia (the west and northwest). The results took a long time coming but they revealed a very low incidence of yellow fever parasite in Zambian blood. There was one last blast when somebody tried to get us to go back and look for the parasite in "nonhuman primates." There were some bad mannered exchanges between Pretoria, Lusaka, and WHO HQ in Geneva, but the reclassification eventually happened. I hope that I, and the minister of health, are forgiven in the relevant places . . . such as the heart of Margaret Chan, Office Number One, WHO, Geneva, Switzerland.

Zambia has three times the land area of the United Kingdom and extremely poor infrastructure by comparison. When I asked how much information we had on record about vulnerable and minority groups generally, it emerged that we possessed only a very partial picture of our own country's 15 million or so people, and that some of that was as much as 100 years old. I gave orders for a big catch-up exercise with the recording and archiving of Zambia's people. I decided to start the archiving of Zambia's people by bringing the Batwa people back to life, or more literally out of hiding and marginalization. The Batwa are the original modern human peoples of southern and central Africa, or so it would seem from the patchy evidence. We have already met these people in Chapter 2.

I called Mulenga Kapwepwe to discuss this issue. Mulenga is a daughter of Simon Kapwepwe, the childhood friend and fellow freedom fighter of Kenneth Kaunda who was later imprisoned for forming a political party and planning to use it to seize power from Kaunda. She has, unsurprisingly, deep feelings toward Zambia's hidden sources of spiritual life and a sense of mission where recording our culture is concerned. We gave a contract to a group of young men with their own production company and set them off on the track to Bangweulu swamp and thence in the direction of a reported sighting of "Batembo" hunters close by Chienge town on Lake Mweru, just southeast of the area dominated by the slave raider Tippu Tip in the nineteenth century. "Batembo" means bush people or bushmen and indeed, this group of people was Batwa.

The reaction of the team that we hired—all city boys—was really very interesting. They were unable to contain their excitement at meeting their "ancestors" and could not hold back their tears of joy. From a documentary filmmaker's point of view, this was a very unprofessional attitude, but I am not one of those, and I authorized them to make a film about themselves, seeking out and getting to know the Batwa. The UNDP (the United Nations Development Programme) bought into our enterprise and hired a film crew to make the "professional" version. As you might expect, this was predominately about the materialistic poverty in which the Zambian Batwa live— although they did identify lack of identity documents as a serious cause of worry. I was able to issue instructions on that, particularly as the fabulous Permanent Secretary Peter Mwaba had been transferred to the Ministry of Home Affairs seemingly by the hand of God. The UNDP "straight" version of the film is called *Leaving No One Behind*

© Eddie Mwanaleza

Visiting Kasenga Island in the Bangweulu swamps, home to a Zambia Batwa community, 2014

and ours is entitled *Dancers of the Gods*. Both now seem to be under the control of UNDP. The two complement each other as a "spiritual" and a "material" version of the same thing.

Talking of supernatural beings I found myself increasingly confronted by what we came to call *Ilomba*. In many Bantu tribes, if not all, these creatures are invented to teach you a lesson. You feel like having a rich and relaxed existence so you go to the witchdoctor who, using witchcraft, makes for you an Ilomba. This is a small snake or snake-like creature that performs all kinds of chores for you. Just pick, whatever you want: it weeds the fields, it prints money, it escorts the children to school. And all it needs is a bowl of milk each morning. But as it grows it starts to develop a taste for blood. Your neighbors start disappearing one by one; then one of your relatives goes missing; even one of your children. Kill the Ilomba! Kill it, before you too disappear into the never-return-land of its insatiable hunger.

What I am describing is not far off the thing known as a quango in several English-language countries. To Zambians, a quango is hard to pronounce and also too tame sounding to send the requisite chill down the spine.

Ilombas have official sounding names; and there are hundreds of them. Here is an ancient one: the TBZ, or Tobacco Board of Zambia. Here is a far more modern one called ZEMA (the Zambia Environmental Management Agency); and here is yet another, ERB (the Energy Regulation Board). The list of "statutory agencies" is at least a hundred long; if you looked hard you would find many more.

Of course, "quangos" are a well-known problem in Western governments, and governments set off on crusades to lop them down to size and reduce their blood-sucking talents without absolute success. But my guess is that our Ilombas—with their thirst, their sheer cheek toward the people trying to control them, the relentless spread of their ownership— are bigger and nastier than anything you imagined.

To make an Ilomba you need a source of professional management and professional directors; now where are you going to find such professionals, bearing in mind you want the great majority to be Zambian?

Yes, in the government! The very people who are collaborating with the donors to create new supervisory/regulatory/enforcement agencies/ commissions/authorities are the very people who will become the dwellers in the new house they are building. This conflict of interests obviously bodes ill for the interests of the public. It is not only in developed countries that you find public servants who cannot cope honestly with wearing more than one cap.

The fault in this proliferation of Ilombas lies largely with donors and their consultants. The basic idea is that government is corrupt and/or inefficient, or it can't hire or fire the right sort of staff. So, the reasoning goes, these problems can be solved by setting up a brand spanking new statutory body—a mini-government—with professional staff answerable to an independent board (or better still to the donor itself). Just give them a little milk every morning.

I started a war on Ilombas but it did not get very far in the three years I was in post. But in the process of fighting with people who were better paid and apparently ready to fight me at every turn, I found an opportunity for a fast and so far highly successful policy initiative: put every Zambian on the cellular phone network. If ZICTA, the telecoms authority, could not do anything in Lusaka except build up a real estate empire—the primary Ilomba abuse of power—perhaps they could also do their job as well and establish a cell phone network throughout rural Zambia.

In campaigning throughout the country I had taken meticulous note of the complaints of the rural people and, more importantly, the priority they attached to their perceived needs. A surprising and very marked priority, for those who do not already have it, is cell phone connectivity. Everyone wants cell phone access; the more remote and technologically backward they were, the more so. In fact they yearned for "network" or "signal" more than for the roads Michael was starting to build. After all, a phone was terribly cheap compared to a car, even cheaper than a single round trip on a bus to town. The destination of a phone could be reached instantly. I told this finding to Michael who disbelieved me. He was a little old fashioned when it came to telephones—he used to insist that speech ought to be carried on wires and felt uneasy at the picture of millions of little radio stations yacking at each other across empty space. But I dribbled him and had ZICTA on the job rather fast. The program was—and still is—wildly popular. We have won some by-elections largely on the strength of having linked up the voters to their relatives and to various important institutions such as banks and suppliers.

The vice president of Zambia is also the leader of government business in parliament, which means he or she is more-or-less the prime minister of Zambia (the two titles have been interchanged in amendments to the Constitution over the years). As expected we had not done very well in terms of our parliamentary majority: we were only two seats ahead of MMD, and when the UPND and odds and ends were included we had well under half the seats in the House. This was true even when eight nominated members were added to our side.

After I set in motion the resettlement of the landless, the healing of the sick, the expansion of the electronic information network, and the hunt for the Batwa—and led PF to victory in our little imitation of Westminster—it was now time to gather my wife and "goons" and set off to put the new Zambia on the map. Summertime: whatever was going to kill Michael was not evident yet; copper prices were high; the fish were jumping, if a bit depleted in numbers; and everyone except the jealous had high hopes for our panjandrum's magnificent progress.

But before I could sample the food in Emirates first class Michael called me and vented his frustration. At the start of our government's tenure he and I had exchanges concerning the economy in only a very superficial way. The minister of finance was Alexander Chikwanda, a relative of Michael, and this is presumably why he didn't want me all over the Treasury Department. Chikwanda clearly regarded me as a pest, especially regarding restrictive financial practices that were aimed at stopping investors taking money out of the country. These restrictions have names like "SI33" or "SI155." I made my view clear and Chikwanda, to his credit, openly said he would get me sacked "within the week." Michael showed him the door with a customary Bemba-ism to the effect that you cannot chase the one who fought with you in the field in favor of someone who was just waiting to be fed. "Relationship by common cause seems to be thicker than family blood under this dispensation," he laughed, in what I believe to be a genuinely friendly way. We formed a common, if limited, objective: to keep the rate(s) of interest that bubble up from the Bank of Zambia down through the financial sector to something reasonable. Politics.

But Michael was listening to sundry liars and thieves, taking in stories about "investors" running away with money. My view is roughly that if investors are making a reasonable return, and are not constantly hedging against losses caused by bad government, they will have no particular reason to want to run away, nor to want to bring money in. Put differently: a free market in "investment" would yield balanced supply and demand for money and yield the best in all possible worlds. Trust the market, subject to obvious risks.

"We promised so many jobs; so much money in your pocket; lower taxes . . . and we are not even keeping up with the birth rate. We have even re-based the currency to make it strong."

We argued. "What about tax evasion? Your brothers are up to that!"

"Is there any difference in that regard with the developed countries?"

We argued some more and came to an agreement. I would develop a proper model—an economic model—to enable us to test alternative policies. I explained that at Cambridge there was an economic model made of colored water and plastic tubing that was an analogue model in which physical quantities (depth, volume, rate of flow, pressure) stood for economic quantities (national income, interest rates, consumption, investment, national debt). The machine was designed in such a way that quantities across the two worlds—fluid dynamics and the more abstract quantities of the economy—matched up.

"Can we borrow it?"

"There is one on my computer." (Of course; who plays with actual colored water these days?)

"I thought you said it was a model."

"Well, it's a model of the model if you like."

"Damn nonsense. But let's have a look."

Alas he never saw the model. When I entered his bedroom, computer in hand, glowing in the dark, he was only just *compos mentis* enough to yell at me. I still have the software on the machine, but it might just as well have been interred with him in his two-story tomb. Nobody since has shown any doubt that all may not be healthy in the way we run our economy. We just maximize the value of our kwacha against the US dollar (or something equivalent). What could be wrong about that?

13

Double Dutch Syndrome

ZAMBIA HAS BECOME WELL USED TO A FLUCTUATING INCOME ORIGINATING from the vagaries of world markets, including most particularly the market for copper.

In the old days it was customary for mineworkers to receive Christmas bonuses based on the profitability of their activities in the previous year. A journalist friend of mine, Derek Taylor, came to Northern Rhodesia from Australia before independence on the instructions of his editor to cover the most spectacular example of a Christmas bonus—over 100 percent of annual earnings for white mine supervisors, mostly South Africans, working on the Copperbelt. As they waited for the train that would take them home for the Christmas break they inspected fancy cars—Chevrolets, Mercedes, and even a Rolls Royce—shipped in hurriedly by the car salesmen who could reasonably hope to find some customers longer on money than sense. For the long journey itself, across the Zambezi in a shower of spray from Victoria Falls and down along the edge of the Kalahari Desert, the miners carried their full bonuses in cash. Before departure one of them approached Derek and said words to the effect: "You look like an honest young man—can you keep this for me please? Man, I am going to get drunk and I would hate to lose it." He handed over his wage packet, which the journalist promptly transferred to the insides of his shoes. Eventually the train arrived in Joburg, and Derek went in search of the owner of the money. He found him in a state of utter grief at the loss of his bonus. He could not remember giving it into his safe keeping. The money was duly returned and passed over to him. He said, "Oh!" (not thanks) and walked off an insanely happy man.

At independence Zambia had more money than it knew what to do with. In fact a surge in the copper price, combined with domestication of the copper royalties, boosted Zambia to No. 1 in the GDP growth tables in 1965, despite real economic growth being virtually paralyzed. "We have no shortage of money" was a common claim. But, for all the self-deceit about the boom lasting forever, recession arrived as a consequence of the commodity collapse due to the oil crisis, and we went de facto bust. "The money is now finished," announced Simon Kapwepwe when he resigned from the government. Fixed wage earners such as civil servants suddenly found the value of their wages shriveling—not in a hyperinflationary dust devil (Zimbabwe leads our region when it comes to that genre) but on the order of a rate of half or so of the purchasing power in a year. African politics under strongmen, who have no personal use for money, dictate that the public servant "must sacrifice" in solidarity with the common man, so as the kwacha got weaker, the civil servant got poorer. Kaunda was slow in having second thoughts about his painfully slow but somehow spontaneous policy positions.

An IMF friend—they do exist—tells how he flew into Lusaka from London in the 1980s. He was quickly cleared and found a highly intelligent-sounding freelance taxi operator to take him to town. He was surprised to find the man very well informed and articulate on the subject of Zambia's current affairs, particularly concerning public finances. At the hotel they parted and my pal set about showering and shaving, then strolled across two blocks where he asked for the Permanent Secretary of the Ministry of Finance. He was duly guided and admitted—to find himself facing the taxi driver. "I have to do extracurricular work to educate my children," he explained rather shyly.

By 1991, when I became part of the Chiluba government, the real value of a cabinet minister's salary had sunk to less than one dollar a day. But there had been compensating changes. For authorized travel abroad I was entitled to $430 per day, for my personal use, and payable for every day out of the country, even where it did not amount to work. For example I took two days off to visit my mother in the Cotswolds en route to Paris. I played Scrabble with her from morning to late at night. "Shouldn't you be earning your keep, darling?" she kept asking.

"But I am, mother!"

"And can you come whenever you like?"

"Er, no. It depends on me having something to do abroad and upon the president feeling sufficiently pro-me to authorize the travel."

It is worth a brief aside at this point to recall that we Keynesians do not take inflation very seriously—at least so long as it is not so severe as to disjoint prices and incomes. A 20 percent, even a 30 percent annual inflation figure, would not worry a Keynesian too severely so long as incomes were more or less following the same curve as the prices of goods or of dollars. Where is the real cost of inflation? Unless you are using a commodity—gold, silver—as the currency (which no one does anymore) there is nothing to be gained or lost directly from its movements save by laying bets on its movement. (Then you call yourself a portfolio investor or some such.) However, if there is a severe political constraint to some incomes moving with inflation—such as Kaunda's refusal to recognize the moving target nature of cash and his demand for "sacrifice"—it is little wonder that public servants and other fixed-income earners are terrified that double-digit inflation will return and deposit them in the Land of Less Than a Dollar a Day.

Zambia's challenge with money is to make it uninteresting. The Bank of Zambia and the Ministry of Finance know they are off track if every Zambian with an iPhone is pulling up the exchange rates every half hour. This can only be because the kwacha is not behaving in a boring way. It is being interesting, that is, unstable.

By repute, good people to talk to if you want to stabilize your currency, and with it your economy, should be the Norwegians. Their enormous but fluctuating income from North Sea petroleum over the years has been carefully stashed away in sovereign wealth funds. Norway, as you might expect, puts money aside when things are going well, returning the savings—that is what they are—back into the economy when hard times come again. It is dead boring—precisely on target. Norway? A European economist said to me: It is not so much a country as the name on a bank account. Whatever Munch's screamer on the bridge is alarmed about, it is not the volatility of the Norwegian krone. The Norwegian experts who came to Zambia, paid for by Norwegian aid, try very hard to get us to behave like them but it doesn't always, or often, if ever, succeed.

To avoid being accused of employing idiosyncratic ideas, let us use the *Financial Times* lexicon to enlarge our vocabulary. It is boring. Hallelujah. "*Dutch disease* is the negative impact on an economy of anything that gives rise to a sharp inflow of foreign currency, such as the discovery of large oil reserves. The currency inflows lead to currency appreciation, making the country's other products less price competitive on the export market."

The term *Dutch disease*—which Dutch economists are reasonably reluctant to recognize as theirs—arose because in the 1960s, the Netherlands experienced a vast increase in its wealth after discovering large natural gas deposits in the North Sea. Unexpectedly, this ostensibly positive development had serious repercussions on important segments of the country's economy as the Dutch guilder became stronger, making Dutch non-oil exports more expensive and, therefore, less competitive. This syndrome has been witnessed in many countries across the world, including but not limited to resource-rich commodity exporters. Although Dutch disease is generally associated with a natural resource discovery, it can occur from any development that results in a large inflow of foreign currency, including a sharp surge in natural resource prices, foreign assistance, and foreign direct investment. Economists have used the Dutch disease model to examine such episodes as the flow of American treasures into 16th century Spain and gold discoveries in Australia in the 1850s. (Ebrahimzadeh, 2017)

("Ostensibly positive"—the road to Hell is paved with ostensibly positive interventions.)

Take a look at the graph below of the Zambian kwacha per US dollar over the years, according to Bank of Zambia data.

Kenneth Kaunda once stated that Zambia's problem was that the country was born with a copper spoon in its mouth. For a man with notoriously low levels of economic common sense this is a very insightful and striking image, recognizing that our gift from God is also our curse, or at least our challenge. It tends to be the case that when things are going well in the copper industry other industries are closing down—or failing to open up in the first place. Most of the

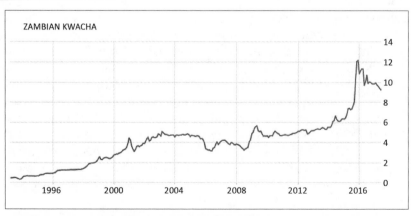

Exchange rate for Zambian kwacha to the dollar, 1996–2016 (Data from Bank of Zambia)

time, when skills and resources are focused on the production of copper and associated minerals, alternative economic sectors—such as agriculture, tourism, and manufacturing—are somnolent or in crisis. It is not difficult to see why. In good times, mining brings dollars in; the kwacha becomes overvalued (dollars are plentiful and cheap). Any attempts to keep the country competitive are in vain, thanks to the plenitude of copper, or coffee, or oil, or whatever it is that God has selected as our "something for nothing." (It is also easy to see how a big one-off debt rebate like the IMF's special assistance for HIPC has the same effect as a commodity inflow.)

If the resource gift of copper were to be continuous and steady, you can make a "feature out of a bug" as they say in the artificial intelligence argot. The copper income will be sufficient, especially if you can find ways of distributing it equitably. This was the model in the early days of Zambia's independence. Government collected the revenues arising from the production of copper and tried to shell it out equitably among all needy citizens. There were subsidies, both visible and implicit. Education was free, food was the cheapest in the world, people hardly bothered to pay tax. Oh happy breed!

Oh, short-sighted homo sapiens! The problem obviously arises when the "boom" sector causing the Dutch disease goes through a hard patch. The price of copper comes crashing down, as indeed happened in 2016, and the engine driving the economy judders to a stop. If only we had more agriculture or tourism, if only we had diversified our economy while we were earning the extra cash, if only. . . . Next time around we will behave better.

The Economist claims to have coined the phrase "Dutch Disease" in 1977 (*The Economist*, 2014). The Dutch economy had been struggling for some years, and their analysis attributed the high levels of unemployment and low levels of investment to an overvalued currency. Booming gas exports had strengthened the guilder, but that industry did not actually employ many people. With low interest rates and a strong currency, Holland was an unattractive destination for investment in any other sector.

Over time, it became clear that the Dutch disease was not limited to that country. Put simply, assuming the local currency is fixed:

> Extra foreign currency enters the country, is converted into local currency, and is spent on goods that cannot be traded across borders (construction, certain services and so forth). As foreign currency is changed into local currency, the money supply rises: extra domestic demand pushes up domestic prices. That, in the jargon, results in an

appreciation of the "real" exchange rate: a unit of foreign currency now buys fewer services in the domestic economy than it did before. The country loses competitiveness" (*The Economist*, 2014).

The remaining issue is whether this is actually a problem—could it be argued that economies must simply play to their strengths, rather than worrying about the peripheral effects on other sectors. Well, it seems that problems start if and when the whole picture becomes too lopsided, and the economy is dominated by a single natural resource commodity. Jeffrey Sachs and Andrew Warner showed that economies abundant in natural resources grow slower than economies without substantial natural assets. They tracked economies with a high ratio of natural resource exports to GDP in 1970 for twenty years, showing that growth was markedly slower than for other countries with a similar starting point (Sachs and Warner, 1997).

I have called this chapter "Double Dutch Syndrome" because our economy, under current management, has two distinct (if equally painful and harmful) economic syndromes. In the first, the mining industry is doing well and crowding out other industries via overvaluation of the currency. Consumers of imported goods are doing well with a strong currency, consuming more than would be the case if surplus copper revenues were to be sequestered in some sober Norwegian kind of way.

In the second phase the "mother industry" ceases to perform. Prices of foreign goods increase in kwacha terms; the only two ways to limit this inflationary effect (with its negative political effect) are:

1. To increase the domestic interest rates directly or indirectly, choking off the kwacha liquidity.
2. To use dollar reserves and/or borrow dollars to take the pressure off the kwacha.

But both these measures damage the prospects for private sector non-copper growth. In fact they selectively target the very cure for Dutch disease, making sure that we will not escape it, by killing diversification. Hopefully, the Chinese or the world economy will recover, the nightmare end, and we will find ourselves back in the arms of King Copper!

For the sake of clarity: A non-copper exporter such as agriculture or tourism, say, has difficulty making a profit and thus growing in either a copper boom or a copper slump. The first is because of classic Dutch disease overvaluation of the domestic currency (aggravated by debt relief and any other manna from heaven). The second is due to overvaluing domestic currency in terms of interest rates—which reduces liquidity for investment—in the name of controlling inflation. This latter situation can be even more damaging to the non-copper sector. In fact, many bankruptcies, especially of farming businesses, are interest-rate induced; the interest rate increase being engendered by a fall in copper revenues.

About ten years ago, Zambia was in a copper boom, with effects amplified by debt relief. The farming sector, the tourism sector, and the manufacturing sector all screamed bloody murder about the effects of overvaluation of the kwacha. Amazingly, the IMF failed to set off alarms about Dutch disease, even though it was very well known basic economics, about which you might be asked to answer a question before being admitted to university to study less trivial economics. But the IMF clearly did not see:

> "Zambia's external position improved markedly, supported by strong copper and non-traditional export receipts and extensive debt relief under the enhanced HIPC initiative," said Mr Kakoza, the IMF representative to Zambia. "The improvement in economic fundamentals and future prospects bolstered market confidence and underpinned a strong appreciation of the Kwacha," he said, adding that economic prospects had continued to improve in 2006. Boosted by higher copper output and prices, a recovery in agricultural production, and sustained growth in construction and tourism, gross domestic product growth was projected to rise to 6 per cent this year. (*The Post*, 2006)

This statement reveals no awareness of the fact that the agricultural industry, outside the magic circle demarcated by subsidies and nontariff barriers, was bound to collapse (for obvious Dutch disease–related reasons) and indeed was making a noise about it. The easiest way to quickly check the competitiveness of tourism in Zambia is to compare prices across the Victoria Falls Bridge. "Sustained growth" indeed!

In fact, the kwacha's sharp appreciation threatened to undo years of patient work building up new export industries—growing flowers and vegetables for European supermarkets and attracting safari tourists. Luke Mbewe, director of the Zambian Export Growers' Association, was reported to comment that vegetable growers cut their output by about a quarter and shed a third of their 6,000-strong workforce. Tourism businesses complained that all their revenues were in dollars but pretty much all of their costs were in kwacha, and hence they were hit particularly hard by the rise in the currency. These new export businesses were severely knocked with a rapid appreciation in the value of the kwacha.

The official response was not terribly sympathetic. The governor of the Bank of Zambia, Caleb Fundanga, commented that appreciation was generally a good thing, helping to keep down the price of imported oil.

Fundanga noted that "we engaged in discussions with the farmers about improving productivity, which is a more sustainable approach than trying to target a particular exchange rate." Note the belief that surfaces among bankers, and other indoor types, that Dutch disease is best addressed through teaching farmers how to maintain higher levels of productivity! What have they been trying to do all this time? And what have bankers got to teach them about agriculture? Note also the mention of the easy option of maintaining sovereign debt management through "an off-shore dollar-denominated account to neutralise the effect on the currency." So where is our Zambian "offshore dollar-denominated account"? And what level are we aiming to hold it at over a reasonable time in the future?

At the time of writing this—more than ten years on—Zambia is in a copper slump, HIPC has blown itself out, and the Chinese bubble has burst. Our currency has lost a lot of value against the dollar, and the slump-induced variation from Dutch disease is clearly visible, even to journalists. This article by Chiwoyu Sinyangwe was published in Zambia's *Post* newspaper:

BANKS STOP LENDING DUE TO CASH FLOWS, HIGH INTEREST RATES
Commercial banks have stopped giving loans because of low cash levels and high interest rates prevailing on the market. And the Bankers Association of Zambia has warned that key sectors of the country will start getting hurt if the current high interest rates and lack of liquidity is allowed to hold for too long.

BAZ Chairman Simatyaba explained that commercial banks in the country had stopped lending because they did not have cash to lend out.

"That is happening at the moment because in order to stabilise the local currency, monetary policy has been tightened and tightening of monetary policy means there is no liquidity in the market," Simatyaba said. "So if there is no liquidity in the market, I will not just give out a loan. So banks are restructuring their balance sheets and not giving out loans because of the tightening of the monetary policy. Funds have been siphoned out to try and protect the local currency."

He said surging interest rates in the country made it very difficult for banks to lend.

"The fact that general interest rates have gone up, the market has gone up and the Bank of Zambia's overnight lending facility is now at 25.5 per cent means before I can consider any client right now for a loan, I must be pretty sure the client is going to pay," Simatyaba said. "I am not just going to issue a loan because a client wants a loan."

He said lack of liquidity in the market was likely to stifle growth the longer it was allowed to hold. "The downside is that economic activity will slow down and that is what the policy is trying to achieve because when there is economic slowdown, then, there is not so much demand for foreign exchange and then it stabilizes."

Like all people who try to control markets, our leaders used to simply announce prices (for dollars, for tomatoes, etc.). The problem with state control of money is that the numbers you are trying to fix (e.g., the rate of the kwacha to the dollar) tend to be miscalculated (there is no market to consult) and also set so as to impress the president and his political objectives or his hopes. Once in the 1980s the IMF et al. forced the Zambian government to hold an auction of foreign exchange every week to try and get to a realistic exchange rate. The starting (official) rate was very unrealistic (the kwacha was far too strong, overvalued) and within weeks had changed its level ten-fold (i.e., weakening by a whole decimal point from two to the dollar to over twenty). When Kaunda woke up one morning and found the rate was still moving he issued an edict there and then—it is said before he had showered—that the kwacha be revalued by a factor of more than two (it went to about eight).

Some people (and this includes most Zambian policymakers for thirty years) felt that the money market should be completely controlled by government (including the central bank) in order to reach the best outcome in the best of all possible worlds. There were many things wrong with the result of applying government controls to money. The black market came into existence to correct the often-insane price setting of the bureaucrats. Much of the time the official exchange rate was several times stronger than its effective value (i.e., a kwacha bought you many more dollars than it was worth but such convertible kwacha were hard to get your hands on). When exchange controls were very strictly applied to try and "kill" the black market, every businessman's objective became to move his money outside the country. Some went to extremes, importing entire factories, for example, at fantastical nominal values, without the slightest intention of ever putting them to work or employing a single night watchman. The actual price of the factory was a small price to pay for having managed to externalize huge amounts of fast-devaluing kwacha.

If you wanted some time off, you could not even get a few hundred dollars to go to Mauritius for a long weekend. Zambia Airways offered cheap flights to a hitherto unfrequented resort on Lake Tanganyika that was in Zambia but was also in an area infested with combatants in the Congo-Zaire unrest who were bent on exchanging their AK47s for bags of mealie meal—which is one way of gingering up a safari.

At the other extreme of the argument there are people, putting ideological knee-jerks before the lessons of empirical observation, who believe that there is no big issue here: just free the market for copper, currency, and everything else, and it will all reach an equilibrium that is the best feasible one in the best of all possible worlds. Alas, very little research is required to show that real markets—even simple markets for things like vegetables—have a strong inclination to be irregular. More complex markets like the money markets are even more erratic. Nor is it possible for money markets to run themselves without government's heavy hand appearing, however self-effacing it may try to be. Government itself, being a spender and saver, a setter of all sorts of taxes, and a fixer of interest rates, quite apart from a promulgator of regulations, is almost invariably the largest and most significant player in the money markets.

One of the features of the structural adjustment program was the commitment to money market liberalization and specifically to a free exchange rate. This commitment was kept, after a little hesitation, and the legal, free-money market lurched into existence. There was a market-determined exchange rate within a year of the MMD coming to power, and all restraints disappeared by 1996. Credit must go to Frederick Chiluba, who certainly lost a lot of sleep over this revolution. Zambia was the only country in southern Africa (if you exclude the Indian Ocean islands) where you could just take money in one currency out of your pocket at a Bureau de Change and put it back in another. We even became something of a haven; South African investors appeared in our cities, not to use our peoples' hard work or our beautiful weather, or to court our lovely women, but to generate profits inside a free currency area. Without going into detail, they were close to laundering money made in South Africa, but which could not be externalized from there other than in the guise of regional investment.

So now we have a free market for money—subject to the rider that the government is also a buyer and seller on the same market. What is wrong with that?

I will attempt to cut a long and convoluted story short by pointing out that there are two "prices" for the kwacha. One is the "cash" price in dollars (or other currency or basket of currencies). The other is the price of today's kwacha in terms of tomorrow's kwacha. This second price is not a reference to the rate of inflation, which can be calculated away for the purposes of analysis, but to the "real" interest rate—the real cost of spending a kwacha now as opposed to, say, in a year's time when it has earned you more money. The two prices: the exchange rate and the interest rate interact with each other. If the kwacha interest rate is raised, many people will hold on to kwacha and others will pay back or defer their borrowing. This creates a reduction in liquidity, which leads to less demand for dollars and thence to a lower kwacha price for the dollar.

Put equivalently: raising interest rates strengthens the kwacha against the dollar.

Now a first-world dweller might think that the interest rate is a small matter—a fine tuning variable controlling a point or two of inflation or devaluation. But in Zambia we are talking about retail interest rates in the vicinity of 25–30 percent for blue chip investments, running to 100 percent for microlending. All this while the official consumer inflation index is less than 10 percent. Take, for example, a mortgage to build a hotel in London. Reputable investors and developers might reasonably expect to arrange a fifty-year loan repayable at 5 percent interest. The same developers, approaching what may even be the same bank with a branch in Zambia, will be pushing their luck if they ask for better than ten years at 20 percent. In fact, today, you would be likely charged more than 20 percent and offered less than ten years to repay.

The picture is one of the time dimension being compressed—everything has to be done in a hurry in Zambia, and future earnings more than a handful of years away are inaccessible to the investor/developer. The future is another country: Do they do things differently there? Among other things the rate of return to banking is very high relative to its level outside Zambia, or outside Africa. Bob Diamond, the former Barclays CEO, has recently been in this country because, he says, banking returns are higher in Africa than anywhere else. He was surprised when he found out. He should have asked me.

I was invited to dinner in Lusaka with the Archbishop of Canterbury in 2016. I was a little apprehensive that I might have to simulate an interest in theological matters but should not have worried. All the twenty-odd religious leaders present had only one topic of conversation: the exchange rate between the kwacha and the dollar (it happened to be slipping slightly at the time). "Why is this topic so interesting in Africa?" he asked. "In Nigeria they could also talk about nothing else." (He was an oil trader in that country for many years). "I think it may be something to ask Freudians about," I said. I will not quote his answer.

Africans tend to be of a "strong currency" tendency. A few weeks ago, as China was attempting to weaken the yuan to maintain its competitive edge, Zambia was desperately trying to strengthen the kwacha. We were doing opposite things to our currencies. We Zambians want to stay strong; they want to stay weak. We Zambians tend to feel that to depreciate against the dollar—the universal currency of reference—is a sign of economic failure.

In fact it occurs to me that what the Chinese have found themselves confronted with is just a variant of Dutch disease and they have been driving down the value of their currency accordingly.

Not so Zambians in the face of Dutch disease. If you don't keep the value of the kwacha up, it means your spouse cannot go shopping in Johannesburg so often; it means your kids that you are educating outside the country are more expensive in terms of your domestic income. You cannot maintain your secondhand Japanese car. You feel proud of a strong currency.

With an overvalued currency and an exaggerated interest rate, the things that governments ostensibly want to see—more jobs, more national income—are just a dream. Investors, including Zambian investors, lack confidence and leave for other pastures (except when they are over-profiting in an import business). Richard Branson asked on a visit to Lusaka last year about the interest rate structure. When told he simply answered to the effect that "you cannot do business like that."

There are a number of studies comparing "Asian tiger economies" with "African lion economies," seeking to find the factors that have led to

"Kwacha stays strong," an advertisement from a local company, touting cheaper prices for imported goods as a result of a strengthening currency

The Post, 5 January 2006

a proliferation of tigers versus a severe shortage of lions. Cecil the lion jokes aside, many factors—the prevalence of corruption or the distribution of natural resources—do not do the explaining. Following the economic history of pairs of similar countries shows up one ubiquitous difference.

African countries are obsessed with "strong currency"; Asian countries are the opposite; they worry that they are pricing themselves out of business, out of growth and out of employment. A very good example is the archbishop's hunting ground of Nigeria. Paired with Indonesia there are almost no key differences that emerge. Except for one: Nigeria's leaders are doing everything to avoid devaluation (even prohibiting imports of components by domestic producers at the present time). Urban high-income consumers benefit from the resulting strong national currency, the naira. But producers, especially rural ones, suffer. With Indonesia it is the other way round; the currency is quickly devalued to keep rural industry competitive and shrug off the dependency upon oil.

Richard Dowden compares Nigeria with Indonesia, another oil producer, which came from a similar economic base. Both suffered dictatorships from the 1960s that both ended in 1998. But when Suharto left power in Indonesia the national output was $221 billion after an average twenty-year growth rate of 7 percent. Adult literacy in Indonesia was almost 90 percent and manufacturing represented 40 percent of exports. When Abacha died, Nigeria's output was $33.4 billion after a 2.5 percent average growth. Adult literacy in Nigeria stood at 60 percent and non-oil exports were less than 5 percent (Dowden, 2008).

So far so good. But Dowden misses the point by hauling in African corruption and goes on to paint a picture of uncaring elites differing in their caring about Nigeria and Indonesians respectively. But we by now know exactly what we are looking at, however the Dutch may resent us for using their name for a disease at the time they got their exchange rate wrong so long ago.

Here is a summary sketch of how it actually works:

1. Money market is cruising along and stable
2. Sudden shock—for example, a fall in copper prices—results in reduction of dollars in the money market; kwacha weakens (it takes more to buy a dollar)
3. Bank of Zambia and the government stabilize the situation by
   a. increasing interest rates to "mop up" kwacha or
   b. throwing dollars (if any are available) at the market
4. Exchange rate steadies but with high interest rates
5. Private investment decreases

6. Bank of Zambia blames it all on "market forces" and rejects responsibility for any adverse effects on employment since its constitutional role apparently confines the Bank of Zambia to stabilizing the currency!

The Big Ilomba indeed. If the model was symmetrical it would look like this:

1. Money market is cruising along and stable
2. Sudden windfall—e.g., rise in copper price or HIPC—results in an increase in dollars in the money market; kwacha starts to strengthen (it takes less to buy a dollar)
3. Bank of Zambia and the government stabilize the situation by
   a. absorbing new dollars (e.g., sequestering offshore)
   b. abstracting dollars (from the market)
4. Exchange rate normalizes (weakens) but with low interest rates
5. Private investment increases
6. Bank of Zambia truthfully blames it all on "market forces" with which it never tampers!

Then at least the free market producers would have a share of the windfall. But alas, the actual model works like this:

1. Money market is cruising along and stable
2. Sudden windfall—e.g., rise in copper price or HIPC—results in increase in dollars in the money market; kwacha starts to strengthen (takes less to buy a dollar)
3. Bank of Zambia and the government do not care to stabilize the situation and do nothing (a strong kwacha is politically good!)
4. Exchange rate strengthens but with high interest rates
5. Productive investment decreases, consumers and importers have a ball, employment stagnates and even falls (the situation is possibly made worse by budget deficit money being redirected to state-owned enterprises, which are hopelessly inefficient)
6. Bank of Zambia blames it all on "market forces" with which it never tampers!

These steps, or lack of steps, accentuate the sort of instabilities that naturally occur when you have our Double Dutch version of the disease. As an investor, local or foreign, big or small, you do not know what is worse: the classical Dutch disease that is bad when the boom is on; or the artificial financial shortage and increased costs resulting from the so-called cure for inflation. The most common consequence naturally is that you close down and emigrate from Zambia or return to the village. We have a town on the Copperbelt called Ndola, which got going as a local manufacturing and mining supplies manufacturing sector. Somehow it squeezed into the gap between "boom" and "bust." But it is now a ghost town, thanks to the Bank of Zambia's "constitutionally" mandated monetary policies.

(The Bank of Zambia is the Ilomba of Ilombas. Not only is it completely independent of government—if that is practically possible—but it claims its remit, as spelled out in the Constitution, includes only the control of inflation. It has nothing to do with employment or growth, which must therefore be the remit of the government. You don't have a job? Speak to the Government.)

Can a country in which consumers are more influential than producers ever thrive? That is perhaps our problem as a nation; we have an ancestral memory that it is our destiny to be buying Rollers and dancing in the Kalahari. We feel cheated when we suddenly wake up and find ourselves in self-inflicted poverty.

Michael and I did not see eye to eye on the blessed or blasted kwacha. The currency had been created in 1968, replacing the British pound at the rate of K2 per £1 (ten shillings per kwacha to suit decimalization). By 2006 the rate was pushing K5,000 to the dollar and we started promising to "rebase" the currency by dividing through by 1,000—that is, knocking off three zeros. This would make 3,000 old kwacha equal to three new kwacha, for example. As soon as we were voted into power the wheels were set in motion and, after a bit of confusion caused by division of "ngwee" of which there were 100 in each kwacha under both systems, it settled down.

"We have created a new currency; a stronger one!" Michael declared.

"Well, yes, we have basically moved from the kwacha to the 'pin' as our currency," I volunteered. Zambians had long since ceased to think in old kwacha most of the time and had invented a currency unit of a "pin"—that is to say a paper clip holding a standard 20 x K50 notes.

"You don't understand," he said impatiently. "It is just not the naming which is new, it is not a pin, it is the new kwacha, which is now stronger." As I listened attentively I formed the impression he felt he had tried to wipe out the shameful past of the currency—it had halved in value fourteen times but he had somehow cleansed it. He got rid of the national shame. Have I got this right?

The behavior of the kwacha was unaffected by the positioning of the decimal point, obviously, and in due course it had a bad week. "What is wrong with my currency?" Michael lamented. "*My* currency?"

"It's just an accounting unit," I said. "If everything goes up or goes down together things just remain the same."

I tried desperately to get us on the same page of the book: "money is not something of intrinsic worth or cost. It is purely a symbolic thing designed to make complex transactions easier."

"You people from Oxford do not understand these things."

"I wish I did. I would be famous. Perhaps I'd get a Nobel prize. And it's Cambridge."

There is much more to say about Dutch disease, currency valuation, and interest rate policy as a profoundly important factor in entrenching poverty in Zambia and elsewhere. Most so-called experts puzzle about how to trigger diversification, while glibly overlooking the fact that credit—when available—costs anywhere above 30 to 40 percent in interest. But that more serious economic analysis is not for this book.

14

Chinese Whispers

I HAVE MENTIONED CHINA HERE AND THERE IN VARIOUS CONTEXTS, BUT such is the depth of interest in the subject of China in Africa that I have decided to give it a fairly focused chapter of its own.

Zambia's first close encounter with China was the partnership of the two countries, along with Tanzania, to construct the Tazara Railway that provides landlocked Zambia with a link to the port of Dar es Salaam. Large numbers of Tanzanians, Zambians, and Chinese were employed to construct the railway; the Chinese were undoubtedly the senior management, though it is not known who used to order the only working locomotive at one stage to travel each morning more than 600 kilometers round trip to collect milk from a farm in Mkushi district and deliver it in Mpika.

Many more Africans were shipped to China, where they learned the management skills (in Mandarin) to run the railway once it was complete. To judge from verbal accounts from several Chinese people, the visiting Zambians did not make a very favorable impression. Their indiscipline and apparent lack of seriousness was, it is said, saddening and even shocking to their hosts. However, the fact that China was going through the Cultural Revolution, in which unfamiliar standards of "seriousness" were being generated and applied makes us wonder whether the critique of our people on Chinese soil can be fairly judged.

The Chinese workers in Zambia were frequently accused of keeping to themselves, both socially and in respect of what they learned about Africa more generally. An extreme example of this was the (alleged) refusal by a Chinese man of the advice from an African that he desist from trying to capture a black mamba to add some variation to his lunch. He was of course killed by the snake, a high-specification member of the cobra family, which has many times both the speed and toxicity of the domesticated farm-reared cobras and adders that are used in China as food and medicine.

So far as I am aware no economic evaluation of Tazara has ever been carried out. Its justification from the Chinese point of view was strongly political—a "monumental" construct representing the determination on the world's largest and poorest countries' refusal to be dominated by capitalism, imperialism, and so forth. Zambia may have hoped that many benefits might flow its way, now that it was effectively brought closer to the sea. But it is hard to see what they were, especially weighing them against a railroad close to 1,200 miles long. Our copper could exit the country and join the world more easily than by truck. Small amounts of fertilizer were sometimes imported from the Middle East. Intermittently there might be a few wagons of mixed cargo and emergency supplies. But the performance of the railroad never approached the million tonnes per annum load required to make it (or any railway anywhere) viable.

The Zambian headquarters of Tazara (there is another in Tanzania) was built at Mpika. Notably it featured a workshop that was the most advanced in southern Africa. You could, I was told, make a whole diesel locomotive from scratch—from iron ore and a few trace elements. As allegedly the first white to set eyes on the inside of the workshop I felt the obligation to throw a challenge; so I asked for a prototype hammer mill—for grinding maize—to be designed and manufactured. It took about six weeks to produce; it screamed piercingly and blew itself to pieces on the first demonstration.

In my capacity as the minister responsible for food relief from 1991 to 1993 I became involved with Tazara in the role of a customer. "Good morning Tazara: I have ordered 50,000 tonnes of maize to be delivered to a suitable southern African port in about two months time. Can you load it at Dar es Salaam and transport it to the Zambian Copperbelt please?" Naturally the answer was yes but the actual daily quantity handled was disappointing—way short of the planned 1,000 tonnes a day. One problem was that Tazara was suffering from lack of maintenance; breakdowns and derailments were routine. Another problem arose from the relationship between the various players in the operation, notably the port authorities at Dar and Zambia Railways that uplifted the imported maize in Kapiri and took it to the Copperbelt. The Dar boys were playing games with demurrage—determined to get their share of the donor-funded cake. Zambia Railways preferred collecting on the longer route into South Africa and therefore had a vested interest in slowing Tazara down. This they did by simply failing to return the wagons that had been sent from Dar. Nowadays the situation has become worse. There are considerable Tanzanian private interests in the trucking industry, and these usually work by effectively sabotaging the operations of Tazara.

It is tempting to join the chorus of old Africa hands chanting, "Is there no limit to the damage Africans will inflict upon each other?" but it is pointless to ask a rhetorical question and leave it there. The problem with the railway is surely connected to the fact that we never paid for it in the first place; we have no "sense of ownership." Formally, it was financed with a Chinese loan to the two governments, but the loan has never been serviced. There are people around who are suggesting that we go back to China for more money to renovate the asset. Unless there were hidden benefits to them, that would be written off by the Chinese as throwing more good money after bad.

Belief in the resurrection of bad ideas is a common thing in Zambia and remarkably persistent in the face of evidence. I don't have a law or "syndrome" named after me, so let me modestly volunteer for this nugget of truth—"Scott's recurrence principle."

After the Tazara construction was finished and the Chinese went home, a few remained, operating privately as farmers or traders. We more or less forgot about them. This remained the case until the waking of the dragon—sorry tiger—and the current economic "going out into the world" of China, some thirty years after Tazara was built. But all the time there was a game afoot in Africa being played between the governments of the People's Republic of China (PRC) and the Republic of China (ROC). Michael and I decided to join in.

Following the fall of "the last emperor" in 1911 the Chinese spent much of the first half of the twentieth century at war among themselves. Chairman Mao's army and the Chinese Communist Party, with much Soviet help, eventually prevailed on the mainland. The Kuomintang (KMT) party of Chiang Kai-Shek was confined to the island of Formosa (Taiwan) and some lesser islands in the South China Sea. Each government claimed to be the legitimate government of all China. Initially Taiwan was recognized by more members of the United Nations than was the Communist government of the mainland. However, over the years, countries recognizing Taiwan have dwindled in prominence, numbering to twenty or so. Taiwan—which has become a very rich country as one of the first of the Asian "tigers"—provides aid to countries whose governments recognize it in the UN. It also, more controversially, became very fond of giving monetary assistance to opposition parties in countries whose government did not recognize it. (The mainland government did not acknowledge that any country could recognize both Chinas.)

Several opposition parties entered into agreements with Taiwan to recognize it in exchange for support. Several parties in several countries came to power thanks, at least in part, to Taiwanese help. Prompted by threats from the mainland, most of these reneged on their deal—not even paying the Taiwanese back. This happened in Zambia, though not in connection with the PF, as revealed by Michael Sata at a press conference:

> The government of Frederick Chiluba was very close to recognising the government of Taiwan but it was new in government. They succumbed to intimidation by Chinese that if you recognise Taiwan, we are going to pull out so they left it from there but that was a collective responsibility.
> "Cabinet agreed, the whole government agreed," Sata said. "In 2001, when I broke away, I broke away with my thinking of this country. The few friends who we went away with . . . I must admit it was not easy to convince this man (pointing to Guy Scott) about Taiwan." (Saluseki, 2007)

(The stuff about my being hard to convince, in view of the fact I suggested we tango with Taiwan, is typical Michael.)

By the time the PF had launched its Long March to power, the scrap between the two Chinas had heated up considerably. Taiwanese political parties have in essence two ways to choose between in adjusting their country's relationship with Big China. The current state of affairs cannot last forever, and one possible evolutionary direction is the Hong Kong model of One State, Two Governments. This is the natural drift— the two countries are becoming increasingly entangled economically, with as many as two million Taiwanese working and managing business on the mainland.

The other option however is to drive Taiwan toward being an independent republic, disconnected politically from its "motherland." Beijing hates to see Taiwan pursuing this line, which its new government espoused in 2003. It was daggers drawn, even in our neck of the woods, as Big China set about purifying the world of Independent Taiwan. Malawi, notably, had inherited recognition of Taiwan all the way back to the right-wing Hastings Banda.

I made the point to Michael that a lot of money was likely to be flowing around, and that we as PF should have a crack at begging for some of it from Taiwan. We might even become one of the few parties that honor their promise to that country.

Michael decided to play his cards face up. He was outspoken regarding his support of forces for change in China, despite this unquestionably annoying the mainland government. He made no bones about Chinese standards of "slave labor," plundering of Zambian resources, and corruption.

Michael's anti-Chinese campaign gained wide support as a result of incidents such as fifty or so Zambians being blown to pieces in 2004 in an explosives factory operated at Chambeshi on the Copperbelt. It was claimed by company workers that the Chinese management team at Beijing General Research Institute of Mining & Metallurgy (BGRIMM) had seen the temperature rise as the wrong ingredients were allowed to mix and had run away without alerting the workers. The identity of bodies could not be established and a mass burial was carried out with the help of a "family" spokesman. The Chinese image was not at all helped when one official marveled about the fuss over "only" fifty people. But the family spokesman produced the most bitter comment. "When we lived by ourselves we thought our chiefs were brutal; when the whites came we saw that our chiefs were relatively gentle people; then the Indians came and we stopped complaining about the whites. Now the Chinese have come and we no longer pay attention to the Indians. Now we have really seen disregard for humans."

Said Sata: "I am meeting the Human Rights Commission at Harvard University and the Amnesty International in USA. So all of them, I am telling them about the invasion of the Chinese in Africa and Zambia in particular. That's human rights." Michael's natural charisma resulted in him becoming internationally famous or infamous in pointing out the failings of the current government with respect to China. He became Africa's spokesman on China to the point where he was invited to attend the formation of a China reformist organization in Boston. After Michael spoke—off-the-cuff on two nights without sleep—they unanimously voted him as their world leader.

The Post newspaper reported the story in a pretty sensational manner. So I responded, and they published a further article the following day:

Patriotic Front vice-president Dr Guy Scott yesterday said there was nothing wrong with party president Michael Sata asking for US $50,000 from Taiwan to continue his mission to discredit China. Reacting to yesterday's *Post* lead story revealing that Sata had asked the Taiwanese government to help him with US $50,000 (about K195 million) to enable him to travel to the United States on his continued mission to discredit China in favour of Taiwan, Dr Scott there was nothing wrong with Sata's request.

"It is perfectly normal for diplomats and politicians to use each other to achieve common cause. The other day I was transported to Taiwan by that island's government and used by them as an example of a pro-Taiwanese African (albeit a white one) in an Africa-Taiwan trade conference," Dr Scott said. "Mr Sata's visit to Harvard, which is likely to be high profile in the United States, is of considerable interest to the Taiwanese.

"Why should they not be invited to contribute to the cost of it? And perhaps even leave some change for the PF party to use in by-elections caused by the dirty tricks of the MMD?"

And Dr Scott took issue with yesterday's *Post* editorial comment, which stated "Sata's view on China is blurred by the dollars being splashed in his face and not by a genuine political stance or ideology."

"Leaving aside the question of whether the dollars actually materialised, this is not a fair deduction. Our misgivings in PF about China's undue influence in Zambia are longstanding and principled," he said. "In fact, the Chinese offered to assist PF in the last few days of last year's election campaign (believing that PF was winning and wishing to obtain some goodwill) and I personally turned the offer down after consultation with Mr Sata.

"You will recall that in the early days of that campaign, some Chinese gentlemen appeared on an MMD platform and one even threatened to withdraw all Chinese investment if Sata became president of Zambia. So much for a 'genuine political stance or ideology'!"

Dr Scott said there was an underlying problem in Zambia. He said although Zambia had become notionally a multiparty democracy, consequential legislation on such matters as party funding had not been passed. He said the ruling party seemed to have unfettered access to money from parastatal companies and investors seeking "goodwill."

"It also has unrestricted use of government transport and staff, not to mention planes and helicopters, when it comes to election campaigns," Dr Scott said. "Who is paying for the fertilizer currently being distributed in the Nchanga Constituency? You and me, mate.

"Meanwhile the opposition is supposed to travel, organise and campaign on what? On the smell of an oil rag? On thin air? On donations from street vendors running away from the police? I strongly believe firm rules are needed on the funding of party activities (including presidents traveling to Harvard or the less well-known Harding University). These rules need to apply to the governing party as much as to opposition. The playing field needs to be levelled."

Dr Scott said until that happened, "We in opposition have to live like dissidents in a One Party State, surviving on the opportunities that present themselves."

"Incidentally, a Chinese equivalent of your excellent journal would not survive one week in Beijing," Dr Scott said. "On the other hand, it is difficult to imagine (since the 2000 Taiwanese elections) there being any impediment to the publication of *The Post* in Taipei."

Sata had asked for US $50,000 from the Taiwanese government for upkeep and costs for his travel to United States' Harvard University where he has been invited by the university's committee on human rights to speak on human rights at a conference themed, "China-Africa: The Yin and the Yang" to be held tomorrow.

"When I met you in 2005, I undertook to do everything within my capacity to discredit The People's Republic of China so that they can concentrate on defending themselves against my attacks and leave your country at peace," Sata's letter to Taiwan's Ambassador in Lilongwe read in part.

"My campaign has paid dividends. The whole world has come to acknowledge my campaign positively. It is this positive campaign which has attracted my invitation to one of the most famous universities in the world, Harvard University USA, which invitation you already have a copy. Harvard University has offered a one-way economy ticket from Zambia to Boston, USA.

"The above invitation is very important for the publicity of your country. I will be accompanied by my Director of Research, a Dr Mulenga. Because of the importance of the above trip, I have obtained a quotation which comes to US $28,612.00 (Twenty eight thousand six hundred and twelve dollars).

"I am therefore humbly requesting support from your government in the sum of US $50,000 (Fifty thousand dollars) to cover the cost of this important trip, upkeep in London and the USA."

Sata further stated that if Taiwan's government approved his request, the money could be wired into his personal account at Finance Bank's Corporate branch. (*The Post*, 2007)

The whole endeavor nearly went completely wrong. On his way to Boston, Michael's passport disappeared in a hotel in London, just as he was due to leave for Heathrow. He calculated that, with a great deal of luck, he could get a travel document from the Zambian Embassy, which would get him back to Lusaka the following morning. Thence he "only"(!) needed a new passport, along with visas from the US and UK embassies, before setting off for Boston a second time. I met him off the plane the next morning, and we went for it. By early afternoon he had a new passport and two visas. I did all the playing around with computers and schmoozing lovely ladies in the two consular departments. By three in the afternoon, he was unpacking his laundry in the middle of the concourse at Lusaka International Airport. He caught the plane and made it to Boston via Atlanta. He phoned me and said: "Thanks for everything. Hey, know what? This is America and this airport has a power cut. Imagine!"

The amazing competence of Zambian bureaucrats to act quickly and efficiently when they are motivated to do so gives me much hope for the future. Examples such as the passport case give me confidence we can actually run a proper country—even an above average one—if only we get the motivations right.

Although they swore innocence in the initial disappearance of the passport, the minister of home affairs and his sidekicks were incandescent with rage that the meeting took place as planned. The replacement passport was seized, only to be returned to Michael by Mwanawasa at their first public reconciliation meeting after Michael's heart emergency.

The Chinese government was piqued by Michael's attacks, most particularly his description of Taiwan as an independent republic. China was easily persuaded by the Zambian government to take a hard line over Michael's open criticisms. "Li Baodong, China's ambassador in Lusaka, said Beijing might cut diplomatic relations with Zambia if voters elected Michael Sata, an opposition candidate, as president, Zambian media reported on Tuesday" (Reed, 2006). Mr. Li even joined in what were effectively MMD government press conferences—even mini-rallies—speaking against an opposition party.

Our anti-Chinese rhetoric was at its peak in the 2006 election lasting to 2008 when the election to replace Levy Mwanawasa took place. In 2007 I went to Taiwan for a sort of poor man's version of the Taiwan-Africa Economic Forum—specializing in being friendly to opposition parties. But I got the impression the Taiwanese knew the game was up. I spent most of the time being amazed at the architecture in Chinese classic style of Taipei and inspecting the snakes (and pretending not to notice the sex toys) in the night market. I am told but did not observe myself that men whose "hard currency" was flagging would buy a cobra, impale it behind the neck on a hook in the wall, cut off the tip of the tail and suck blood from the bleeding stump. This apparently drives men to a compelling lust that can only be gratified by rushing into the brothels along the street and paying for the urgently needed sex partner. I know nobody who admits to having tried it.

In 2006, much to my surprise I received a call from the Chinese Embassy less than a week before polling day. They just had to meet with Michael; the instruction had obviously come down direct from Beijing. But he was on the Long March and did not consider for one second that he would abandon it. "Tell them we will meet after elections." What if they charter a plane and meet you in the bush? He put the phone down.

"Sorry," I said, "the only alternative you have is to talk to me." Eventually we met and the story was as plain as could be. The Chinese had somehow garnered information that we were winning the election and they had believed it. Now that it was actually about to happen we were asked to name our price for abandoning our support for Taiwan. It was as simple as that. I tracked down Michael and briefed him. "On no account do any deal," he ordered. "But it's free money," I protested and some of it would be nice to have considering how short of cash we are close to polling day.

"No deal!"

After 2006 (which we lost; the embassy didn't call again for a while), our political use of China and Chinese investors as targets somewhat went off the boil—although it did reignite occasionally when something egregious happened, such as the shooting of a dozen or so workers by owners at the Collum Coal Mine in 2010. Inspection of the mine revealed a lack of first aid availability and protective clothing.

The Taiwan angle had very much altered with a change of government in Taipei (and a return to One China), as well as the abandonment of relations between Malawi and Taiwan next door to us.

We stuck to our guns on such matters as safety, labor laws, tax compliance, and many other areas where we had evidence of laxity. But such stuff makes for sleepy campaigning.

After we were elected in 2011 we were fortunate (or the beneficiaries of planning?) to have a new Chinese ambassador, Zhou Yuxian, who was not associated with the MMD government or campaigns. This made the diplomatic transition from enemies to good friends easy. It also allowed us to look behind the bamboo curtain into the great variety of organizations clustered as "Chinese." We had not realized the extent to which the Chinese firms differed from one another in their ownership and management, for example. And we did not fully understand what their objectives were. (To make money obviously, but are they taking a long view or a short view; are they interested in flat-out expansion or are they just holding onto their options for another day?)

I had a good idea when a Chinese American sociologist—CK Lee, a well-known specialist on China in Africa—turned up in my office on about the fourth day after my installation. She was desperate to get access to the various large mines in Zambia to do a comparative study of Chinese and other kinds of mine owners. Not surprisingly they were reluctant and bureaucratic and it took me to arrange access for her from my perch near the top of the tree. She worked on several mines and assembled her insights. Passing them on to us was of course part of the deal. I now had access to what was happening behind the scenes and it cost nothing at all. The main Chinese investment in Zambia is through a company that is owned directly (more or less) by the Chinese Communist Party. This means it is a serious operation (if a bit short on humor) in contrast to, say, the notorious Collum Coal Mine, which was owned by a family of brothers with no background in mining operations, never mind in foreign countries. This academic-government partnership system worked well, although on occasion my office felt like a candle-to-moths for doctoral students wanting to get through the tunnels of government.

The Chinese subsector of the mining industry is not spectacularly large—operating in Zambia there are mining companies based in Switzerland, Canada, Canada again, and India. However, according to Dr. Lee, the Chinese holding is likely to expand more or less indefinitely while others collect their winnings and call it a day. The Chinese seem to have a low interest–long payback period mentality. This, as we have seen, enables development that is otherwise going to be disabled by a short time horizon.

We have also won some insight into the Chinese portion of the construction industry. Here the outstanding feature is the long-term and apparently "soft" financing that comes through, say, the Bank of China. Even if we, Zambia, wish to organize our own financing, we are up against the short payback period. Our floating a eurobond on the Western commercial markets gives us only ten years, whereas a loan tied to a road or stadium requires that we *start* paying after ten years.

Of course, if you do the discounting to get net present cost you will find that the Chinese are overpricing to compensate for the generous terms of the loan. But at least you can build something, even if it is burdensome to your children to pay the loan back. Rule of thumb calculations indicate that Chinese financed capital projects cost about double what they would if paid for in cash.

However in the agricultural industry, our government is behind in understanding the "little south China" that is building up. Even the Chinese Embassy does not know how its citizens end up farming in Zambia. How many are they? We do not know. Are their products safe? We do not know.

The level of xenophobia in Zambia—where many tribal groupings have some sort of migrant history within historical times—is relatively mild. To some extent, the "low quality" of the earliest investors from a new source of immigrants tends to boost xenophobia—especially if they do not speak English and cannot explain themselves. It is really a cause of agitation to unemployed Zambians if Chinese—or Africans from elsewhere, or certain other countries—seem to end up competing with Zambians by, for example, selling street food identical to the local style. What do we get from them? Matters improve when serious professionals put in an appearance and create jobs that just were not there before.

I visited Beijing two months after taking office. Wynter wanted me to go along with what was essentially his expedition to make friends with our (or at least his) fellow "socialists." It was cold, smoggy, and altogether a very peculiar experience. The VIP dispatcher at Beijing airport almost used a tape measure and calculator to figure out how long my limousine should be. I was soon ensconced in a five star hotel penthouse overlooking the Forbidden City. Driving to the Great Hall of the People the traffic was stopped to let us zoom down the short stretch of road. I phoned Charlotte, waking her from her sleep with news that "I am driving down the highway round the Forbidden City and Tianamen Square all by myself in the rush hour!" "Likely story," she said, "let me sleep!" She later claimed she thought I was making it up.

Our hosts had been born and brought up in a One Party State, a permanent institution supposedly. The nearest "multiparty" point of commonality was the teachings of Sun Yat-sen, the doctor, political theorist, and first post-emperor of China, whose 100th anniversary of ascension to power was in 2011. There are statues to him in mainland China as in Taiwan. I had taken the trouble to bone up on his political science, which rests upon a five-way separation of powers (as opposed to the three-way system we have adopted widely in the West and its former colonies). If you feel a little ill at ease in the Great Hall of the People, built with ceilings high as giants and trying to eat a giant's dinner involving fourteen dishes, take my advice. Raise your glass and say: Sun Yat-sen!

15

Good Neighborliness

A MAJOR REASON FOR APPOINTING ME AS VICE PRESIDENT WAS SIMPLY public relations—to have a white man representing Zambia at high international levels. Michael was fully aware that people, however politically correct and indifferent to racee, could not at least help but notice and ask questions about what they had noticed. As far as he was concerned Zambia had stood in the back of the crowd for too long, and he wanted to bring it to the forefront. Since the people of Zambia, including most of those in the opposition, appeared to approve of me almost unanimously, this was an easy option. The fact that I could answer questions with ingenuity and vigor in parliament, understand economics (up to a point), chair meetings effectively, and so forth were welcome but secondary reasons for making me the VP. His widow told me that he was inordinately proud of his achievement in being the first independent African leader to promote a white so high up the ladder. (He, of course, would not tell me this to my face.)

Charlotte and I would get to see the world and meet interesting people. The cost to us was a modicum of jet lag and boredom. And it was sometimes invigorating to drop and scatter names like bread for ducks. "I had an argument with Bill Gates the other day . . ."

Once in a while we had small misunderstandings with the rest of the world. In transit at Dubai Airport the protocol officers led my aide de camp off to the royal suite of the airport hotel for a sleep and offered me a chair to sit in. They must have Googled Zambia and decided that the first black man out of the plane had to be the vice president. That meant the white man must be his security officer. The white woman? Well, we sorted it out and had a good laugh all around.

The first little trip I took was on a scheduled flight to Malawi for a Southern African Development Community (SADC) meeting. The apron at Lilongwe Airport was covered in armed men in dress uniform and Zambian and Malawian dance troupes.

"Could the vice president come to the door for disembarkation!" said the PA system. I smoothed down the rumples in my only suit (I bought more later) and headed for the exit. "Sit down, sit down, make way for the vice president," the other passengers kept telling me, but I eventually attempted an elegant disembarkation, inspected the guard of honor as if I knew what I was looking for, danced with and tipped the dancers, and climbed aboard the motorcade. It is quite a shock to find yourself traveling at speed on a normally congested road being cleared—all six lanes—by motorcyclists. My first reaction was to feel like a fraud and to beg the driver of the limo to be more gentle with the other road users. But the sentiment passes, believe me.

Michael had an issue with the president of Malawi, Bingu wa Mutharika. A couple of years earlier Michael had slipped across the border to meet Bakili Muluzi, a former president of Malawi, from whom he hoped to organize campaign assistance from the Taiwanese (say some) or from some other sources (say others). Zambian intelligence (probably) had news of this, and asked President Bingu to return Michael to Zambia. He was accordingly bundled into a car on arrival at the airport and driven home across the border. His cryptic briefing to me as I left was to somehow square matters up "diplomatically."

I called a press conference in Lilongwe and told the story that my president was not coming because he had been insulted and hurt by Malawi's president, and he was waiting for an apology. Until it was received, the most senior Zambian who would deign to speak to Bingu or visit Malawi was me; bad luck, chaps. Was this diplomatic enough?

I received a joyful message from Joyce Banda, the Malawian vice president, at that time daggers drawn with Bingu, saying, in the Chewa language: "Welcome to Malawi, what kind of white man are you? Call that diplomacy?" I swore to be more careful in the future.

At the reception for the heads of state that evening I was walking toward Robert Mugabe to renew my acquaintance after many, many years when a BBC News report distracted my attention. Zeinab Baddawi was in full spate on a topic of the day. "She's Sudanese you know," came a kindly avuncular sort of voice from behind me. I turned to the speaker, who turned out to be President Omar al-Bashir of Sudan.

A crazy thought formed and hung there a second or two. Maybe I could make a fortune as a bounty hunter for the International Criminal Court, the ICC, which was currently seeking the arrest of two people standing almost within arm's length of me (I was not sure of Mugabe and the ICC but figured someone must want him). Then I realized there had to be some sort of white flag arrangement in order for international discourse to take place. Damn. So I shook al-Bashir's hand warmly and said: "It's a great honor to meet you, Sir, do you know my old friend His Excellency Comrade Robert Mugabe?"

Somewhere in St. Peter's record system, I hope, is a note to the effect that I was cleared for diplomatic operations that involved being nice to rogue individuals and traveling to rogue states. I certainly hope so, because I came to meet and visit enough of them.

The press pack quickly got wind of the fact that Mugabe and I were as close to first name terms as protocol allows and decided they wanted a photo of us in each other's arms. Luckily for them, the two of us were sitting near each other in the conference tent since our countries both began with Z. The photographers started creeping up on us. Mugabe noticed he was being stalked and demanded: "What do you want?" I said I thought they wanted a picture of us shaking hands and embracing each other. He leapt up and we did the needful, the internet sparked, and there we were on Africa's front pages.

A few days in office I was off to the Africa Cup Final in Gabon where Zambia was in the final against Cote d'Ivoire. We had agreed, Michael and I, to rehabilitate the (then) eighty-eight-year-old Kenneth Kaunda; Chiluba had derided him as a scapegoat for the poverty into which the country had sunk, and Mwanawasa had parked him at some distance. But by now he had been out of the picture for twenty years and had attained ancestor status. The combination of him and me would be even more difficult to ignore than me alone. So we hefted our former president on to a jet leased by a mining company and shot across the rain forest into a different Africa. Michael dislikes soccer and indeed any sport other than vote chasing; I can get quite involved in a good game; but Kaunda always insisted on being called "Zambian soccer fan number one" when he was in power. And so we rechristened him.

In 1993 most members of the Zambian national football team were killed in the crash of a military transport plane off the coast of Gabon, shortly after takeoff from Libreville airport. The final word on the cause of the accident has never been released (not even to vice presidents) and one can only assume the truth would be deeply embarrassing to someone who was at some time powerful enough to ensure that the truth would never come out. The badly mutilated bodies were brought ashore by divers on a beach in a residential area of Libreville, and memorials were erected in Lusaka.

The 2012 Zambian team, camped in Gabon, were taken to lay flowers and murmur prayers on the spot where their predecessors' bodies had been recovered. From verbal reports it is clear that their visit of homage moved them very deeply. Some could not talk for hours afterward.

In the evening of the day of the match, Charlotte and I dutifully presented ourselves at the presidential palace, where names started dropping like Ivorian strikers diving for penalties. Not only were half of Africa's French-speaking presidents there, but people kept introducing themselves, name-dropping themselves it seemed. We had "Sepp Blatter" (thud) and even "Pelé" (double thud). To do justice to the big event, President Bongo had hired the kitchen staff of the best hotel in Johannesburg, along with their canapés and sushi ingredients, Krug champagne and like stuff, and flown them to the match.

I was led down to greet the teams and was very struck by the fact that our players (with the exception of the goalie and two other defenders) were markedly shorter than the star-studded West African team of giants, who looked sorry for us already.

The story of the Zambian victory, deep into penalties, is too well known to bear retelling in detail here. A gripping video documentary called *Eighteam* was made about the whole event, even reaching Cannes; it's really worth the small sum it costs to watch it online. The story lives on in the hearts of all Zambians and many others across the world. The high point during the main body of the match was the save by our goalkeeper Kennedy Mweene of a penalty kick from Didier Drogba. Mweene mocked the failed strike by covering his eyes with a hand of spread fingers (in a gesture obviously meaning "how long have you been blind?"). Half the people I spoke to after the match swear they saw two players in the goal mouth when the penalty was saved—Mweene himself and the ghost of our legendary goalie Efford Chabala, who died in the 1993 crash. Only the most literal minded Gradgrind would bring himself to argue with the illusion of ancestral spirits rising to the occasion and tipping the ball over the crossbar. It would be like taking issue with Homer for arranging for the goddess Aphrodite to help her favorite mortal Paris in combat with the near-immortal Achilles. In short, it would be arguing with poetry; you are doomed to lose, though that doesn't stop some people from trying it.

Pelé gave it as his opinion that the match was the most exciting he had ever seen. The most exciting Pelé had ever seen? He repeated the comment, with emphasis.

We arrived in Lusaka the next afternoon with the team. Since the moment of victory the previous day, crowds had been gathering and hunkering down for the long night. The airport itself was effectively under occupation, with the apron crowded and even the taxiways accessible to the public. At some stage the various telecommunication and lighting towers were taken over by the better climbers. There was no hard-nosed law enforcement, perhaps because the enforcers themselves were hysterically happy.

The first plane into Lusaka the following morning had been the British Airways overnight flight from London. After touchdown the pilot could not turn the plane around with all the people chasing it up the runway. It had to roll to the very end of the runway and wait for some order to be imposed. The first lady, Christine Kaseba Sata, was on the flight and phoned her husband with an account of the chaos. The inspector of

© Charlotte Scott

Arriving back from Gabon with the Africa Cup of Nations, 2012. This crowd was on the runway, with no semblance of airport security. Notice the people who had climbed the tower and were on the building.

police lost his job over the shambles. Order was established—but only up to a point. If the team is not on this one then it must be on the next! Even the solitary fire engine with its normally po-faced crew sprayed each plane that landed with water, in case it was "the one."

Back in Gabon the immigration authorities were having a bad morning. They were exhibiting what seemed to be a sulk and delaying our processing at the airport. Hence it was almost eighteen hours between our winning the match and our landing; hundreds of thousands of Zambians were short of sleep, a factor that made them only more enthusiastic to greet the team. In the chartered plane carrying us it was hot, and once we were down, the South African crew opened the cockpit windows to cool themselves. It worked better than they expected as a full-pressure jet of water from the fire engine immediately soaked them and their instrument panel.

Charlotte and I got out first and decided to take a motorcade ahead of the team to hopefully relieve some tension on the part of the crowd, since it was bound to be another hour or more before the team itself could be wheeled through the crowd on gun carriages—the only vehicles other than tanks that could stand up to the great upheaval along the way.

The Zambian sense of humor was in good shape: "For Sale" said the first placard, "Former Footballer Didier Drogba"; "20,000 kwacha (crossed out and replaced by) 10,000 kwacha."

Sports fans throughout the world gather to welcome their conquering heroes. But this was on a different level. It was not even a reprise of the presidential inauguration; it was an enhanced version, and the celebration somehow blended into a passionate memorial for our fallen heroes of twenty years earlier. At the showground it proved impossible to silence the vastly overquota crowd and all the team could do was climb onto a chair, one by one, holding the Africa Cup on high. We were chivvied out of the event as night fell and the fears of uncontrollable happenings in the dark became a factor to the "close party" of bodyguards. But the magic prevailed into the night and no life was lost (amazingly, actually, given that a wall collapsed under the weight of people who had scrabbled up in search of a better view). Life without some voodoo is not real life.

(We would have won any election in any part of Zambia easily on the day the Africa Cup came to us. President Ouatera of Cote d'Ivoire wryly said to me after the match that a victory to his side would have toned down the civil strife in his country.)

Back to Malawi, where meanwhile Bingu wa Mutharika had suddenly died of a heart attack. The Malawian constitution specified that his vice president should automatically take his place and rule until the next general election. The vice president was originally elected as the "running mate" to the president. This is exactly the American system; what's wrong about it? Whoever drafted it had not foreseen a key African problem: what if the president and his vice had fallen out politically, to the point of their becoming members of different parties?

This is what had happened. Joyce Banda had been chosen for the electoral advantage she would bring to Mutharika's campaign three years earlier. Despite her status she was subsequently sidelined, given no post in cabinet, and left in isolation. She responded by forming her own party, resulting in procedures to remove her from the vice presidency. But critically, these were unfinished at the time of Bingu's death, and the constitution read like nonsense—declaring that the presidency must pass to a member of the opposition!

Two tendencies established themselves. The "Mutharika" group was led by Bingu's brother Peter. This sought to ignore the constitution as meaningless in the context and to instate Peter as president. The other group took the constitution as biblical in its inflexibility and supported Joyce Banda. Peter's group gathered at his house; Joyce's group gathered at hers.

There are many versions of what happened in those few days. I have heard one side in great detail, the night before Bingu's funeral, as Charlotte and I had dinner with Joyce and her husband. Perhaps in time I will hear the other side and even have something to say about it—but for now, I think discretion is in order. The funeral itself was a tense affair, with newly inaugurated Joyce seated adjacent to vanquished Peter. The crowd seemed equally divided as we sat through an extremely long outdoor service, and interment in a rather flashy mausoleum. As dusk, the visiting VIPs were allowed to leave, while the formalities continued into the night.

Joyce was only the second woman to make the presidency in Africa (after Helen Johnson Sirleaf of Liberia). It would have been nice if she had had a further full term under her own electoral steam. It would also be nice if we had ended up on the right side, supporting her. But the strength of the Democratic Progressive Party, Peter's party, in the government networks was too much for her. From our point of view it was also difficult to support her since Michael had tit-for-tat commitments with Muluzi (who was promoting his son as a candidate) stretching back to his ignominious removal from Malawi by Bingu and before. Although our initial contacts had been extremely friendly, particularly in Charlotte's case, relations between Joyce and me were soured last time we met. She expressed her bitterness at Michael's betrayal. But if she reads this, I hope she realizes that we still look forward to seeing her again in future.

In the Southern African Development Community we are supposed to help each other with our political problems, simply speaking. The major source of such problems over the past few years appears to be Zimbabwe and its style of managing elections. Remember, Zim is not a one-party state, but it has managed to be a one-president state for thirty-five years, with the liberation party ZANU-PF ever in charge and only obliged to even power-share for one term. Complaints from the opposition are standard fare, and pressures from further afield are also significant. When handing out responsibilities we small countries comparable in size to Zimbabwe—that is, Mozambique, Zambia, Angola, and Malawi—have always thought the job of smoothing affairs in Zimbabwe should be left to us. South Africa and its supporters, however, think that South Africa, a much bigger state by most measures, should lean on the much smaller and weaker state to its immediate north.

Robert Mugabe is not keen on being leaned on by anybody and the point was reached about two years ago when some urgent face saving was required all round. This was needed on the part of SADC generally and its biggest member specifically. In our collective SADC view, Zimbabwe also needed to be more conciliatory. In a Maputo meeting I made a proposal that would affect all these desired outcomes. Zimbabwe would delay a general election by one month to allow the opposition to inspect voters' rolls and do other things SADC was complaining about. Yes, we took note that the constitutional court in Zim had ruled that the election must go ahead sooner, but surely, if the government itself were to join the opposition in pleading for the extension, then the court would consent. After all, which court grants a divorce if all parties agree not to ask for one? It was not as if a short delay in the election date would make any difference to the result, which was an overwhelming victory to ZANU-PF. Mugabe agreed and we all patted each other on the back.

Then Zimbabwe reneged, without quite seeming to. The court refused to play along, insulting SADC in the process, leaving us all looking slow-witted, and the election proceeded. This taught me that Mugabe and his team were not interested in earning political brownie points. Perhaps they actually liked being the bad boys on the block and were perversely keen on black marks. Come to think of it, they were remarkably similar to the Rhodesian Front government of Ian Smith in this regard. Perhaps there is an insight about compulsively imitating former colonial oppressors to be extracted here.

The press is an important agent in enabling leaders and voters to understand themselves and each other. I mean here the *real* press and not the computerized social media in which the proportion of truth to falsehood is totally indeterminate. But it seems that the "real" press, including some giants of Fleet Street, has taken up playing the social media game, trying to compete in terms of sensationalism and neglecting to understand complicated issues or to present real evidence.

We started quite well with the international media; I survived a "Hard Talk" session with Stephen Sackur and exuded puzzled charm on a BBC documentary about tax evasion by copper companies.

But there were deliberate hatchet jobs as well. *The Guardian* newspaper interviewed me. As their reporter proceeded I became worried for the young man's career. It was surely going to be the most boring dialogue that never saw publication, so I gingered it up. The result was a story in which I described the South Africans, regardless of race, as "backward," generally berated them as arrogant, as well as declared that I hated them. I suppose it is my fault again for trying to play the teasing *chimbuya* (traditional cousinship) in a medium that does not transmit tone of voice unless the writer has the skill and takes the care. But regardless of the subsequent fracas, I believe I saved the man's career.

For those who missed it: South Africa has only been independent for twenty odd years, and most people remember apartheid. Zambia has been independent for fifty years and has had legislation against discrimination for nearly sixty. Compared to us, they are behind—or backward, or "historically challenged," which is what I was saying. And now they lord it over countries that risked their own stability and sacrificed their own prosperity to bring South Africa into the twentieth century before the twentieth century got finished. And yet they do not even call themselves Africans. "Africa" for South Africans begins at the Limpopo (they say to me, "so you're from Africa"). They lionize Nelson Mandela, but they forget that the rest of the continent is replete with examples of once-jailed freedom fighters who steered people of different races into reconciliation and were well deserving of Nobel prizes and the like. It's just that it happened earlier and most of them are dead. I could go on and on. If someone gives you the chance, how can you not?

The Guardian is a paper that takes itself seriously. Its founder C. P. Scott (no relation I think) laid down the motto: Opinion is free, facts are sacred. The journalists immediately modified this to: Opinion is free, facts are expensive. But I am sure they take themselves seriously enough to expect that they had brought about my political demise. Alas for them, my comments were warmly greeted across the region, and in South

Africa particularly. Of course, the Zambian opposition in Zambia tried to use my undiplomatic utterances as ammo but that is to be expected. There may have been some humorless people among South Africans and their friends who thought I was endangering good relations among the southern Africans, but mostly the response was surprisingly positive.

South Africans asked: Why does it take the vice president of Zambia to say these things, when we should say them for ourselves?

I am told working relations between South Africa and the embassies of the region improved greatly. And Winnie Mandela gave me a hug.

I was in the UK when the story was published; on my return I went to see Michael who commented: "I did not appoint you for your diplomatic skills; next time you see Zuma tell him I agree with you."

There is a science fiction short story I once read in which time travelers contrived to meet up by independently selecting a date and place of exceptional interest and importance. They all duly turned up at the crucifixion. If a second venue were required, perhaps the choice would be Nelson Mandela's memorial service at the FNB Stadium in Johannesburg. It was an unreal experience, bearing little obvious connection to Mandela's politics or traditions, featuring celebrities in hallucinatory quantities, some of them perhaps time travelers in fancy dress. You could not turn your head without seeing someone you recognized, except that the first instinct was that person was wearing a rubber mask. "Gosh there's someone dressed as Bill Clinton; no, hang on, it has to *be* Clinton!"

Having fought our way up the stairs to a VIP box—that's Charlotte, KK, and I—we found ourselves in the company of almost every world leader you could care to mention in an unusually jumbled grouping. Robert and Grace Mugabe; the crown prince Haaken of Norway (who we knew from a visit he paid to Lusaka) and a great range of other royals; the entire UK front row of Major, Brown, Blair, Cameron, Clegg, and Miliband; and a similar collection of Obamas, Bushes, and Clintons; Sonia Gandhi; Hamid Karzai; and so on. The PA system, in spates, introduced the visiting dignitaries—including Zuma, Obama, and many others. The crowd of ANC party members and some opposition cheered each name dutifully—until it came to Mugabe. Then they really cheered their heads off. For all the talk of reconciliation the fact remains that all over southern Africa, including in the rainbow nation itself, he is extremely popular. Whatever the case may be among Zimbabwean refugees and in the opposition, the fact is that Mugabe is seen to have brought self-respect to Africa, by telling the West, and the British in particular, just where to get off. He gets thundering applause even from an audience of university graduates in anglophile Malawi. But were the time-traveling glitterati too engrossed in taking selfies to notice?

It was soon evident that we were under the eye of the world; SMS messages fluttered in from the most unlikely places: "Hiya Mr. Vice President, tell Obama we love him"; "What you doin' with Hillary you old silver fox you" and so on. The crowds of non-VIPs in the bleachers, and there were many thousands, meanwhile booed Zuma and showed to anyone with time to learn that South Africa is politically contentious as well as vibrant . . . and full of uncertainties.

Most egregious introduction: "Allow me to introduce my wife, her name is Michelle." Most egregious political advice: "Mr. Vice President, you old dude, if you ever get invited to eat kebabs with this guy take a food taster with you."

There was a small panic when KK went on walkabout, or was taken on a walk about by persons unknown. Luckily a nameless woman brought him back just in time to stop the manhunt.

We overshot Lusaka the following evening and landed the Challenger jet in Nairobi. This was the fiftieth anniversary of independence, and considerably more relaxed than the last time I had been there. On that previous occasion, the new president and vice president there were about to be sworn in, and we all wanted the political situation stabilized as soon as possible. For one thing the opposition was making noises about a rigged election, and more important, the International Criminal Court had a bone to pick with Uhuru Kenyatta, the new president, and his sidekick William Ruto over electoral violence five years earlier. That could seriously destabilize things and we of the neighborhood rushed in holding hands to protest at phony justice directed seemingly at Africa. As the dignitaries filed in, Jesse Jackson, the US freedom fighter, brushed me aside to take over as KK's adjutant, calling out to new arrivals: "Here he is, Kenneth Kaunda, he's the man, he's the man." I was completely sidelined until President Kikwete of Tanzania arrived and said to me: "Hi, Guy, who is this fellow?" (referring to Jackson).

A few weeks later, at the VIP lounges in O. R. Tambo airport, I asked a waitress to get some drinks and she took ages returning. She had been ambushed, she said, by a man with an American accent who asked her: "How is Mother Africa?" She had taken a long time to make up enough stuff that he let her go. I asked her to show him to me and we crept around until we spotted him: Lo! It was the man, it was indeed the man!

From the fiftieth anniversary, we tanked up the faithful Challenger and headed south again, overflying Lusaka. This time it was the real funeral of Nelson Mandela, a family affair with only a few thousand guests, in his home village of Qunu in the Eastern Cape. The funeral was very moving in many respects, completely making up for the celebs, booing, and duff sign language interpreter that dominated the stadium event in Johannesburg. But Zambia—the home of the ANC, and the front-most of the frontline states—was again left off the list of speakers in favor of Malawi, which had in fact been the only country in Africa to maintain diplomatic relations with the apartheid regime. Joyce Banda spoke brilliantly, but even so the omission injured any right-thinking Zambian to the core. Kenneth Kaunda rose to the occasion and insisted on giving an impromtu speech in which he completely abandoned all the careful politically correct protocols and started hammering on about the "Boers" and about how little the young know about anything. When Cyril Ramaphosa stepped toward him to indicate that his time was up, KK berated him, repeatedly demanding, "Who is this young man, who thinks he can tell old men to stop talking?" Once we all settled down again, the funeral proceeded according to plan. This time he did not go on walkabout, and we made it back to Lusaka uneventfully.

© Charlotte Scott

With Kenneth Kaunda at Nelson Mandela's funeral in Qunu, December 2013, with unintended photo-bombing by Prince Charles

16

The Not-So-Rough Guide

WITHIN DAYS OF BEING SWORN IN, AND IMMEDIATELY AFTER THE MALAWIAN jaunt with Mugabe, al-Bashir et al., it was time for my first CHOGM—Commonwealth Heads of Government Meeting—in Perth in Western Australia. As a Zambian with some sense of history I was inclined to be enthusiastic about CHOGM; as I have already explained it was the 1979 CHOGM that stopped the war in Rhodesia and brought about majority rule in that country as it became Zimbabwe. As I packed for Perth I wondered, What will we do this time round?

CHOGM first and foremost seems to be an occasion on which the host country shows off. It seemed that half the security forces of Australia had been shipped to Perth. Everyone from anti-terrorist specialists to traffic police was crowded into corridors of the hotel. Since Zimbabwe was not present, Zambia sat next to Australia on the round table, which meant Julia Gillard and I had the opportunity of exchanging greetings and jokes with a southern hemisphere flavor. The spouses were carted off in a bus with the Ozzie "first bloke" as their guide and had a jolly good few days. After a photo opportunity (there was an endless stream of them), we the delegates were boxed up in a small conference room with luxurious leather chairs and fed only the very finest in seafood and wine.

What with the jet lag and the soporific throbbing of the security helicopters overhead, I fell into a deep sleep. I awoke to a posh English voice asking, "Are you all right, old chap?" It was David Cameron. When I told this story to a group of Labour MPs they got the punch line before I did. "Yes, you thought you had died and gone to hell!" they all shouted.

I thought, in the days I was working with computers and IT, that the leaders of the world would stop traveling and take up teleconferencing. But it seems we're traveling like never before, with entourages like never before. It's very uplifting, I admit, to meet the actual people you see so much of on TV, but does that make a sparrow fall anywhere in the real world?

David Cameron gave a speech on the agricultural industry in the "southern hemisphere," by which we may assume he is talking about the "third world." The report had been compiled by the Commonwealth secretariat and dealt with all the technical factors anyone could think of: lack of irrigation, underuse of fertilizer, lack of infrastructure, and so forth. You have to say something at these affairs so I made a point, which I have since come to make at many forums. There seems to be an assumption made by most first world experts that the problems of the developing world are technical; that they have to do with lack of finance, lack of investment, lack of knowledge, and all those other easily identifiable "limiting factors." But in fact the real problems in the south are political—not technical. In Zambia as I spoke there were in excess of two million tonnes of maize that should never have been grown, because there is too much for people to eat and no way of getting it onto the world market at a reasonable cost. The maize was doomed to rot and it existed only because there were political forces at play to do with getting peasants to vote in a certain way (unsuccessfully as my presence bore witness). And Mr. Cameron and others should not snigger at the inclusion of politics in agriculture, for their European Union is infamous for its Common Agricultural Policy, which variously subsidizes people to grow nothing, or to grow far too much of something, depending upon what political forces the Europeans in power are trying to take into account. (Indeed, it was because I had tried to implement technical solutions—and failed—that I switched my attention to the politics of development, with the result that I had become a politician and been sent packing to Perth.)

In the tradition of peripatetic prime ministers, I had the Zambians of Perth rounded up and invited to complain about their lot. They were surprisingly numerous and generally very happy to be in Oz. Most were students but quite a number were working there. (They had some moans about not being allowed second passports, which I will not bore the reader with). Why are you happy? Because we find that we fit in easily. So perhaps there is something, something intangible but nonetheless very significant about the "Commonwealth thing." And actually this book is turning out to be largely about things that are intangible yet that seem to make the world go round. What has Zambia lost with the passing of Michael? It is surely something elusive but enormously important.

A "foreign investor" made his way to my hotel one morning; he looked somewhat familiar and I gazed curiously at him for a while before he let me off the hook. "We were at school together," he said.

The coincidence of meeting the same person in two different lives seems to be a matter of remote chance until you think about it. If central African history had progressed without war and political upheaval between schooldays and the present, the number of whites brought up in the region now investing and working in it would be considerable and unsurprising. But, as the paradigm in force is that growth will come from foreign investors, the field is skewed in favor of outsiders (in respect of taxation incentives, importation of capital goods, importing foreign managers, etc.). So what the local investors are doing is registering their companies in other countries like Canada, living somewhere exotic like Western Australia, taking citizenship in say Ireland, and then happily proceeding with their business in the country they grew up in: paper "foreign" investors.

I found the story encouraging in one sense: it confirms that not all emotional bonds with their homeland have been loosened. I was however unhappy that smaller, necessarily Zambia-based investments were evidently discriminated against by the incentive structure. The international group that my school pal is running counts its Zambian assets in billions of US dollars; whereas he could not afford to spread himself out and become a "foreigner" if he was dealing in mere fractions and small multiples of a million.

Still, you live and learn and may CHOGM be praised for my inadvertent further education.

We met Queen Elizabeth and Prince Philip at dinner. I must confess I anticipated one of the duke's famous gaffes when he met a white vice president from Africa, but he just looked a bit puzzled. If this did anything to shake my faith in the Commonwealth this was corrected when we received Princess Anne in Zambia almost a year later. She knows exactly where she is and what she is trying to achieve. In Zambia's case she remembered in detail staying with the Kaundas in the 1960s. She also does a nice line in self-deprecating humor. I was explaining how the Chinese process African politicians at Beijing's airport; they seem to award us points and then make up a motorcade of the right length and strength for the status of the person concerned. If necessary the lower-scoring VIPs are pulled off to make way for the more senior ones to go ahead, blasting down the six-lane drag to the

Forbidden City. Yes! she exclaimed, they pulled my motorcade off to give way to the vice president of . . .

"Zambia?" I enquired.

"Unfortunately not, it was Djibouti. Imagine that: Djibouti!" And she did a mock sulking royal stamp of the foot. "Didn't they know who I was?" I was so charmed I nearly became a royalist on the spot.

Charlotte and I were similarly taken with Prince Edward who came out to do something relating to youth and Duke of Edinburgh awards. Contrary to the impression sometimes put about by the media, the kid is seriously good at his job and a thoroughly nice person to boot. What is wrong with that?

The CHOGM of 2013, held in Sri Lanka two years later, had some rather dubious flavors to it. The Sri Lankan tough man Mahinda Rajapaksa—currently unemployed—gave us a great show, with everything from the world's best-dressed elephants to its best food, but the continued friction between the two sides in his civil war, despite the peace agreement, was difficult to understand. It seems that both Jacob Zuma and I independently approached Rajapaksa and proposed an Africa-headed "Peace and Reconciliation Commission" to let out some of the bile—daily evident in the media. Rajapaksa did not accept our proposal. With several countries absenting themselves it became one of those international conferences where the host takes center stage and is preoccupied with seeking support for its own interests—very far from the spirit of a "Commonwealth family" meeting.

Sri Lanka was made even less family-like by the absence of Julia Gillard and the presence of her replacement Tony Abbott, who declared that he could not sign the communiqué on climate change without losing votes at home. "Then just don't sign!" the secretariat told him. Now what kind of a meeting is that? What has been concluded? Why did we meet at all, let alone fly first class?

International conferences are two a penny. I had just come from a Non-Aligned Movement meeting convened in Iran. It had seemed the Iranians wanted to get everyone's approval for their taking a hard line on Israel. I say "seemed" because I could not understand the simultaneous English translation in its entirety. Enquiry revealed that the Iranians are good at producing multiple translations—different translations in different languages—to confuse conferences. Apparently it is a trick developed in the Soviet Union. Quite how and why it works to anyone's advantage is still a mystery to me.

Perhaps in compensation for poor verbal communication I was shown some solid symbolism. I was shown a robotic model of a dove without wings but with electrons orbiting in their place. Next to it was an actual recovered final stage of a suborbital rocket with a stuffed monkey inside it, and next to it a model of a uranium enrichment plant. Now what were they trying to tell me?

An Iranian journalist asked me what I thought of his country. I just managed:

> *"Myself when young did eagerly frequent*
> *Doctor and saint and heard great argument*
> *About it and about but evermore*
> *Came out of that same door as in I went."*

"Ah! You know our Omar!" Phew, I picked the right country.

Another strange thing I still do not understand are the rumors that tend to be passed around within and between delegations to international conferences concerning a supposed heap of money that the host is intending to divide out among the guests. "Apparently the US government has climate change money they want to give us" was common currency at the United States–Africa Leaders' Summit in August 2014.

Another cache of money for the alleviation of poverty was supposedly available for the plundering in Bolivia (Bolivia?!) at the G-77+China Conference and was believed in so sincerely that one country took up the whole of business and first class in a 737 with its delegates (I counted over forty of them). How could anyone believe in unpublicized free real money, let alone free real money distributed on the basis of size of delegation to a conference? Of course, it might suit the delegation members to have this noble task to justify the cost of sending them; and it may suit the hosts or organizers who want a successful conference to leave open, however slightly, the possibilities of serious money talk with presidents or their Number Twos. Japan, China, and the United States for example like to boast to one another about the attendance figures at their Africa-focused conferences—all of them are pretty close to 100 percent. But would they actually spread rumors to encourage leaders to attend when otherwise they might not?

Surely not?

No golden rain actually materialized in Bolivia but a new line in gossip took its place. The G-77 group has quite a number of members, a subgroup, which are landlocked. I was happily informed that Zambia's turn to chair this dry subgroup of members had arrived. See you in Vienna then! Forward with the campaign for those with sea coasts to compensate those without (to which group despite all efforts Malawi still belongs.) Alas, Michael's dying illness put an end to that.

My last entanglement with the Commonwealth prior to Michael's death and my early retirement started when a young man of subcontinental origin appeared in my office. When I looked at him more carefully I saw that he was wearing a Stewart tartan kilt. He was Minister for Europe and International Development Humza Yousaf, the Scottish scion of a Glaswegian family of Pakistani origin. I had not been intending to attend the Glasgow Commonwealth games but the temptation was too much to resist.

I VISITED THE SCOTTS of Carluke at the jam factory that used to belong to my family. I had never seen it, but I knew my great uncle Robert had stowed away on a ship and smuggled strawberry plants out of California to improve the yield in Scotland—clearly carrying a persistent gene in the family male line. I collected a ton of mixed jam from the current operators of the factory—call it "back rent"—and gave it to the Zambian team. They obligingly ate it in front of STV cameras and said things like "no wonder our vice president is so sweet and strong if he was raised on this excellent jam." They got about one bronze medal more than expected, and I saw footage of them getting off the plane in Lusaka carrying boxes of Scott's best low-fruit high-sugar jam.

The Scottish journalists treated me as a returning hero, following me to Livingstone's birthplace and foaming at the mouth about "the two doctors." They also asked me questions about Zambia's attitude to gay marriage, to which I replied that we had not got around to thinking about it, but would do so once the current Zambian crisis in child marriages and mortality was on the wane. I think Dr. David might have approved my prevarication, however it's true to say that other commentators did not.

THE MOST BIZARRE DESTINATION for the world's only white African vice president was North Korea. It was another old link from the days when both Zambia and North Korea were members of the Non-Aligned Movement. The occasion was the sixtieth anniversary of the winning of the Korean War by the North—or perhaps that should be "winning." The Soviet Union and the United States divided Korea along the 38th parallel at the end of World War II under a friendly arrangement before the Cold War set in. The South was run under an American umbrella of less-than-perfect democracy, the North on lines that were congenial to Stalin, in whose army their chosen dictator Kim Il Sung had fought. Kim sent his troops across the border with the tacit support of Stalin on 25 June 1950. Three years later on 27 July 1953 a ceasefire was declared along a front approximating the 38th parallel. This was after the war had oscillated back and forth and had become obviously unwinnable, involving armies of the two Koreas, the United Nations (mostly US troops), and the Chinese "volunteers" of Mao Tse-Tung.

The Zambian government was invited for the sixtieth anniversary "victory over the USA" that terminated the multiethnic bloodbath. I have no idea why Michael decided that Charlotte and I should attend. Zambians are traditional allies of NK from the Non-Aligned Movement days, true, and their army instructors had been to Zambia and shown us how to perform the goose step and other tricks. But very few countries found that reason enough. Perhaps Michael had the vague idea that we might get the North Koreans to come and provide competition for the Chinese when tendering for construction work in Zambia. An alternative reason was that the NK ambassador in Pretoria worked hard on persuading the Zambian accredited to South Africa—a cousin of Michael's—and that settled that. Anyway, we hit Amazon for a suitcase full of paperback books on *The Korea I Knew, The Most Secret People, The Purest People,* and such titles, and we set out for four nights in Pyongyang.

The customs form handed out on our Air China flight from Beijing warned us of items banned on entry: "weapons, killing devices, narcotics, poison, GPS, cell phones, and publishings of all kinds." So it was just as well that we were diplomatic visitors, not missionaries or secret agents.

We were greeted at the airport by lines of ladies wearing traditional *hanbok* dresses made from garish polyester, waving bunches of plastic flowers. We were whipped into town in the back of a vintage stretch Benz limo, taking the opportunity to get to know the officials.

I was a little puzzled as to how to interpret the agricultural scenery, which featured a blanket of dark green maize covering every inch of land in the countryside and in the suburbs of Pyongyang. The usual Western story is that their inefficient and underfunded socialist system leaves crops unplanted or unmaintained. What I saw was more like a desperate response to a shortage of good well-watered land and growing time. Fertilzsing, spacing, and weeding looked to be pretty adequate, but it was certainly too hot and the growing season too short for high yields. Temperatures rapidly rose through the day and cicadas sawed in a reproductive spasm, competing to make it through the so-called summer before the annual north Pacific ice age set in. (The extremely severe winter that cracks down every year is the consequence of there being no Gulf Stream–type current to bring warm waters closer to the coast.)

Our friendly and extremely adhesive guides had some spectacular talents. They even gave us a choice of what accent we would like them to use when they were speaking to us in English. One man fetched up an accent whose ground zero must have been less than a mile from the house where Charlotte grew up in south London. I haven't encountered such extraordinary standards of interpretation anywhere else.

We were shuttled into a luxury government guesthouse with open telephone lines (I called Michael on direct dial; he answered but the conversation has escaped me). There were ten-course meals of Michelin restaurant standards (well, maybe not quite but close), and every suite was fitted out with bottles of high strength spirits containing drowned snakes whose purpose (I enquired to be sure) was to boost the male drinker's libido.

The main streets of Pyongyang are broad and well kept, but somehow didn't look quite right. It took a few outings to start spotting reasons why this was so. One oddity was the traffic police at major intersections, standing on podiums with hands held up to stop the traffic, apparently providing the same "green light" treatment that we had already enjoyed in Beijing, Perth, and other cities. But there was no traffic in sight; nothing to halt. Oh, the minders told us, yes, we don't actually encourage private cars. Evidently not; there were none, though army trucks rolled through once in a while. Another factor contributing to the overall strange sense was the lack of commercial signage—no shop signs, no adverts, just giant portraits of the Great, Dear, and Supreme Leaders. Of course, we were soon told, there is no private sector, . . . not even selling ice cream cones; . . . none at all. Along the streets, loud speakers bark out propaganda and patriotic tunes all day. At night, most of the windows in the blocks of apartments that line the streets were in darkness.

A fundamental principle of Zambian travel (actually it is a widespread African principle) is that the voyager should bring back gifts for his or her family. Important peace conferences have been sabotaged by this "traveler's gift principle" and numberless development cooperation meetings have been brought to a halt by delegates leaving the proceedings prematurely to go shopping. My party went shopping en masse at one point, leaving me to single-handedly hold a discussion with North Korean companies, and then they came back empty-handed. Alas, there was nothing to buy in all of Pyongyang, or so it would seem. They were left having to raid their rooms for snake-in-the-bottle, or tiger-bone-in-the-bottle, or to hope they would get a shopping break in Beijing.

As visiting dignitaries we watched the famed Arirang Performance in Pyongyang's 150,000-seat national stadium. Here I met Kim Jong Un and blurted out an improvised message from Michael, but he was not interested. His arrival at any public function is signaled by a special anthem—a fast military fanfare with some musical allusions to "Here Comes the Bride." Upon hearing it, everyone leaps to their feet, aligning their bodies directly toward the stout young man wearing grey, shouting "hurrah! hurrah!" and clapping vigorously. The anthem ends as suddenly as its starts, and we all sit down.

I suspect Kim was a little disappointed at the turnout of foreign visitors. He had the Ugandan vice president, apparently expressing the appreciation of Museveni for some special training given to his army, then and still now embroiled in war in Somalia—so that made two African states. The only European was a senior member of Berlusconi's party in Italy. What did we chat about? The use by the Japanese army of Korean women as "comfort women"; he was very concerned that the Koreans would stay embittered on this subject forever. There was a senior member of the Syrian government—something to do with arms procurement, I felt reasonably confident. And there was someone from South America who was a huge fellow with a resemblance to a cured ham made from an elephant's thigh. He did not speak much, and seemed to be very sure that he didn't want to speak to me.

But there was one guest of honor who made up for the rest of us: Vice President Li Yuanchao of China. North Korea is utterly dependent upon China for its survival. It is such a poor country that elementary basics like cereals and fuel are supplied by China as free aid. Even so, they are both heavily rationed. From China's point of view it is of great importance that their small ally does not bring the neighborhood into bad, mad repute. Chairman Mao sent his Red Army to stop the United Nations (the Americans) from crossing the Yalu River and entering China at the end of 1950. Over one million Chinese troops—who were underequipped in the extreme—are estimated by good sources to have died in the Korean War. This is far more that all the other categories of combatant put together. They have paid for North Korea in blood and have no wish to see it patently fail or make the region look unstable. So when North Korean leadership makes aggressive sounding noises against Japan or the West, or lets off bombs or rockets, it is just their reminding China that it is time for some more economic assistance. It's diplomatic blackmail. That is my amateur diplomatic interpretation anyway.

The Arirang is a precision affair. On the ground, gymnasts, acrobats, and dancers tell the story (or a version of it) of North Korea in fifty chapters, accompanied by a loud patriotic soundtrack, with the crowds roaring in approval. Behind, many rows of young people flip colored boards in rapid succession, a human mosaic producing an animated backdrop of pixel-by-pixel precision. Whenever any image of the Great, Dear, or Supreme Leaders appeared in this sequence, which it did quite often, the entire stadium leapt to their feet again, back to "hurrah, hurrah," and the clapping. Both Charlotte and I counted the rows of kids needed to create the backdrop, and agreed on a figure of over 25,000; we believed the person who told us that 100,000 people take part in the show overall. We were later told by a North Korean diplomat that the children who participate are on average 5 cm taller than their peers. He seemed to believe truly that this was because their participation in national glory inspires them to grow. We had already read the anti-NK version of this fact—that basic food is rationed in the country and it shows up in the stunting of "nonpatriotic" citizens. That explanation is, at least, biologically rational.

Every element of every display or ceremony we saw was militarized. Whether it was fireworks, ballet, opera, or folk dancing, the defeat of the United States by North Korea was the theme. The actual main event was the parade of military toys and soldiers, which was almost superfluous. But we had to go and see it anyway. Charlotte and I were split up: I was ushered up to the top of a large building overlooking the huge square and parade group, finding myself again in the company of Kim Jong Un. Hundreds of thousands of people filled the square, the women in shiny pink *hanbok*, the men in identical suits. Each person had a bouquet of plastic flowers in each hand, holding them above their heads, and waving them back and forth without stopping, for two hours. For boys who like toys, the show featured early on a new weapons system in the shape of a fleet of agricultural tractors pulling agricultural trailers each carrying a version of a Stalin Organ—the famous battery of Katyusha rockets. In theory you could harvest wheat, kill capitalists, and get home to harvest more wheat and feed it to some socialists—all in one day.

The parade got more grand—from ground troops to trucks, trucks to tanks, tanks with small guns to tanks with very big guns, followed by a range of rockets from implausibly small things shown off by civilian manufacturers of domestic appliances to huge ICBMs, which, if they worked to spec, would surely be the very terror of the earth. The flypast followed a similar pecking order though it was not so impressive if you knew that the advanced jet aircraft were Russian machines. Next came giant floats devoted to the leaders and escorted by thousands of civilians waving yet more plastic flowers. Wives don't carry much clout in North Korea, and Charlotte was stuck out in very hot sun, watching the parade at street level and mocked by the midday shriek of the cicadas. She had a better view than me of the flower-wavers—many of whom were overcome and weeping at a glimpse of Kim Jong Un, some eight stories above them.

We had brought along a ZNBC news crew to film the seemingly endless regiments of goose-stepping soldiers, sailors, pilots, and artillery crews. For close to two hours not one marcher had taken a step out of line or time. The editor on the crew, Effie Mpande, was so impressed that she compiled five minutes of solid marching, bringing each block of marchers into line, one after the other, in a hypnotic rhythmic sequence. When ZNBC showed it in Zambia she was inundated with callers asking: "Are those real people? You could not get real people to do that! They are robots!"

We visited the dead leaders, each embalmed in the former presidential palace; we were invited to bow to their feet, shoulders, and head as we were marched solemnly around their waxen bodies. They were surrounded by huge exhibits, including personal cars, trains, and boats, along with several rooms of medals and awards. Kim Il Sung had a lot of medals from Stalin and Mao and even one from Kaunda. Kim Jong Il's included a medal from the Derby County show and another one from a Yugoslav building company.

As we drove away from the mausoleum we noticed groups of young people squatting on the extensive swathe of lawn around it, apparently picking at the blades of grass without the help of any implements. "They are voluntarily trimming the grass out of love for our leaders," said our interpreter.

We were given the whole tour. We attended the opening of the museum of war—a truly vast new museum, glorifying the North Korean victory and vilifying the United States (but playing down the role of the Chinese as mere volunteers). We were taken to a dolphinarium, a particular passion of the Dear Leader, who apparently advises on dolphin training. They told us 727 (i.e., 27 July, the date that the Korean War was "won" in 1953) species were represented—not one more, not one less! We went to the Juche Tower, home of the Juche Idea, the political ideology of North Korea. To be honest, we tried but failed to understand Kimilsungism or Kimjongilism, and the reader will have to look elsewhere in their struggle for enlightenment. The view from the top of the tower was interesting though, as we saw behind the facade of the main streets to the hundreds of run-down apartment blocks behind.

As we left a massive firework display en route for a state banquet on our third night in Pyongyang, Charlotte realized she had her dress on back to front. No matter; the experience of the previous few days was so bizarre that sequins down the back rather than the front was hardly an issue. For a banquet, in a country where food is notoriously short, we were served chicken with quail's egg, glutinous rice cake, squid pieces, fruit and vegetable salad, pork dumpling soup with mushrooms, mung bean pancake, sweet and sour fish with apple, duck stuffed with rice, giant fishball in soup, cold black noodle soup with beef, as well as watermelon and ice cream. By each plate was a pack of 7:27 cigarettes, the Supreme Leader's favorites (27 July again). Sweet wine, clear spirits, and beer are served simultaneously, with a custom of downing shots of spirits in the company of people who come to your table wanting to share a toast. Fortunately for us, we were not as popular as the Chinese vice president; it would have been hard to keep up. I recall just one conversation: "Is your former president still alive and waving his handkerchief and dancing?"

When I got back I apologized for not taking KK since I didn't know he was so famous is that neck of the woods. "Why did you go?" I asked. "To help them make peace." "And?" "They didn't want peace so I left and never went back."

The last event we attended was a concert in a massive hall, seating around 10,000 people, most of whom seemed to be in military uniform. A vast orchestra, choir, soprano soloists and a group of tenors belted out against a huge film backdrop. The footage of the brave Korean troops started off fairly cheerfully, accompanied by some patriotic opera. As the show went on, however, it all got nastier and nastier. The volume rose, the tempo increased, and the tenors sang "ha, ha, ha," barbershop-style while the film depicted US soldiers being crushed by tanks, bayoneted, and blown up. The audience cheered and cheered again, further frenzied by the presence of the Supreme Leader, leaping to their feet to clap and shout hurrah. We went back to the guesthouse, crying off the cultural dancing program scheduled for that evening.

I tried extremely hard to persuade our hosts to let us to travel to Beijing by rail from Pyongyang—that is after all how NK's leaders like to travel. However, our request was refused. Perhaps if I had not looked so much like an American spy it would have been more successful. So we had no choice other than the state-owned Air Koryo. Despite it being the only one-star rated airline in the world, and declining the proffered spam sandwich and glass of water, we arrived safely back in Beijing— back from a place that even Stalin would describe as shockingly Stalinist to what now represented for us an acceptable standard of normality.

"Welcome home," said the head of the Chinese security detail.

17

Slow Death

FOR MANY MONTHS, IN FACT ALMOST AS SOON AS WE WON THE ELEC-
TION—come to think of it *before* we won the election—the social
media were telling stories about Michael's state of health. The *Zambian Watchdog*, a scurrilous electronic "news" sheet, in particular produced long screeds of diagnostic waffle that must surely have come
from a medical student with a book, calling into question the condition
of every presidential organ. Sometimes the coordination was not up to
the rate of invention, and we got stories of him chasing young girls
around the grounds of State House while simultaneously bedridden in
a near comatose condition. But some of the mud stuck, perhaps on
account of the comparatively recent death of Levy Mwanawasa while
in office, and people started to worry.

If I was late to start worrying about his condition, it was because I
knew his temperament too well and had learned to enjoy the shock it
evoked in many people. If he suddenly cancelled a planned trip, in or
out of Zambia, some took it as evidence of ill health—I just wrote it
off as Michael indulging his aversion to the prospect of boredom. He
had me, the only white vice president in Africa, to make his fellow
heads of state sit up and take notice—so why endure too much ceremony and pious expressions of concern for a better world? Come to
think of it, his instincts were to keep Zambia out of commitments to
over-aggressive peacekeeping missions and other adventures in foreign
lands. He did not mind helping neighbors like Malawi (after the death
of Mutharika) with fuel or Zimbabwe with maize on credit. Nor did he
change the long-standing tradition of Zambia being a haven for all

refugees. But he was terrified at the prospect of Zambia becoming inextricably caught up in other people's squabbles. He was adamantly averse, for example, to giving assurances about involvement in the Rwanda-Burundi-Congo-Uganda area, normally referred to as the Great Lakes region. He was all too aware that its complex issues of ethnicity and history put it on a par with the Middle East in terms of being a trap for well-intentioned intruders. So rather than leave Zambia himself and go to a meeting in which he would be pressured to make commitments, he just sent me, or someone even more junior, to say that we were not empowered to agree to anything but would consult. He would leave it to those looking for a continental legacy—such as President Zuma or President Kikwete of Tanzania.

But a point came where he absented himself so often, even from routine cabinet and other administrative meetings at home, that there had to be something going on. My colleague Emmanuel Chenda and I, still sprightly students of the Academy and with perfect confidence that there had been but a glitch in the diary, went to remind him of a meeting due to start an hour earlier. We were guided to his bedroom where we found him in his pajamas, with the lights off and the curtains drawn, wanting to know why we were disturbing him on a public holiday. He thought it was Sunday. We told him it was Monday. He told us to call off the meeting. "How are you, your excellency?" one of us asked.

"Get out! Are you a doctor to ask me how I am?"

A few weeks later he was delayed in turning up to another meeting. I phoned him and received an apology, along with instructions to chair the meeting myself, since I was the only person qualified under the Constitution to take over chairmanship from him. This situation became increasingly the norm. The boss was definitely ill. But from what was he suffering? Cancer, heart disease, you name it; all were dragged out and listed in the rumor mills. Alas, I could get nothing from Michael apart from the assertion that he was fine: "There is nothing wrong with me." But he was plainly in poor physical shape; the pitch of his voice was rising and the skin around his mouth was showing some sort of deficiency.

There was, in PF, an "anonymous" initiative aimed at discrediting top leadership with, of course, the view of replacing it. That is what you expect in Africa, and it is only different in degree from what you might expect in Europe. The attack is seldom direct but aimed at someone close to the Big Man. In the case of PF, from late 2012, the ostensible target of discontent among the rank and file of the PF was Wynter Kabimba, the secretary general. I was not a suitable target since I was still crippled by the parentage clause of the Constitution and was popular for having (in common belief) engineered the PF victory. Wynter on the other hand was a more likely target for cadre discontent since he was the party secretary and thus open to being resented for never being sufficiently generous with money or for being the one whose job it was to initiate and finalize disciplinary cases. He is also not a Bemba (well, strictly speaking he is 25 percent Bemba but apparently this doesn't count) and unable to clutch at the straw of ethnic solidarity.

So it was Wynter's lot to be the object of "coffin" marches, where cadres plus some rent-a-crowd paraded a coffin with his name on it and shouted allegations to the effect that he was the one who was plotting to tumble Sata from the throne and replace him. As is normal in this variant or episode of a game of thrones, "evidence" of a very dubious standard was adduced anonymously to show Wynter's guilt beyond doubt.

Graduates of the University of Fibbing collected like birds of one species, keeping all others away from the water in the birdbath.

For more than a year Michael did not seem to care about the witch-hunters stalking Wynter; nor did he seem to place any credence on the evidence against him. And Wynter seemed perfectly relaxed in his twin positions of minister of justice and secretary general of the party. But the pressure continued, and one can only assume that Michael's continued illness was deepening and depriving him of the strength to resist paranoid tendencies.

A characteristic of paranoia is that what ought to work against it tends to perversely work with it. Perhaps to convince Michael and the rest of us of his loyalty, Wynter applied money and extra effort to his countrywide reorganization and strengthening of party structures. This was immediately translated by his libelers as "he is reorganizing the party to give him the position of president at the next general conference." Michael eventually became prone to give some credence to such stuff and he even went so far as to ask me to accompany Wynter on a few of his reorganizational trips and judge his motives. I did accordingly and discovered nothing suspicious, though Wynter was more popular than the coffin marches were designed to suggest. I duly reported my "findings." End of episode? Not in Zambia.

There are experts in Kremlinology of the African sort who will wring every possible angle out of a story. Since Michael's death, a popular variant of the Wynter/coffin marching story is that Michael himself was behind the plot against him. In other words, goes this theory, the paranoia and stuff came at the beginning and Michael pulled all the strings leading ultimately to his firing. Even if this twisted web of a tale were true, it does not dispense with the plotters—it only brings their influence earlier into the story.

In July 2014 a parliamentary by-election was held in the very non-PF area of Western Province. Since 2011 we had developed considerable abilities in swinging the membership of parliament in favor of PF. We were no longer "hung." Some of our victories had to do with me in a helicopter run on very tight schedule (up to ten rallies a day) but mostly it was the work of Michael's Academy as a group—the originals. The battle for Mangango turned into a fight between the Academy (sometimes called by our enemies the "cartel") and the rest of the PF (known by this time as the "clique"). Their scenario was that we—the Academy—would run the campaign for the PF and inevitably lose it, at which point the clique could run to Sata and denounce our lack of relevance. Sylvia Masebo, the secretary for elections, moved bodily into the constituencies and ran the campaign to perfection. The rest of the Academy joined in. We walloped the opposition in unlikely circumstances. What did the clique do? They went to Michael and said, "Wynter has been boasting that they no longer need you to help them win an election! You are expendable."

Never for doing things by halves, it was now time for some more forgery. We had not had a decent forgery since we were charged all those years ago with defaming Mwanawasa. A professional liar cum laude poured the poison in Michael's ear to the effect that there had been an exchange of emails between plotters who planned to remove him from the presidency using Clause 36, the one that provides for removing a president no longer able to hold office. The purported emails were produced, confirming that the government would be in the plotters safe hands within days. *The Post* reported:

> The emails, which appear to come from faked accounts, show correspondence regarding mass corruption among Kabimba [and his supposed fellow plotters]. Given that the emails are so explicit in their details and created under unusual spellings of the account names, a common observer could see that they are not authentic—nevertheless, this served as sufficient evidence to President Sata to fire his longtime ally Kabimba. (*The Post*, August 2014)

I happen to have had reliable confirmation that the emails were a set of forgeries, and Michael should not have been taken in. But he was on the very edge of reason. After two days he put out the message: I have fired Wynter. This was at the end of August and close eyewitnesses are of the view that this was the end of Michael's battle with himself—

he had less than two months to go until his death. In a confused moment it is said that Michael phoned Wynter, who had immediately rusticated himself to his game and cattle farm an hour's drive from Lusaka. "Where are you? Why haven't you reported for work?" he asked.

There was around this time considerable pressure being brought on our increasingly confused president to chuck me out along with the beleaguered Wynter. I am told there was even a typed, ready-to-sign order removing me from the vice presidency. When it was brought to him, Michael put it to one side of his bed and said something to the effect that "I will think about it." He showed it to me later, and asked me whether I thought he should sign it. The objective of those with the agenda was clear enough—to obviate the need for a transitional ninety-day government run by me as per the Constitution. Heavy fibbing was also used in an attempt to oust me—for example Michael was fed a story that Wynter and I had driven to a small town south of Lusaka in order to drink and generally celebrate his impending death or removal from office. Dealing with Michael at this stage was like dealing with two people residing in one skin—one moment he would laugh the lies off, the next he would be throwing the same concocted accusations at me. It was the tendency of the liars to go clear over the top that saved me. When the story was fed to him that I had become the king of ivory smuggling in Zambia he burst out laughing and sanity prevailed—of a sort, for a while.

Could we—the Academy, the good guys—have done something to short-circuit the accumulation of hyenas around a weak, sick, and stumbling man? In this situation the spotted hyena does not whoop but indeed laughs, for all the world sounding like an Englishman in his pub.

The Zambian Constitution makes some provision for the situation in which the president is suspected to be physically or mentally ill. It says:

36. [Removal of President on grounds of incapacity]
    (1) If it is resolved by a majority of all the members of the cabinet that the question of the physical or mental capacity of the President to discharge the functions of his office ought to be investigated, and they so inform the Chief Justice, then the Chief Justice shall appoint a board consisting of not less than three persons selected by him from among persons who are qualified as medical practitioners under the law of Zambia or under the law of any other country in the Commonwealth, and the board shall inquire into the matter and report to the Chief Justice on whether or not the President is, by reason of any infirmity of body or mind, incapable of discharging the functions of his office.
    (2) If the board reports that the President is incapable of discharging the functions of his office, the Chief Justice shall certify in writing

accordingly and shall table such certificate, with the report of the board before the National Assembly who shall on a motion, passed by a two-thirds majority—

(a) ratify the decision of the board, and thereupon the President shall cease to hold office; or

(b) reject the decision of the board and cause a further inquiry into whether or not the President is incapable of discharging the functions of his office and shall thereafter decide on such questions by a two-thirds majority vote, which decision shall be final.

(3) Where the cabinet resolve that the question of the physical or mental capacity of the President to discharge the functions of his office shall be investigated, the President shall, until another person assumes the office of President or the Board appointed under clause (1) reports that the President is not incapable of discharging the functions of his office, whichever is earlier, cease to perform the functions of his office and those functions shall be performed by—

(a) the Vice-President; or

(b) in the absence of the Vice-President or if the Vice-President is unable, by reason of physical or mental infirmity, to discharge the functions of his office, by such member of the cabinet as the cabinet shall elect:

Provided that any person performing the functions of the office of President under this clause shall not dissolve the National Assembly nor, except on the advice of the cabinet, revoke any appointment made by the President.

(4) A motion for the purposes of clause (1) may be proposed at any meeting of the cabinet.

At first glance this may sound well thought-out, but it is not in practice much use for solving the problem of a sick president—particularly when you could not be sure about the word "sick." The original drafters must have envisaged a situation in which the president's condition was well-defined and patently and persistently debilitating. A coma, for example. But the situation was that nobody was prepared put a name to Michael's condition let alone provide a prognosis. It is easy to imagine various ridiculous confrontations that might ensue. What was needed was some kind of crisis that would bring serious people to see the problem in a common light. When might this arise?

Michael had three important obligations lined up in September and October. The way he handled these might provide a clear way forward. The first was the ceremonial opening of parliament that has a function not dissimilar to that of the queen's speech in the British house—in particular it announces key government policies and policy shifts. There is no provision in the Constitution for the vice president or anyone else to stand in for the president. This was scheduled for Friday 19 September and was eagerly (not to say nervously) awaited by the whole country, since it would expose Michael on radio and TV for the first time in weeks. After that, in the last week of September, he was scheduled to attend the UN General Assembly in New York. He could have ducked this by using me, but it would not have looked good given that he had made a point in the previous two years of attending personally. Thirdly, there were the fiftieth anniversary of independence celebrations due on and either side of 24 October. How do we hold these without him?

Here is the opening of parliament, as reported in *Hansard*, omitting some of the passages of the formal speech that Michael managed to read.

The House met at 1000 hours
[MR SPEAKER in the Chair]
NATIONAL ANTHEM
PRAYER

———————

TIME OF THE PRESIDENT'S ADDRESS
THE VICE-PRESIDENT (DR SCOTT): Mr Speaker, I beg to inform the House that His Excellency the President of the Republic of Zambia, Mr Michael Chilufya Sata, will be arriving at 1025 hours to declare the causes of his calling the House to meet today.
I thank you, Sir.
(Business was suspended at 1014 hours until 1106 hours.)
His Excellency the President entered the Assembly Chamber escorted by Mr Speaker.
(*Assembly resumed*)

THE PRESIDENT'S ADDRESS
HIS EXCELLENCY THE PRESIDENT (MR M. C. SATA): Mr Speaker, I would like to introduce two people. The first is the woman on my lefthand side who has made me live up to now. I have not died yet.
(*Laughter*)
HIS EXCELLENCY THE PRESIDENT: All hon. Members have seen the tallest man in the House, the Minister of Education, Science, Vocational Training and Early Education, Hon. Dr Phiri. Where are you? Please, stand up. [Dr Phiri is of short stature]
Dr Phiri rose.
(*Laughter*)
HON. MEMBERS: Stand up!
(*Laughter*)
HIS EXCELLENCY THE PRESIDENT: From Cape to Cairo, we only have one white man who happens to be His Honour the Vice-President. Now, I am not very sure whether I have two vice-presidents, one in my house and one outside.
(*Laughter*)
HIS EXCELLENCY THE PRESIDENT: However, the one I am introducing is the white one, Dr Scott.

His Honour the Vice-President rose.

HON. GOVERNMENT MEMBERS: Hear, hear!

HIS EXCELLENCY THE PRESIDENT: Now, you have to be very careful with
that muzungu because I imported him to come and help us with rural
development in Mpika. I also imported his current wife. I wanted to
introduce the one in charge of the District Development and Support
Project (DDSP).

From there, he proposed and married Charlotte Scott. Congratulations, Dr
Scott.

(*Laughter*)

HIS EXCELLENCY THE PRESIDENT: We have a replica here of Dr Kenneth
Kaunda, Col. Panji Kaunda [his son, an MP]. Just look at his head.

(*Laughter*)

HIS EXCELLENCY THE PRESIDENT: I once came to this place seventy-four
years ago. The person who sat next to me is the one I am introducing
now. I would like to introduce Mr Shamenda and our new president
as we read in the newspapers, 'President' Kambwili. [The seventy-
four year period is evidently a confusion, Chishimba Kambwili is an
MP and minister with avowed presidential ambitions.]

(*Laughter*)

[*continues reading official speech*]

Have you seen you, young girls? Every time you are sitting, you are being
disturbed by these young girls. [reference unclear, perhaps people in
the gallery]

(*Laughter*)

HIS EXCELLENCY THE PRESIDENT: So, President Kambwili, be careful.

(*Laughter*)

[*continues reading official speech*]

HIS EXCELLENCY THE PRESIDENT: Looking at the people seated in front of
this House, right behind me, I can see that the courts are on holiday
because I have seen many lordships in here. So, do not go to court
today, Dr Scott, ...

(*Laughter*)

HIS EXCELLENCY THE PRESIDENT: ... because all the Judges are here. So,
the Clerk of the High Court will adjourn your case to next year. This,
especially, applies to Hon. Lubinda who is a troublemaker.

(*Laughter*)

[*continues reading official speech*]

HIS EXCELLENCY THE PRESIDENT: Last week, my wife received a phone
call from a woman who was a district governor seventy-four years
ago. She said, "Madam Kaseba, I am living in abject poverty." So,
madam was wondering why this woman was living in abject poverty
when she is abject poverty herself.

(*Laughter*)

HIS EXCELLENCY THE PRESIDENT: She wanted support by way of assisting
her with money to start up a business. My wife promised to call her,
but has not called her to date.

(*Laughter*)

[*continues reading official speech*]

HIS EXCELLENCY THE PRESIDENT: Sir, let me state that construction works are on-going at Robert Makasa, Paul Mushindo and Palabana universities. As regards Chalimbana, Mukuba and Kwame Nkhrumah universities, additional infrastructure is being put in place. I, therefore, direct the hon. Minister of Education, Science, Vocational Training and Early Education to accelerate the construction of this infrastructure and start the process to operationalise these institutions in the shortest possible time.

Who is the hon. Minister of Education, Science, Vocational Training and Early Education?

(*Laughter*)

HON. OPPOSITION MEMBERS: Stand up!

HIS EXCELLENCY THE PRESIDENT: Stand up, tallest man.

(*Laughter*)

Dr Phiri rose.

HIS EXCELLENCY THE PRESIDENT: We had the tallest man at one time in this Parliament, Mr Chindoloma. Every time he stood up, I would hear hon. Members calling him to stand up.

(*Laughter*)

HIS EXCELLENCY THE PRESIDENT: So, the same thing applies to John. Who is that one in a white hat? Can she stand?

Prof. Luo rose.

HIS EXCELLENCY THE PRESIDENT: Where does she come from?

(*Interruptions*)

HIS EXCELLENCY THE PRESIDENT: Does she come from Mandevu or Muchinga Escarpment?

(*Laughter*)

HIS EXCELLENCY THE PRESIDENT: That one is a trouble maker from Chinsali.

(*Laughter*)

HON. MEMBERS: Hear, hear!

(*Interruptions*)

MR NTUNDU: Gwembe University.

HIS EXCELLENCY THE PRESIDENT: Who wants Gwembe University?

MR NTUNDU: It was a promise.

HIS EXCELLENCY THE PRESIDENT: We gave you a university. I will go and tell your people in Gwembe that I gave you a university, but you are still making noise.

(*Laughter*)

His Excellency the President: I do not need to beg for transport from voters like you do. I can fly from here and take my wife with me.

(*Laughter*)

HON. MEMBERS: Hear, hear!

HIS EXCELLENCY THE PRESIDENT: If I do not want to take her with me, I will gather handicapped children around Gwembe and send her there because she is a friend of handicapped children. So, hon. Member of Parliament for Gwembe, be careful.

(*Laughter*)

HIS EXCELLENCY THE PRESIDENT: The biggest problem we have at the moment is a critical shortage of accommodation and classrooms for

students. Therefore, the Government has a programme to build 4,160 bed-space student accommodation at the University of Zambia, 3,200 for the Copperbelt University, 1,280 for Mulungushi University . . .
Dr Phiri, do you know where Mulungushi University is?
DR PHIRI: Yes, sir.
HIS EXCELLENCY THE PRESIDENT: The Mulungushi University is the only one where we have a female chancellor. When young people look like Shamenda, this time, no one wants to talk to them.
(*Interruptions*)
HIS EXCELLENCY THE PRESIDENT: . . . and 960 bed spaces at the Evelyn Hone College of Applied Arts and Commerce. I do not know where we are going to put the 960 beds, but anyway I cannot talk about Mulungushi because I will just be punished. These people meet privately and I am just informed about the outcomes of their meetings. You have to be very careful when you are in power. Doctors say that if we have health centers with health facilities, we are going to start treating people from these health centers, including white people like Dr Guy Scott. After all, the medicine we take came from white people.
(*Interruptions*)
HIS EXCELLENCY THE PRESIDENT: Mr Speaker, to mitigate the shortage of skilled health personnel, the Government has been rehabilitating and constructing training institutions. To this effect, two new training institutions are under construction in Senanga and Lusaka at Levy Mwanawasa General Hospital. For this one in Senanga, we will have to teach people the Lozi language first. They must be able to say, "eni sha." (Yes, sir/madam), and the chancellor will be Hon. Wina. When she is in Senanga, she really walks like a typical Lozi woman. Have you seen the way she is looking today?
HON. MEMBERS: Stand up!
(*Laughter*)
HIS EXCELLENCY THE PRESIDENT: Hon. Wina, can you stand up.
(*Laughter*) Hon. Wina rose.
HON. MEMBERS: Hear, hear!
(*Interruptions*)
HIS EXCELLENCY THE PRESIDENT: So, if you want to take your children to Senanga University, you must be nice to Hon. Wina.
[*continues reading official speech*]
HIS EXCELLENCY THE PRESIDENT: Mr Speaker, I thank you for giving me this opportunity to deliver my speech for the official opening of the Eleventh National Assembly. I wish to thank everybody who listened, and as per tradition of this House, I am leaving the whole speech with the Hon. Mr Speaker.
HIS EXCELLENCY THE PRESIDENT: Mr Speaker and Madam Clerk of the National Assembly, I now declare this House officially opened.
Mr Speaker, I thank you very much.
HON. MEMBERS: Hear, hear!
His Excellency the President left the Assembly Chamber.
(National Assembly of Zambia, 2014)

What had I just witnessed? I was seeing clearly, and what was revealed to me was a man's potency being stripped from him, layer by layer. He could hardly read a sentence; the numbers have taken flight in their ultimate protest at unskilled handling; nothing but habit was left to propel his sexual fixations and corny jokes. But he fought back; all except his real enemies tried to help him fight back.

But you had only to shut your eyes and the degeneration of Michael's judgment, concentration, and energy was quite evident. Meaningless numbers, inappropriate comments, and disconnected narrative. Nonetheless Michael had come to parliament, made jokes, recognized people, and left—all without falling over. The taxi drivers were not taking fares—instead they gathered around radios in the taxi ranks listening to their hero; here and there TV sets were perched on walls or suspended from ceilings; nurses neglected to change sheets and bags; miners downed tools. There's our man! Yes, he looks a bit weak but he will soon recover . . .

One crisis survived (only just); two to go.

Alas, the UN General Assembly was a disaster. Michael failed to appear for his scheduled slot and, somehow, the story got into the "serious" press that he had died in his hotel room. The fact that he was still alive, and indeed not even hospitalized, was soon out on the wires, but the nasty incident gave support to suspicions of serious ill health.

Also it must have been obvious even to Michael by this time that he was not in any shape to handle the strain of the independence events. He was booked into a hospital in London and a story was hastily concocted to accommodate the fact of his absence. The ceremonial tasks were allocated between me as the vice president and Minister of Defense Edgar Lungu, who I was told had been appointed acting president during Michael's absence for medical purposes in London. It was like Hamlet without the prince. What are we "celebrating" when our leader is—by now obviously—seriously sick? Though we did get one good Zambian joke out of it: On Independence Day in 1964, a white man lowered the flag and handed it over to a black man; this year, 2014, a black man lowered the flag and gave it to a white man. In 2064 a white man and a black man will together lower the flag and give it to a Chinese man.

The fiftieth anniversary of Zambia's independence came and went. A few days passed, and I was awoken from sleep by my aide de camp, the attorney general close on his heels. I was asked to make a phone call to London and heard that Michael had been discharged from his hospital bed and had gone back to the Connaught Hotel, preparing to pack and return to Zambia. He was feeling, he had said, fine. Then he was suddenly not so fine: he had chest pains and clearly needed to return to the hospital. Upon arrival he died. Nobody asked for a post mortem at the time.

Nobody?

Really?

"Your Excellency," said the attorney general, "Good morning."

Epilogue:
A Quick Presidency,
and After

I<small>T TOOK ME A RIDICULOUSLY LONG TIME TO REALIZE THAT</small> M<small>ICHAEL'S DEATH</small> was at hand—that it could actually happen. Zambia had, after all, been visited by the prolonged death-by-stroke of Levy Mwanawasa in 2008. For the death of another sitting president to be so close to hand was terribly unlikely. It might seem that only fake news, and the full involvement of Schrödinger's high-speed cat, would possibly produce such a repetition of events. But it did eventually become clear; however terrible the prospect, it was happening.

Half a Government

One day in the middle of 2014, I plonked myself down in Michael's darkened bedroom and tried to tell him the truth. The women who had been looking after him, including soon-to-be widow Christine Kaseba, were quick to vacate the room—they were expecting an explosion, perhaps. I told him I had heard rumors that he was not eating and other stories to the effect that he had cancer. One source of my information was an Israeli institution, the other British. Despite my status as vice president, and my long-standing personal friendship, I had received no information at all from the Zambian side (government or family), despite numerous attempts to find out what was going on. By this time he had stopped attending meetings and other functions, making it automatic by the Constitution that I should chair cabinet meetings and stand in on occasions where Michael would usually be expected. But he was still the president, and we needed him to brief us all and if necessary to stand to one side while he recuperated; in fact the Constitution demanded so.

But it seems that is not how it happens. The system of the extended family protects the dying sufferer from nonfamily members, treating outsiders as possible opportunists. Within their own families, even medical professionals, it seems, are part of the obfuscation of truth. The problem was that the truth was also hidden from those who cared about him and would do their damnedest to keep him alive if such a miracle could be brought about.

Michael was not in a benign mood. As soon as it was clear that I wanted to discuss his condition, he was livid and demanded to know what my sources were. Had his relatives revealed the deadly threat, or was it the professionals? Sneaky little officials from our diplomatic missions in countries where he had sought treatment? The servants? I told him I was sick of being called a liar by everyone—claiming to the world on the BBC Africa Service that he was quite well, and just resting—and so I had made my enquiries. It was my responsibility, I considered, so long as I was his number two. "I am running this government," I said, "You are not competent right now." I shut my eyes and waited for the bang. He later told me that my enemies had reported that I had been celebrating with others, drinking champagne in anticipation of his death. I asked what conceivable advantage my loss of his presence on this earth would give me. He looked as if he took my point, but reverted to his crabbiness: "To hell, I am firing you; now go home."

"You are seventy-seven years old and you know very well the lies people make up to serve their purpose! How can you believe such a bullshit story?"

Michael started calling, and a couple of servants appeared and were dispatched to root around the bins. Two empty bottles of champagne were duly produced.

"See," he said, "you have the evidence! And do not tell me they are someone else's since we are Africans; we do not drink champagne." This, he would have noticed if he had looked around himself on a pretty regular basis, is categorically not the case.

I think I made a mocking snort and continued: "I am not going home; it is much better you survive and I die here. I am expendable, you are not," and so on.

"As for champagne . . ."

"Very well, so be it."

"By the way: how would Idi Amin have treated you, raising taboo issues? Your fellow Europeans asked that question when I first appointed you."

A policeman marched me out to the gate of the presidential residence, a gloomy place in the corner of State House, infested by unpleasant sounding peacocks. "Good night, sir, look after the Boss. And yourself."

I NOW KNOW WHAT I did not know at the time—Michael's cause of sickness and death. Since he died in London, his death certificate became publicly available. So, when I was none the wiser some months after his death, I obtained a copy for the princely sum of £9.25. And, especially for readers in Zambia, I include it (see p. 232).

Carcinoma is cancer; the rest is detail that those of us who are not medics can Google. I have no comment, other than to say that those who had knowledge of his condition could and should have made some very different decisions.

IT BECAME INCREASINGLY OBVIOUS to me—even without information and with my optimistic temperament—that Michael was in trouble, and with him, the rest of us. A few days after his scrap with me in his bedroom, he arrived somewhat unexpectedly at a meeting at State House. His face was discolored around his mouth and his walk was a mixture of stagger and slide. We stared at him as if he was a stranger; worse still, he stared at us in the same way.

Michael turned directly to me and told me he was going to fire me before he even sat down, and that he would appoint Emmanuel Chenda to my position. The casual tourist may not at first notice the danger that was casting its shadow . . .

There was an immediate ruckus, with his announcement disturbing greatly the people who had been anticipating Michael's demise, caused by the following logic: Guy Scott, under the Constitution, since his parents had not been born in Zambia, was generally assumed ineligible to stand as full president. This was the result of Chiluba changing the Constitution in 1995 to exclude Kenneth Kaunda from any further elections (beyond the six terms he'd already had) as explained earlier. In the event of Michael's death, even as acting president, there was still no realistic prospect of me being able to stand as president.

Emmanuel, on the other hand, was a "real Zambian." If he became vice president and subsequently acting president, it would have been quite likely that the advantage of this position, and Michael's apparent blessings, would allow him to assume the PF leadership and likely become the next president. Whatever maneuvers were already in place— at an advanced stage, I am now sure—to determine the succession of

CERTIFIED COPY
Pursuant to the Births and

OF AN ENTRY
Deaths Registration Act 1953

BBF 908160

DEATH	Entry No. 276

Registration district Westminster	Administrative area
Sub-district Westminster	City of Westminster

1. **Date and place of death**
Twenty-eighth October 2014
King Edward V11 Hospital For Officers, Beaumont House, 8/10 Beaumont Street, Westminster

2. **Name and surname** Michael Chilufya SATA	3. **Sex** Male
	4. **Maiden surname of woman who has married** ————

5. **Date and place of birth**
Sixth January 1936
Zambia

6. **Occupation and usual address**
President Of The Republic Of Zambia
Husband of Christine Kaseba SATA Medical Doctor
Plot 1, State House, Independence Avenue, Lusaka, Zambia

7.(a) **Name and surname of informant** Akalalambili KALUWE	(b) **Qualification** Causing the body to be buried

(c) **Usual address**
Zambian High Commission, 2 Palace Gate, London W8 5NG

8. I certify that the particulars given by me above are true to the best of my knowledge and belief

A Kaluwe

Signature of informant

9. **Cause of death**
I (a) Bronchopneumonia
(b) Metastatic Transitional Cell Carcinoma

Certified by Simon Hughes, MB

10. **Date of registration** Twenty-ninth October 2014	11. **Signature of registrar** Anne Regis Deputy Registrar

Certified to be a true copy of an entry in a register in my custody.

……………………… { Deputy

*Superintendent Registrar
*Registrar
*Strike out whichever does not apply

Date 22.01.16

System No. 511050149

CAUTION: THERE ARE OFFENCES RELATING TO FALSIFYING OR ALTERING A CERTIFICATE AND USING OR POSSESSING A FALSE CERTIFICATE. ©CROWN COPYRIGHT

WARNING: A CERTIFICATE IS NOT EVIDENCE OF IDENTITY.

Michael's death certificate

Edgar Lungu would have been dealt a serious blow if Michael had gone through with his announcement. I am sure Michael knew that, and was perhaps playing around with the people who had been bullying him and lying to him about champagne bottles. But he didn't act; he told me to stay in my seat. Michael left shortly afterward, and Emmanuel and I went for a coffee together, sharing our sadness for our struggling boss.

To STRESS A POINT: some "bush" constitutionalists, and even some very eminent ones, have argued that there was a realistic prospect of my becoming a constitutionally valid presidential candidate within ninety days. However, our courts often do not solve any problem in as few as ninety days, even where there is no political controversy. After three years we had still not promised to repair defects in the draft constitution document. Had I sought to assert my right to stand, the issue could have lain unresolved in the courts long after a definitive judgment would have been required. A coup, constitutional impasse, or even a civil war was a possibility.

ZAMBIA IS GENERALLY NOT very racialist. In fact I think many people were quite proud of me on that very basis ("it works like magic!" in attracting outside interest and giving the government credibility). But there is one definite limitation that became apparent: the top job. If you go from being just the vice president, like me, to looking like someone who might end up as the actual boss, then there is a problem. Zambia would have broken an invisible barrier. Magic would turn into a serious threat. Everyone else in Africa would laugh at us. They wanted me out so as not to cross the invisible line, and they'd have preferred to have their candidate in, to have the advantage of being VP when Michael died. But they did not want to insult Michael or risk his ire—a scary prospect, even in those last days and weeks.

So while they might not have wanted me as acting president, the majority of those present was confident they could remove me if required on the parentage technicality; they *really* didn't want Emmanuel Chenda, as his grip may have been much more tenacious. There was a sudden outbreak of fake cries that "we want Guy!" designed to torpedo Chenda. Oh bullshitters!

I've referred several times to "them"—by that, I mean people who were thinking about succession, rather than hoping against hope for Michael's recovery. While I had been worrying about his health, it was now plain that others were galloping ahead—so far ahead that I didn't even see them clearly in the dust and the distance.

I kicked myself over a conversation that I had held with Michael at least a year earlier when he was still very much on the ball. During one long meeting, the mid-morning tea break fell in the midst of a difficult item that one or two people were resisting. He stayed put while the seats emptied; he did not need to signal me to stay put. When we were just the two of us he asked: "What is the quorum of this meeting?"

"The President plus one, shall we say?" I replied. He hit the table and declaimed: "Good. We've won, that's fine, next item."

Outside in the overgrown grounds, with the famously accurate urinating vervet monkeys, a number of minibuses with thugs or "cadres" were deploying in the parking area as if readying for battle. Warlords on the inside looking out, currently taking coffee or tea, were presumably aware of the deployment of their battalions. But no one even pretended to be looking. "What on earth is this street fighting threatening to break out 100 yards from here?" I asked.

"*Mwana* [kid], you went to Oxford, and you do not deal in cadres. Do you have cadres in England? Who in this country can put these people in order if not me? You?"

I looked at him, and could not hold back a sob. He was so weak.

I told Michael: in Oxford—and my actual university of Cambridge—the cadres are called "fellows." They can be very intolerant toward other people, including their fellow men; they are bullies by their very nature, sometimes in very crude ways. So I know a bit about the use of bullying, I claimed bravely, but perhaps my example failed to convince him. I should have kept a straight face and reminded him that it was the two of us jointly who had cleverly out-maneuvered a malevolent character, Billy Phiri, during the 1991 campaign that ejected Kenneth Kaunda from State House. I had rocks thrown at me by Billy (at that time a powerful chap in a far-flung district) and his goons in the name of UNIP (KK's party) in 1991 when we went campaigning in the remotest communities in the Luangwa Valley. When the same Billy, in new political clothing, drove a fleet of buses through my constituency in 2011 on behalf of the outgoing MMD, who was it who recruited a scratch army made up of Congolese punks to put him out of business? Or at least reduce his influence to a manageable level?

Thugs, or party cadres, had played an essential part in the conduct of the 2011 elections, both presidential and parliamentary, albeit ultimately unsuccessful. The police could not be relied upon to protect voters, journalists, opposition members, or polling center officials since they were under the thumb of the ruling party.

But post-2011, PF did nothing more to keep matters in hand. I thought I could redirect my few amateur thugs to more productive activities, but before I knew it they had grown to thousands. Where did they come from? Never mind the Congolese, what about the thousands of "PF family members"—young girls giggling together with shaven heads, sweating in plastic Chinese protective riot suits, quite capable of grievously assaulting passersby with no more hesitation than scoring a goal in netball. This was new. It was a truly Mafia family–type structure, and even the police were frightened. It was likely that only Michael could have curbed the behavior of the gang leaders, and with his failing health, the sense of looming chaos was growing.

I should have pressed Michael for information. Who are these particular ruffians in the State House car park? Who is financing this cadre war and for what end? If you are such a street fighting field marshall tell me where this violence is coming from, and why is someone rumored to have died in a clash between minibuses on the road to the airport just yesterday? I had heard talk of a scheme to get him to appoint Edgar Lungu as the PF presidential candidate, who was by then the minister of defense as well as holding several other posts. He was seen as an Easterner with strong Bemba links (hence amenable to the two largest tribal voting blocks) but weak enough to need some independent input for unknown others to control. Smug was I—I had the apparent support of Michael, and he gave me reassurance whenever I wanted. And I had no idea of the depth of preparation that in retrospect must already have taken place.

Weekly and then almost daily international press cuttings started appearing, speculating that Michael was dying (a few times this took the form of premature early announcement of fact) and a white man may have already taken over. Despite my own considerable and determined state of denial, I considered my options and sat down with two documents—the Constitution of the state and that of our party. These prescribe very clearly what to do when the president died, and I would follow what they said.

Night Birds

On the night of 28 October 2014, just under three years after our glorious victory, three years from the start of the end of racial discrimination in politics, the phones started to ring around the world. My ninety days of marginal worldwide fame or infamy were about to begin, though I was still a few minutes from discovering the fact definitively. I have read every document relevant to what happens next. The written word's role is performed, but many night noises remain unexplored in detail, as prescribed by the best hunters.

I was fast asleep as an empty motorcade departed the unlived-in official residence of the vice president and made a fast run to our farm. It was toward the end of the long dry season—the hottest time of year—and restless thunderheads were making irritable, growling forays southward from the equatorial rain machine. Charlotte and I were sleeping with our bedroom doors open to the garden, after we had located an intact mosquito net and intimidated the dogs into uninterrupted sleep (shut up, shut up, *SHUT UP*, good dog), more restful than the official mansion, where we had never once slept. Stephanie, Charlotte's sister, was taking time out from her home at the ambassadorial residence in Brussels, fast asleep in the spare room.

My ADC, Daudi Sikanyika, senior superintendent, was very keen on guns, and liked to adorn the guardroom at our gate with stuff that would look good at an arms fair. This particular night, I distinctly recall, he had planted a North Korean two-stage handheld antitank grenade launcher (or some such thing), which he assured me could penetrate a thumb's length of armor plating. "It looks dangerous. You don't want anyone firing it accidentally," I had commented. "Yes," he agreed enthusiastically, perhaps missing my note of concern.

Mr. Sikanyika came into the garden and woke us up. I staggered out of bed. Now what is so important? Carelessly, we had left our mobile phones on silent, so we'd missed all his calls. It was nearly 1:00 A.M.

"Well, what is it?" Though I knew the answer even as I asked the question.

"You must phone London." Michael was in London, in the hospital.

"The president is dead, Your Excellency."

The attorney general materialized.

"Good morning, Your Excellency."

Under the Zambian Constitution as it was at that time, when a president dies in office, the vice president becomes acting president, and a presidential by-election then follows within ninety days. Simple, right?

"You had better stay close, AG," I said. "I am sure you know why."

"There is going to be an unseemly process of succession, Your Excellency. Indeed a fight, I would guess. Perhaps even deserving to be called a coup, but right now it's all very unclear."

"Thanks for the reassurance."

A black storm cloud sparked with lightning and cleared its throat for a menacing cough. The nocturnal nightjars started their fearful prayer ("Good Lord deliver us!"). The ghost bird—the buff-spotted fluff-tail—mocked us with its melancholic moaning. A tree hyrax ran and jumped through the patch of forest in our garden. It screeched and cried, "Your friend is dead; what are you going to do now?"

"Where is the secretary to the cabinet?" (Roland Msiska was SC then, and also a doctor. We'd never had an insightful discussion into Michael's health.)

"The air force is fishing him out of Livingstone as we speak."

There is no limit to what your shocked mind can cook up on a thundering night in Africa while you are waiting for time to start moving again. And even a shallow sleep beats talking politely to people whose minds are greedily munching on the prospect of wielding new forms and degrees of power and wealth. Whatever happened next, there would be no escape from confrontation—for the next ninety days.

Appointed by the Constitution: Acting President

The Constitution of Zambia was extremely clear. On the death of the president, the vice president becomes acting president. I became acting president when I was fast asleep; I found out about it perhaps thirty minutes later.

However, there were some who were not keen on this idea. It would have been *so* much more convenient to have your presidential candidate as acting president during an election. It's not only for the kudos; there are practical benefits that come with being president, such as the services of the air force and other handy entitlements.

As it happened, Michael had appointed Edgar Lungu to act as president in his absence when he was whisked out of Zambia, unannounced and not mentioned to me, about a week before. At the time, I know that he was not at all lucid. Perhaps he had a sudden moment of clarity, but personally I doubt he really knew what he was doing. Anyway, regardless of any appointment while the president is alive, the moment he died, the constitutional provisions applied, and the baton passed to me.

Despite this, there was a stand-off for some hours. Edgar Lungu convened a meeting of cabinet members at State House. They announced the death of the president, without so much as inviting me to the meeting, and tried to argue that Edgar was Michael's chosen successor and as such should remain as acting president. I was not present when the attorney general and Emmanuel Chenda arrived at State House and busted up that debate. I do know, however, that—rather later in the day than should have been the case—the heads of the Defense Forces lined up and saluted me.

The issue of my qualification to be acting president grumbled on for several days. There were some fairly hotheaded statements about whether I had unjustly snatched Edgar's "instruments of power," or indeed whether he had graciously decided to hand them over. These Battle-of-Bosworth-style stories focused on some physical representation of power—but these were a work of fiction. Expert after expert declared that the Constitution was crystal clear on the succession, with alas no mention of any crowns, scepters, or special bits of paper. The grumblings died down in time, overtaken by more pressing issues.

The more critical question is not who the Constitution appoints as acting president, but what it allows him or her to do in that position and whether the job comes with much actual power. There is one huge constraint—an acting president may not appoint or dismiss anyone among the huge range of posts that fall directly under that office. So, with a limited tenure and no realistic prospect of being either the candidate or indeed the winner of the next election, an acting president can be a pretty lame duck.

A one-legged duck is, however, not totally incapacitated. It can always hop. I presided over Michael's funeral, which lasted an entire scorching November day, and was attended by dozens of senior leaders from Africa and beyond. Mugabe was chairing the SADC at the time, and he and his wife, Grace, therefore played a prominent role. Ructions on the day were limited to a handful of louts, and the program overran by hours.

After that, the job went on. I managed to keep a lid on some of the worst attempts to misuse state resources for the forthcoming elections. I swore in some ambassadors and judges, and I did the daily job of a president.

But the consequences of lameness grew over time. In particular, the actions of several ministers and senior officials seemed to abandon protocol, custom, and common sense. People came and went from their offices, from cabinet meetings, from Lusaka, and indeed from the country, without regard for how the Zambian government is meant to conduct itself. A number of civil servants absconded from their posts to work on Edgar's campaign, while others spent their days peering out of Cabinet Office windows and making threatening phone calls to everyone they thought may be planning to visit my office. I myself received many

Photographer unknown

Michael's widow, Christine Kaseba, consoled by Charlotte Scott and Grace Mugabe

threatening messages from within Zambia, and indeed from the leader of a neighboring country (deeply concerning, but possibly fraudulent).

There were more significant breaches of the law and the Constitution that happened in this period. The actions of some people influenced what happened then and what continues to happen. However, I am bound by the State Security Act, and I cannot give a partial account as it would be rather lopsided. So the good reader, or the good historian, will have to wait a while; a full account exists, and it will be made available at some time in the distant future.

Party President

While details of the affairs of state are subject to legal restrictions, the political machinations are not. And, as observed by many during this period, it was pure politics that occupied much of my ninety days as acting president of Zambia, and of the party I had built, with Michael, from nothing.

The problem was essentially very simple. The party constitution specified that a new president (of the party) could only be determined by a "national conference." This is a large meeting, with a defined attendance comprising around 1,500 members gathered from across the country. The nomination of candidates and the usual voting takes place. Before voting, legally unqualified candidates are eliminated but there is no elimination of legally valid candidates. Also, there must be a sufficient spread of support countrywide to avoid tribalism. This was the system that was mandated by the PF constitution, and so I was determined to use it. Among the reasons for this was that I knew Michael had insisted on the "large number of voters" and "cross-country" process to avoid future presidential candidates being chosen at a closed door meeting ("in the dead of night," he said), this being the same way that Chiluba had used to bypass him.

Just as a gang of my colleagues had been ready to disregard the Constitution and nominate Edgar as acting president by acclamation, so they were determined to avoid this national conference. In early November, they convened a meeting of MPs, described by the party chairperson, Inonge Wina, as a means of "coming up with a suggestion" of how to adopt the presidential candidate. Overlooking the party constitution, she said they would "accept nominations from provinces on which format they prefer in choosing a candidate." To start the ball rolling, the MPs in attendance signed an endorsement of Lungu as the PF candidate.

I tried to ban the meeting, and then I refused to accept the petition, which was obviously irrelevant to the party constitution. Riot police surrounded my office. My side was certainly in the minority, but in my view we were obliged to follow the party constitution.

As we grappled with the issue of whether there would be a national conference, there were tit-for-tat sackings between my side and theirs. It was me who started it, when soon after Michael's death I tried to defuse the emerging chaos by sacking Edgar as secretary general of the PF. I wasn't terribly impressed by the staged riots and sweaty denunciations of my actions by well-known characters. But my action was premature, before Michael's funeral took place—not a good judgment on my part. I upset the Sata family and had to reinstate Edgar. At that stage, I was only beginning to understand the extent of organization that had gone on before Michael's death. In the weeks thereafter, the sackings and suspensions went on. We all sacked each other on various charges, quoting various authorities, but all to little effect and barely worth recounting.

Having realized that a national conference was inevitable, and following a court judgment to that effect secured by a party member, the Lungu camp realized they had better stop protesting and start trying to guarantee their victory.

The simplest way to victory in any election is to ensure that the voters are on your side. By late November, the PF secretariat was deep into the job of compiling lists of eligible delegates, drawn up in accordance with the constitution. Under severe pressure and threats, the team worked under tight security, around the clock, to produce a credible register of voters.

Much use this was, though, as the Lusaka accreditation process was hijacked and turned into a violent shambles. In the same hall where Michael's body had lain in state just weeks earlier, the worst of the thugs took over the lists, the police, and the issuance of credentials. One colleague, perceived to be against Lungu, was detrousered and physically thrown out. I peered into the conference hall from the adjacent room on 28 November with horror; I have witnessed significant chaos and a fair amount of violence and lawlessness, but this was an unimaginable inferno. I was reported as saying cadre power and thuggery had taken over the process. "What we found today was cadres breaking into buildings, taking election materials and tearing them up. Attacking people, intimidating people operating the accreditation [system] into accepting people who are not bona fide members of the Party" (Sichone, Moonga, and Sichikwenkwe, 2014).

I went back to State House and cancelled the Lusaka accreditations with just three days to go. The correct lists would have to be used at the conference venue, Mulungushi Rock, some 100 miles north of Lusaka. I insisted that if we could not have a proper process, we would not have a candidate in time for the registration of candidates for the presidential election, which was due in less than three weeks.

By this stage, the PF secretariat had received nominations for PF presidential candidate from seven aspirants. Edgar was one, Michael's widow Christine Kaseba was another, and the most prominent of the others (at the time) were two relatively young candidates, Michael's son Mulenga Sata, and his nephew, Miles Sampa. Delegates were called from around the country to the national conference with the task of choosing between them. In the days before the conference, reports started to arrive that delegates perceived as non-Edgar supporters had been prevented from traveling. Among those that set off, one bus filled with delegates from the south was attacked on their way through Lusaka and hacked with machetes. These were not cadres looking for a fight; they were middle-aged and older party members who suffered greatly from the beating they received. We knew exactly who had inflicted the violence, and I ordered the police to make arrests and restore order. I said at the time: "A busload of delegates . . . was ambushed at a flyover in Lusaka by cadres from

Intercity but nothing has been done about it. . . . As I stand here, as so-called Head of State, nothing has been done because of political interference" *(The Post,* 2014a). They ended up at Government House, the official VP residence, where they were cleaned up and fed before proceeding to the conference.

Mulungushi Rock rapidly became overrun with unknown and unregistered delegates. The entrances were manned by thugs, who chased away many who were entitled to attend. The atmosphere was febrile; the appearance of any leader not in the Edgar camp could have triggered any kind of response. I was in the presidential guesthouse in nearby Kabwe, waiting for confirmation that the accreditation process was acceptable, at some level at least.

No such news came. I waited and waited with the colleagues who had supported my position on the party constitution. I heard reports that Inonge Wina was declaring the conference was ready to open, apparently quite happy to overlook the presence of so many ineligible, unknown people. Sylvia Masebo (PF chair of elections and one of the bravest politicians I have come across) marched out of the guesthouse, commandeered some police from the presidential guard, and drove off to Mulungushi. She faced down the instigators of chaos as well as the thugs, which was a serious risk even with the cops around her. She insisted that the PF constitution determined that only the acting president could call the conference to order, and only once she had herself signed off on the accreditation of voters—which she was not about to do—and declared that the party was ready for election of a candidate. A *Post* reporter noted that "the move by Masebo was not taken well by those behind the illegal elections that she had stopped. They hurled unpalatables at her while advancing toward her, forcing police officers to fire two gunshots to scare the angry mob" *(The Post,* 2014b). She left.

Despite her similarity to Lupita Nyong'o's performance as Nakia in the *Black Panther* movie, Sylvia's intervention did nothing to stop the proceedings that day. Under Wina's leadership, candidates were called to come forward with the required 200 nominating delegates. Of all the candidates, only Lungu was there. No one else could have turned up without serious risk to life and limb. So there was only one candidate. He was declared to be elected unopposed.

We didn't give up. I declared the election null and void, for all the reasons I have described. The next day, we had another try—with proper accreditation of delegates, all of the candidates (except Edgar), enough food for everyone, and a peaceful election process. After so much stress, it was a very relaxed event, with a live band and dancing while the votes were counted into the warm evening. Miles Sampa was declared the winner.

So, we had two presidential candidates from two consecutive conventions: Edgar Lungu and Miles Sampa. Lungu appeared to be intent on simply insisting that he was the candidate; he certainly had force on his side. Acting PF Secretary General Bridget Atanga and Sampa took a case to court, intending to determine the validity of the two conventions. It was struck out when Edgar appointed a new Secretary General, who signed an infamous "consent order"—a declaration submitted by both parties agreeing to end a court case. Neither Sampa nor Atanga signed; the parties consenting were all from the same side. Sampa sought to appeal, but the judge did not hear the case in time.

We got to the nominations for the presidential election, starting on 17 December and spread out over days. As a founder of the PF, and as president, I decided to go. I think the team who had been battling against me so intently for weeks had expected me to get a terrible reception from the crowd, but that was far from the case. In the game of "take turns to stick your head out of the window of the supreme court and see how loud they cheer," I was certainly no worse than second place.

The campaigning proceeded. Lungu left the country on trips to Zimbabwe and Uganda, I assumed to seek support. He didn't ask me if he could leave, as protocol required, and he didn't tell me what happened.

I eventually decided to support the presidential campaign. Somewhat half-heartedly, I flew out of Lusaka to address meetings across the country and came back home every evening. I felt that the party I had founded with Michael had strayed very far, very fast, from what we had intended. People who I had supported, nurtured, mentored, campaigned for, given shelter, and helped out of personal difficulties had treated me as well as our legacy with the utmost contempt. My faith in loyalty and trust had been very badly battered. But I thought it was wrong to kill off what we had worked for, and I had hope that somehow the party could still continue with its mission of change for good. When Rupiah Banda, our MMD adversary from 2011, started campaigning for Edgar, I should have realized that we were more likely to U-turn than to soldier forward.

Charlotte cleared our things out of Government House, where we had never stayed in any case, and we counted the days. In the election on 20 January 2015, Edgar won narrowly by just 27,000 votes over his rival Hakainde Hichilema. HH, as he is known, protested irregularities that may have been present. Even so, I felt fairly happy that I had controlled some of the more egregious abuses of the electoral process.

Just for completeness, let me outline why the option of removing myself from the whole nightmare was unattractive to me. It might have been straightforward to resign from the cabinet, the party, and the acting presidency. It would surely have been straightforward to get my doctor to write me a sickie ("Guy is not well today and would be better keeping away from politically induced stress"). The trouble is that quitting would simply have been cowardly and would have resulted in more chaos if I ran away. In short, when it comes to the crunch, it is very difficult to face the prospect of failing to do what I know is written in black and white in the state Constitution and what my boss and instructor had made abundantly clear he expected.

If you want to avoid the rough road, you shouldn't have gone into politics in the first place.

Handover and Run

A few days after the election, we duly assembled at the 60,000-seat stadium (built with Chinese money at something like $1,500 per seat) for Lungu's inauguration. I felt I had lost, as my party had conducted itself disgracefully, and abandoned Michael's high personal standards of conduct. But I was greatly relieved to be able to step away from the impending fiasco, which was the likely legacy of the habits that the PF had displayed in the preceding months.

I stepped from my motorcade (goodbye forever after today) clutching the so-called instruments of power I had been given. After such a fuss about instruments of power in the aftermath of Michael's death, we had no choice but to invent some and make a show of handing them over. The secretary to the cabinet thought it might be advisable to manufacture something suitable, so he gave me a copper tray embossed with an elephant, made in Zimbabwe, along with (so far as I can remember), a map of Africa with Zambia shown in pink, a flag, a copy of the state Constitution, and a pen and pencil gift set emblazoned with the insignia of one of the local hotels.

President Robert Mugabe gave a speech in which he thanked me; President Kenneth Kaunda also thanked me. More than that: when he was admitted to hospital as a precaution for heat stress, I went to see him on the way home. He commanded me to hold his hand, and declared "Thanks to the Lord for you." I would have forgotten these easy compliments had Edgar Lungu not gratuitously neglected to say anything similar. We went back to State House for a lunch. It quickly degenerated into a debacle quite unlike anything previously witnessed there, as busloads of cadres invaded the area designated for invited diplomats, shoving them off their tables.

A few days later I walked into the Johannesburg cardiologist's waiting room. "Hey, Doctor Scott, how was the gin and tonic?"

"Gin and tonic?"

"That you drank to completion of the ninety days!" They'd seen a TV interview, in which I'd been asked for my plans following the elections.

"Oh, I had forgotten!"

Performance and Legacy

The three years that our government had sought to give Zambia a shove in the "correct" direction, and begin washing off the mud of corruption, can hardly be a simple matter of a "successful" versus a "failed" venture. A country the size of Texas, with maybe one-fiftieth of its per capita income, is certain to pose a serious challenge. But we wrought some progress even if it is somewhat complex, and I maintain that Michael Sata left a legacy that made Zambia better than he found it.

That said, whatever can be done can as easily (or more easily) be undone. And it would have been very hard to prepare for or protect against some of what has taken place since that election in early 2015, and the general election that followed in mid-2016.

The case of Zambia's forty-two secondhand fire engines became known to everyone who has heard of Zambia—or at least cares about it. It seems so straightforward that it appeals to everyone, especially those who do not want to delve into more complex issues. In December 2015, Inonge Wina—mentioned above, and now my successor as vice president—reportedly announced that government had spent K40 million (perhaps worth about $4 million, but it's hard to be exact as the kwacha was wildly fluctuating at the time) on firefighting equipment, including forty-two fire engines (Chishala, 2015). The whole issue then went quiet. Nearly two years later, fire engines were back in the news. Still forty-two of them, but by then costing $42 million.

Even with spare tires and smart new uniforms, there is simply no fire engine, new or secondhand, big or small, that cost $1 million. Well, perhaps a specialized machine designed to cover a high-security area of an airport or a high-tech manufacturing installation, but that is not what we have been told, nor what we have seen. As a nation, we have all now become experts in the price of fire engines and on whether these occasionally spotted tenders are anything other than refurbished old junk.

Perhaps even more worrying than the possible extraction of tens of millions of dollars is the treatment of those who have raised questions about the issue. My favorite civil society activist, Laura Miti, and her six fellow protestors were locked up over a weekend and have faced a prolonged case simply for standing outside parliament holding placards demanding accountability. One of her co-accused, a musician popularly known as Pilato, later fled the country after receiving threats over his new song "Koswe Mumpoto" (rat in the pot), which has been interpreted as criticizing Edgar Lungu and his ministers. In it, he sings that the ruling elite are behaving like rats that steal food and eat it, including things that they do not need.

Others too have faced lock and key. HH was charged with treason following an incident in which Lungu's motorcade deliberately overtook his (which did not follow protocol and pull into the ditch). It was never clear why Lungu's security decided that overtaking over fifty vehicles that were unlikely to give way was anything but provocative. After four months in maximum security, with the threat of a death sentence, it took the shuttle diplomacy of the Commonwealth secretary general to persuade Lungu to drop the charges and release HH. Other opposition leaders have been locked up on similarly flimsy charges, prevented from talking on the radio by thugs, chased, harassed, threatened, and attacked.

Perhaps more worrying are the increasing difficulties that we face in hearing what is happening to Laura, Pilato, HH, and all the others. The independent media has struggled to operate, whether through various forms of intimidation, heavy-handed interventions by regulatory agencies, or harassment of advertisers and vendors. In Lusaka, independent and outspoken Komboni radio (having given good coverage to the opposition in the 2016 elections) had its license withdrawn on the grounds that it was "not professional." When it was finally reinstated some three months later, the proprietor, Lesa Kaoma, was stripped and beaten by five policemen when she sought to regain entry to her premises. To add insult to injury, having tried to defend herself against the officers as they attacked her, *she* was charged with assaulting *them*. After the case dragged on for six months, she was eventually acquitted; the magistrate said he thought the police had been overenthusiastic in their duties.

At the heart of the independent media in Zambia lies *The Post* newspaper. *The Post* started as a weekly in 1991, some months before the first multiparty election that saw the end of KK's presidency. The founders— Fred M'membe, Mike Hall, Masautso Phiri, and John Mukela—exposed stories the regime would rather have hidden, and the paper went on in that tradition for the next twenty-five years. With the exit of the other founders, M'membe and his journalists became the focus of rage for Zambia's successive presidents. There were arrests by Chiluba (for calling him a thief), Mwanawasa (for calling him a fool), and Banda (for forwarding him unpublished photos of a woman giving birth in the street during a health workers' strike)—a hat trick, all ending in acquittals.

Lungu announced his intention to "fix" *The Post* during the Mulungushi debacle in late 2014 (Zambia Reports, 2014). The combative talk continued, and by 2016 the offices had been locked by tax authorities, and journalists were working on the roadside. As court cases and counter-cases were heard, it appeared that the proprietors had regained control. But Fred M'membe, his wife Mutinta, and the managing editor Joseph Mwenda were arrested at the paper's offices, allegedly beaten during the altercation, and charged. *The Post* continued to publish a limited number of copies, but soon the pressure became too great (Greenslade, 2016).

Over the decades, I have often been on the right side of *The Post,* and sometimes very much on their wrong side. Their position was sometimes hard to understand, and they had stubbornly held views that were sometimes perplexing. But their role was remarkable, and Zambian democracy is much worse off without them.

The experiences of Lesa Kaoma and the fate of *The Post* sends a clear threat to all would-be independent voices in the media, and self-censorship soon becomes the order of the day. I am aware of several pieces of very good investigative journalism that no one will dare publish. Two new publications continue *The Post*'s traditions, seeking to maintain the hard-won presence of independent media in Zambia. But their future is far from certain.

Feast and Famine: Deals and Debt

There is much to say about Zambia's economic position in the years after Michael's death. It is certainly the case that Michael wanted to borrow money—he wanted to borrow to invest in critical infrastructure and to fix the problems caused by many years of neglect. He wanted the railways to become a competitive and practical means of moving goods and people. With a population that doubles every twenty years, he was aware of the huge need for catch-up in the provision of schools and clinics. He wanted universities in every province. Some of his projects were questionable—the proposed roads through two national parks are good cases in point—but in general, he wanted to invest in good, pro-poor social and economic projects.

This is all expensive, especially in a large, fairly sparsely populated, landlocked country. There is a case for borrowing, but the costs of that borrowing have to be as cheap as possible, and implementation has to be very efficient. Without this, the whole venture quickly goes wrong.

In Michael's day, it was a challenge to keep on top of projects, costs, and contracts. He cancelled expensive vanity projects of no benefit to ordinary Zambians, notably a new airport and a new State House. Getting well-priced contractors to do a decent job required extreme vigilance; the propensity is toward very high prices for pretty shoddy work, or indeed no work at all.

Under Lungu's government, however, there has been increasing consternation about the levels of borrowing, intended projects, and the costs and quality of delivery. The debt appears to be spiraling out of control in return for very little.

Africa Confidential, a London journal, has been following Zambia's growing debt crisis with interest. They have reported that the country's precise debt is (worryingly) unknown. Officials have put it somewhere between $15 billion to $25 billion, and *Africa Confidential* believes it to be at least $20 billion, or 100 percent of GDP (the rule of thumb and African norm being around 40 percent) (*Africa Confidential*, 2018). Lungu's first finance minister, technocratically oriented Felix Mutati, says that he was not aware of all the loans contracted during his tenure; his successor, Margaret Mwanakatwe, appears far less likely to pursue a zealous pathway. In 2018, around 30 percent of the budget is financed by borrowing, and the debt to commercial banks has tripled since 2016. Probably the only feasible way to manage the spiraling impact of all this borrowing is to consolidate it under an IMF package. Perhaps unsurprisingly, the IMF will not conclude a consolidation program until the brakes are applied (less borrowing, get rid of money-losing state-owned ventures), and the government is not willing to follow their advice (contracts galore, state-owned ventures as handy cash-cows). Far from entertaining austerity, Lungu is keen to spend. Consequently, the situation is getting worse, and the cost of Zambia's borrowing is rising.

The most egregious issue is the extent to which projects are over-priced, unproductive, or both. The Lusaka airport was revived, at an eye-watering cost of some $360 million (against industry estimates of less than a third of that price). Following the fire engines, other expensive procurement exercises abound, including a whole set of questions around ambulances, Ndola airport, expired drugs, road contracts, and so on.

Zambia has been here before. The debt relief era peaked around the turn of the century. Zambia's debt was written off in 2005, at $3.9 billion. In the same year, GDP was $8.3 billion, and the write-off was equivalent to 47 percent of GDP. The international Jubilee 2000 campaign made powerful arguments for a massive write-off in developing countries' debt; these arguments will be much harder to repeat for some time to come, at least in Zambia. The effects of frivolity, apparent corruption, and carelessness of the current administration will continue for decades to come.

Full of Sound and Fury

Although my time in government came to an abrupt end, the PF did not. Depressing, annoying, tragic it might be, but that is all too usual in a political career. Common or not, however, the player will always reflect back and wonder whether it adds up to a bag of beans.

I am convinced that Michael and I shared a common goal and a genuine desire to break the mold of Zambian politics and improve the lives of citizens. We were fed up with big-man politicians (and some

Photographer unknown

Michael and I decided to abandon some opposition unity talks in 2006. Our driver had nipped out to get lunch, so we left on foot. I cannot track down a high-quality version, but nonetheless this grainy photo remains my favorite depiction of my political life with Michael Sata.

big women too) who tell lies to the ordinary person and hand over Zambia's future, her potential, and her assets to the first person to come along with a half-baked idea or a fat brown envelope. We wanted quality, and we wanted to build a future for the land we both loved. We wanted to do governance differently and to make Zambians truly citizens of their country. We wanted to get rid of second- and third-rate institutions and to end the neglect and abuse of the many by the few.

I believe one of the reasons that Michael appointed me as vice president was to make a point about Zambia. He wanted to show that Zambia was not at the end of a list or the bottom of a pile, populated by people who will do and say what they are expected to. He wanted to make a point that we have our own thoughts, plans, and identity, and our own views and priorities. He wanted people to listen and to show that we can say things they might not expect us to. There were indeed a few times when I said things that were not expected, but his point was neither about (a lack of) diplomacy or indeed about race. It was about showing that, in Zambia, we could do things the way that we wanted to. If that involved having me as vice president, which in many countries would be impossible, we could do that too. Michael told many visitors, including George W. Bush, that he and Obama were the only black presidents with white vice presidents.

It was a natural follow-on from the "*don't kubeba*" campaign that brought us to power. The campaign called out conventional, sleazy political tactics. It insisted that voters need not behave in the way that had been expected of them: Give them a cheap T-shirt, and they'll vote for you! Ha, ha, ha! *Don't kubeba* was a wake-up call, urging people to recognize the cheap tat for what it was and why it was being dished out in such quantities. It said to people, "Don't be treated like a fool! You are entitled to laugh at this, and even to play this game—but then show them that you are not a child."

But it seems there is only so much that you can do in terms of bringing real change of the sort that we had wanted. There are systems at play, behind the throne, some of which have endured since KK's days. There are family systems, tribal systems, systems of obligation and of government, and of course systems of vested interest. There are many who are in the pay of such systems, and others who are in their debt. These systems—together "the system"—have a very strong grip, and the system resists being broken. It binds many Zambians, certainly the elite, and it requires you to be bound to it. There is very limited tolerance for those who threaten it. And every time this system feels the wind of change—in the early days of Chiluba's government; when

Michael won the presidency—the hatches are more firmly battened down against future threats.

Michael wanted change and to show that more progressive, better politics could prevail. He wanted to break the system and replace it with something that would take Zambia, and Zambians, forward. I wanted that too, and his vision accommodated me, as a maverick, pro-poor, patriotic Zambian white man. But he couldn't manage to create that change, not sufficiently, not in the time available, and certainly not as his health failed him.

For now, the system has reasserted itself, and the cracks in the mold have been sealed shut. No more space for me, then; people who I worked with for years, people I know well and who I helped get established in politics, spit their venomous "he must go back to Scotland" into the television cameras. But we have helped the process along, leaving behind more seeds of change than were there when we started, to sprout again when the time comes.

Bibliography

Africa Confidential. 2018. "Zambia: A Swirling Fog of Debt." 59, no. 10 (18 May).

Bayley, P. 2014. *David Livingstone: Africa's Greatest Explorer.* Stroud: Fonthill Media.

Chishala, F. 2015. "Invest in Firefighting Kit, VEEP." *Times of Zambia*, 23 December.

Chitiyo, K. 2007. "Ian Smith's Policies Led to 50,000 Deaths: He Was Worse Than Mugabe." *The Guardian*, 23 November.

Davenport-Hines, Richard. 2015. *Universal Man: The Lives of John Maynard Keynes.* New York: Basic Books.

Dowden, R. 2008. *Africa: Altered States, Ordinary Miracles.* London: Portobello Books.

Duggan, C. 2009. "Ex-Zambian Leader's High Life Awaits a Verdict." *New York Times,* 21 June.

Ebrahimzadeh, C. 2017. "Dutch Disease: Wealth Managed Unwisely." International Monetary Fund. Accessed at imf.org/external/pubs/ft/fandd/basics/dutch.htm#author.

The Economist. 2014. "What Dutch Disease Is, and Why It's Bad." 5 November.

Financial Times. n.d. "Definition of Dutch Disease." ft.com/lexicon. accessed 14 August 2018 at http://lexicon.ft.com/Term?term=dutch-disease.

Greenslade, R. 2016. "Zambian Authorities Use Tax Law to Silence Opposition Newspaper." *The Guardian*, 4 August.

Hoas, I. 2007. "Zimbabwe Called a Sinking 'Titanic.'" Reuters News Agency, 21 March.

Keynes, J. M. 1919. *The Economic Consequences of Peace.* London: Macmillan.

———. 1924. "Alfred Marshall, 1842–1924." *The Economic Journal* 34, no. 135: 311–372.

Larmer, M. 2010. *The Musakanya Papers.* Lusaka: The Lembani Trust and the African Books Collective.

Lea, D. 2013. "We Did It." Letter to the *London Review of Books* 35, no. 7 (April).

References to *The Post* articles may be incomplete or missing, as at the time of finalizing this book, *The Post* archive had disappeared from the internet.

253

Livingstone, D. 1900. *Missionary Travels and Researches.* London: John Murray.
Lusaka Times. 2014. *Video of Vedanta Boss Saying KCM Makes $500 Million Profit per Year.* 13 May. Accessed at www.lusakatimes.com/2014/05/13/video-vedanta-boss-saying-kcm-makes-500-million-profit-per-year/.
National Assembly of Zambia. 2014. "Debates, Friday, 19 September 2014." Accessed at www.parliament.gov.zm/node/537.
The Post. 2006. "Zambia on the Recovery Path." 8 May.
———. 2007. "News Report." 23 October.
———. 2014a. "News Report." 11 December.
———. 2014b. "News Report." 30 November.
Reed, J. 2006. "China Intervenes in Zambian Election." *Financial Times,* 5 September.
Sachs, J., and A. Warner. 1997. *Natural Resource Abundance and Economic Growth.* Center for International Development and Harvard Institute for International Development. Cambridge, MA: Harvard University.
Saluseki, B. 2007. "I'm Not Ashamed to Deal with Taiwan, Zambia Is a Province of China, Says Sata." *The Post,* 1 November.
Serpell, N. 2014. "Zambians Don't Care About Our New President's Skin Colour." *The Guardian,* 30 October.
Sichone, C., C. Moonga, and P. Sichikwenkwe. 2014. "PF Accreditation Process Halted." *Times of Zambia,* 28 November.
Smuts, J. 1930. *Africa and Some World Problems.* Oxford: Clarendon Press.
Williamson, J. 1989. "What Washington Means by Policy Reform," in John Williamson, ed., *Latin American Readjustment: How Much Has Happened.* Washington: Institute for International Economics.
Zambia Reports. 2014. "Lungu Threatens Lawsuit Against Post." 5 December. https://zambiareports.com/2014/12/05/lungu-threatens-lawsuit-post/.
Zukas, S. 2016. Personal communication.

Index

About the Book

As Miles Larmer writes in the foreword, *Adventures in Zambian Politics* is unlike any political memoir you have ever read.

It is . . . A political history of Zambia from colonial times to the present. A revealing insider account of politics and government within a modern African state. A story about race in Africa. A chronicle of the rise and fall of two improbable political allies who wanted to change Zambian politics: Michael Sata, whose convoluted political career led him to become president in 2011, and Guy Scott, Sata's vice president and, after Sata's death, acting president of Zambia. Not least, it is a pleasure to read.

Guy Scott's absorbing narrative of his career and Michael Sata's in the chaotic world of African politics tells a uniquely Zambian story. But it is also a special contribution to our understanding of democracy and democratization across Africa.

Guy Scott was acting president of Zambia after the death of President Michael Sata. Prior to that he was vice president (2011–2014) and has also served as minister of agriculture and an opposition leader in the Zambian parliament.